A

BOOK

The Philip E. Lilienthal imprint
honors special books
in commemoration of a man whose work
at University of California Press from 1954 to 1979
was marked by dedication to young authors
and to high standards in the field of Asian Studies.
Friends, family, authors, and foundations have together
endowed the Lilienthal Fund, which enables UC Press
to publish under this imprint selected books
in a way that reflects the taste and judgment
of a great and beloved editor.

The publisher and the University of California Press Foundation gratefully acknowledge the generous support of the Philip E. Lilienthal Imprint in Asian Studies, established by a major gift from Sally Lilienthal.

A Time of Lost Gods

A Time of Lost Gods

*Mediumship, Madness, and the
Ghost after Mao*

———

Emily Ng

UNIVERSITY OF CALIFORNIA PRESS

University of California Press
Oakland, California

Library of Congress Cataloging-in-Publication Data

Names: Ng, Emily, 1983- author.
Title: A time of lost gods : mediumship, madness, and the ghost after Mao /
  Emily Ng.
Description: Oakland, California : University of California Press, [2020] |
  Includes bibliographical references and index.
Identifiers: LCCN 2019042708 (print) | LCCN 2019042709 (ebook) |
  ISBN 9780520303027 (cloth) | ISBN 9780520303034 (paperback) |
  ISBN 9780520972636 (epub)
Subjects: LCSH: Tang-ki worship—China—Henan Sheng. | Mental
  illness—China—Henan Sheng. | Ghosts. | Henan Sheng (China)—
  Religious life and customs. | Henan Sheng (China)—Rural conditions. |
  China—Social life and customs—1976–2002. | China—Social life and
  customs—2002-
Classification: LCC BL1812.T26 N4 2020 (print) | LCC BL1812.T26 (ebook) |
  DDC 299.5/1—dc23
LC record available at https://lccn.loc.gov/2019042708
LC ebook record available at https://lccn.loc.gov/2019042709

29   28   27   26   25   24   23   22   21   20
10   9   8   7   6   5   4   3   2   1

To my mother, father, and grandmother

CONTENTS

PROLOGUE: WE NEVER SHOULD HAVE MET

Her words from our final conversation ring in my head for days, months, and now years: "We never should have met." She was the first spirit medium I met in Hexian and in some sense also the last—last not in chronological time but in a closure of mythic scale that returned as a stinging reminder in the encounters that came thereafter, staining their very emergence with its foreboding tale of the limit.

I meet Zheng Yulan, a spirit medium in her early sixties, on a crisp autumn morning, accompanied by my host, Cai Huiqing. Zheng Yulan's home altar room is lined with visitors awaiting their turn on long wooden benches, the ceiling caked in black soot from decades of incense burning. After concluding with Cai Huiqing's inquiries on behalf of her family, we move through a hurried and generic reading of my own life trajectory. Sharp and fiery, Zheng Yulan, I hope, might be my first guide to mediumship. But, given her seeming indifference toward me, the prospect of working with her is starting to appear unlikely. As the session comes to a close, and Cai Huiqing and I stand up to leave, Zheng Yulan glances up with an afterthought at once pointed and nonchalant: "Do you have a mark on the front of your chest?" Taken aback, I nod, checking the edge of my high-necked sweater, which should have covered the keloidal scar that enigmatically appeared one year prior without clear cause, as I was formulating the project that would lead to this writing.

She sits me back down and launches into a reading radically different in tenor than the first. The scar was a marking left by an unseen entity who guided me without my knowledge to her altar, she says. That I appeared at her altar is thus not an accident. It is a fated encounter, an echo of otherworldly desire strung together by bodily signs and immanent operators, deciphered in retrospect—the scar, the project, my host, her altar—a chain of events whose relations become apparent, at least to human perception, only through a mode of "afterwardsness."[1] It also marks a future unknown, as the entity whose allocation I was living out could not be named. This knowledge would arrive, Zheng Yulan says, in due time. Moved, I consider this a felicitous encounter, an opening of the sort I had hoped, through which I might gradually come to learn about mediumship.

My hope starts waning soon enough. As I return to Zheng Yulan for subsequent visits, she grows increasingly apprehensive. She has little interest in engaging my questions. My presence comes to feel excessive, intrusive, out of place. She begins greeting my entrance with a chuckle, saying, "Here *again?*" On my second to last visit, her altar is quiet, with only one visitor departing as I arrive. The gods, she says, were away, convening, and she has been losing clients. I ask why the gods were meeting. She shakes her head and insists, "Heavenly secrets are not to be divulged."

"To be honest, I don't feel too well. I'm not someone with a good temper," she muses on and drifts into images I realize my appearance conjures for her. "If you don't harm them, they harm you, am I right? If you don't strike at them, they strike at you. Isn't it the same as the Japanese demons? We in China were invaded by Japanese demons, and aren't we still on bad terms with them? Isn't *this* the same?" She laughs a loud, theatrical laugh.

"Righteous deities remain righteous. Chairman Mao said that one can't allow thieves to rob and steal. If they enter your home, is it not the same? China is an impoverished nation . . . and you? You are in America. You will marry into America. This, then, all becomes hard to say." A tingle zips down my spine with her chuckle.

"I've heard that those who assist two nations don't have much time. This is *ming,*" Zheng Yulan continues. In classical Confucian renderings as well as contemporary mediumship, *ming* carries simultaneous meanings of divine command, allotment, destiny, and lifespan. In other words, the double agent, which she perceives me as being, is not long for this world, cosmically speaking. Shaken, I try to talk myself out of this narrowing vision of my place in the world, explaining what it means for me to take on this project, to be situated between nations in ways different than what she was implying. I say that I myself am a child of these boundary-making processes, and to come to Hexian was, in part, an effort to retrace and think through the aftermath of these fissures. She has little interest in my justifications.

"One can only walk forward; there is no retreat," she insists. "You must also walk forward. As you were assigned this duty, you must complete it properly. Write your novel. See those propagandists out there? They're all mad. Once you're wedded to America, you'll be just like that." She bursts into laughter once again.

Later that night Zheng Yulan phones Cai Huiqing to say that I need not visit her anymore. She relays a story to Cai Huiqing of a young woman from a nearby village who studied abroad in the United States and married into a family there. The young woman gradually lost touch with her hometown, even with her mother and father. It was an allegory of diasporic betrayal, of daughters who sever loyalty and ties to the family and to the nation, lured as they are by the demonic West. When I later speak to others in Hexian about this, the image Zheng Yulan was evoking would be clear to them: Cold War–era agents from Taiwan and from overseas, Chinese in appearance but foreign at heart.

Visions of the demonic imperialist West and its array of agents marked the struggle over images following Cold War bifurcations and contending dreamworlds. As we see in the chapters that follow, such images, along with Maoist and reform-era slogans and iconography, absorb and are absorbed by the languages and rituals of contemporary mediumship. Such otherworldly forces and personae seized me in the crossing of gazes, myself a specter of the uncanny and suspect figure one was always-already waiting for—the returnee researcher, the treacherous daughter. This comes after the geopolitical fracturing of Chinese worlds across unequal treaties, land concessions, and severed alliances.

The battle fought in Zheng Yulan's singular act of refusal of my ethnographic incursion thus gestures toward struggles of a cosmic-historic scale, of a China and a United States brought face to face once again, this time through the figures of the anthropologist after diaspora and the spirit medium after Mao. The corporeal presence of the ethnographer in this sense is a conduit of the other side of historical forces, restaged at the site of refusal.[2] It was a painful repudiation at once unexpected and overdetermined—a divine thread that drew me in only to—or precisely to—shut me out. This act of refusal carried past collisions of otherworldly sovereignty into the historical now, etching another trace. My decision to write of this incident—and by extension all else in this book—simultaneously enacts a betrayal through the very transmission of messages across what the mediums deem enemy lines.

Multiple readings of Zheng Yulan's change of stance toward me are possible. Perhaps her initial comment on the fated status of our meeting was meant to speak to our coming into acquaintance but not to invite further engagement. Perhaps my style of inquiry during subsequent visits—more like a researcher than an apprentice—placed me on the wrong side of cosmopolitical lines. Perhaps she grew concerned in a more earthly sense about the risks of dealing with a foreigner, given the political sensitivities surrounding mediumship, though I have my reservations about a solely secular interpretation.[3] And perhaps no single reading exhausts the forces that conditioned this unfolding.

No matter the reasons, this closure offered an introduction to the fraught scene of mediumship in Hexian, in which one may be inhabited by spirits on various sides of history—there is no neutral space from which to engage. Fortunately, the loss of clients seemed to be temporary, and Zheng Yulan's work resumed a short while after. But this series of events and Zheng Yulan's words taught me the stakes of this work at multiple levels. My later encounters with mediums and others at the temple square would be less sharply confrontational than these with Zheng Yulan, but they were immersed in the same airs of cosmopolitical suspicion and continuous need for renewed discernment. As Mao put it in his 1926 analysis of class in Chinese society, "Who are our enemies? Who are our friends? This is a question of the first importance for the revolution" (1967, 13). As with that of Zheng Yulan, Maoist revolutionary imaginaries would be central to cosmological accounts more broadly in Hexian. I was, as far as I could tell, placed variously across the divide in my time there and can only hope that what Zheng Yulan called my novel and my duty as a propagandist does not merely betray those who entrusted me with their visions.

FIGURE 1. The Chairman. Drawing of Mao on yellow fabric, with corners of the stars of Communism to the sides in red, from the temple square in Hexian. The script on the watermelon reads, *junling* (*jun* meaning military; *ling* meaning divine command). Photo by the author.

Introduction

The China of China

Flicking sunflower seeds from an unfinished pile to a finished one, Xu Liying is killing ghosts. I sit with her on the metal-framed hospital bed, the pile of seeds growing one by one on the white sheet.

"When Mao descended to earth, he did not want to. But they insisted, saying he must be sent down." To descend to the ordinary earthly world *(xiafan)* marks the movement of a deity or spirit from the heavens.

"Once Mao took office, he banned religious faith. After he reincarnated as a human, he smashed all the temples, no?"

She is referring to the destruction of religious infrastructure during the antisuperstition campaigns of the Maoist era, commonly considered among the most violent of modern secularizing policies. Yet, in Xu Liying's rendering, these orders for temple smashing were not given by the earthly party-state, as is usually assumed.

"Heavenly command was given from above, telling him to smash them all, keep none of them. They were filled with demonic spirits!"

With the presence of Mao on earth, harmful spirits vanished, Xu Liying explains. But with his death and the advent of economic reform, thousands upon thousands of ghosts, along with false, corrupt gods, swarmed back into the scene.

"This god, that goddess, all from a fake family . . . swindling people, extorting people, duping people, deluding people." This, according to Xu Liying, is why there are so many people in the psychiatric ward today. "You cannot see [the spirits], you cannot touch them, and you wind up in the hospital."

Mao was sent in a moment of crisis, Xu Liying continues, when China was on the brink of destruction at the hands of foreign powers. Now, decades after what she feels to be his premature death, she continues toiling for the revolution, culling

1

away demonic spirits, one by one. "The Southern Heavens, the Northern Heavens, the Middle Heavens, they have all been corrupted!"

According to Xu Liying, given the severity of moral decay today, across heaven and earth, the human race is headed toward an end time, toward a world aflame. Upon the arrival of this apocalypse, those living at the edges of the world will be burned and annihilated, trimmed like the outer branches of a large tree. This periphery Xu Liying speaks of is associated with foreign nations—the United States and Japan in particular, given their participation in invasions.

China, on the contrary, stands at the center of the universe, the root of the tree, and thus will be the last to be demolished. Henan Province, the heart of the Central Plain region, stands at the center of China. Hexian, in the middle of Henan, is thus the very center of the center—the *guodi*, the pot bottom.[1] Given this, Xu Liying says, this region will be the place from which the last humans will be chosen, and, even within the county, only the few virtuous ones will be kept.

As the rice gets flung out of the edges of the pot, the bottom of the pot will be where the rice sticks and remains.

Only after this burning and culling of the world, she explains, will the revolution reach its aim—that of true socialism.

SPECTRALIZATION OF THE RURAL

Despite variations on divine details, spirit mediums who frequented Fuxi Temple in Hexian agree: it was upon Chairman Mao's death that the ghosts returned to haunt. Just across the road, in the psychiatric unit of the People's Hospital, patients lament accursed lives, tracing etiological paths through tales of dispossession, kinship, and betrayal. South from the hospital, a Sinopec gas station sits atop what was once known as the "ten-thousand-man pit" *(wanrenkeng)*, where bodies of the poor and the treacherous were flung, throughout decades of famine and revolution. This is a story of stories, a story after too many stories have been told, a story told when no one believes in stories anymore—not the anthropologist, not the reader, not those they meet in person or in text. It is in the movements between these scenes of doubt and distrust, one reading the other, that the words here take place.[2]

The story here is set in a time. It is a time, I was told, when villagers feasted day to day beyond the wildest imaginations of Maoist cadres past, a time when money could buy anything and everything. Yet, in spite of the general sense that rural living conditions in Hexian have vastly improved since the economic reform era, it is also a time when the village was "still" the village, and the future was yet again elsewhere.

Soon after my arrival in Hexian, during a chance encounter on the street, an elderly man advised me without provocation: "Young one, hurry up and leave this place. There is nothing for you here. There *is* nothing here. This place is poor, and poor places are *lai*—amoral, unreliable, deceitful. All our young people go to the

South. You'd better head south too. Hurry." The South he evoked was that of south-ern China, particularly the cities of Shenzhen, Dongguan, and Guangzhou, where many youths from Hexian, and Henan Province more broadly, migrated for work. What was it about this time that made this place a space of impossibility, a place from which future generations must so urgently flee?

What was it, in turn, to remain?

. . .

Once part of the "cradle of Chinese civilization" and the center of the cosmopoliti-cal universe, the landlocked, heavily agricultural province of Henan has been recast through a spatial-temporal mapping of those "left behind" in a contempo-rary geography of value. Now, in place of a civilizational center, Henan is more potent in the national imaginary as a land of poverty, backwardness, charlatans, and thieves, evocative of the famines of the 1940s and 1950s under Nationalist and Maoist rule, and of the HIV scandal of the 1990s, when villagers contracted the virus from blood plasma sales for cash.

Drawing on Marx's account of capital's ghostly, vampiric qualities, Ann Anag-nost writes of this blood economy as an effect of the "spectralization of the rural" after the reform era, in which value was drained from the bodies of peasants by state discourse and policy, rendering the rural an evacuated space (2006, 513).[3] In this book I approach the cosmological accounts of spirit mediums in Hexian to provide another rendering of this spectralization, in which ghostly presences swirl amid the hollow of an emptied center, producing a different sense of the "post" Mao.

While images of abjection color Henan from without, and in another way from within, those I met from Hexian also speak with pride of their hometown and home province, of the significance of its lengthy history and the sense of divine regional protection provided by the Fuxi Temple in the county seat. They were the proud, loyal soldiers and supporters of Mao's revolution, capable of enduring the bitterness of war and famine in service of the nation.

Those who return from distant cities reminisce upon sight of the soft, yellow soil—soil of their childhood foods, soil of China's breadbasket. Wedding feasts abound week after week, with heaping tables lining alleyways and filling restau-rants. Expansive two- and three-story houses multiply in village after village. Paved roads increasingly cut across fields of wheat. In the center of the county seat, a large, gleaming mall and hotel, myriad businesses, and new high-rise apartments together create the feeling of a small urban skyline at night. Hexian thus partakes in the widespread rise of postreform rural urbanization, in which distinctions between city and village are mutually blurring (Guldin 1997; Kipnis 2016).

Yet, despite the growing abundance residents have felt since the 1990s and the first decade of the 2000s, there is still a sense of scarcity in local employment oppor-tunities and of underemployment for those with higher educational attainment or forms of aspiration driven by metropolitan imaginaries. Amid a "politics of desti-nation" in which power is marked by upward and outward movement, departure seems ever the horizon in such places as Hexian, particularly for the working age (Chu 2010; X. Liu 1997). In 2012, when I first arrived in Hexian, China's urban pop-ulation at large, for the first time, had become equal to and began to surpass the rural. Within Hexian that year, over three-quarters of the residents were formally categorized as rural. Yet it was extremely common for one or more members of the family to be living and working away from Hexian for part or all of the year.

With low selling prices of agricultural products and rising costs of agricultural production (not to mention the rising cost of living), most I met in Hexian con-sider a life of sole small-scale farming on their allocated plots unsustainable. Within a given family it is common for several of the working age to depart, some returning seasonally to help tend to their family plots, some commissioning neigh-bors and kin to work their land while they are away. The sense of hollowing amid outmigration thus sets the scene for the questions of madness and possession I address here and what it means to stay (Scheper-Hughes 2001). Approaching con-temporary rural China through its hauntings, this book asks, as Jacques Derrida (1994) does in *Specters of Marx*, albeit through the languages and rituals of medi-umship: what ghostly forms remain of socialist visions after the "collapse"?

AFTER CHAIRMAN MAO'S REIGN

A Time of Lost Gods draws on a year of research in 2012–13, and again in 2018, in the county seat and surrounding villages of what I call Hexian, especially across the Fuxi Temple, the county People's Hospital, and the home altars of spirit medi-ums. It also recalls some of my encounters elsewhere in China, to bring forth imaginaries shaping such places as Hexian from without. The chapters that follow pivot around a set of tensions, between a reconstituted rurality and an ambivalent urbanity, a mournful psychiatry and a shaken cosmology.

These tensions come in a time marked by a certain "afterwardsness," with rela-tion to what those in Hexian call "the time when Chairman Mao reigned."[4] The phrase takes on a doubled character in this book. A commonplace saying, "the time when Chairman Mao reigned" is the setting for wistful tales of a more fair and virtuous time. Among those who engage in spirit mediumship, it also speaks to an otherworldly temporality, an exceptional interval of divine sovereignty, after which the cosmos collapsed into chaos. This book is an attempt to convey what it is to experience the present as a postscript to such an interval.

At the same time, among those I spoke with during my time there, there is a sense that the new world—the promised world of the socialist vision—has yet to arrive, across waves of policies that have pledged to improve the rural lot. Out of this there emerges a matter-of-fact sensibility of self-preserving cynicism, in parallel with obstinate if fragile visions of a pristine era to come. The present thus feels caught between what could have been and what still might be.

The twofold significance of the Chairman's reign gestures more broadly toward what I call a cosmic or spectral doubling: the capacity for manifest phenomena—words, images, things, persons, occurrences—to carry force and significance across (at least) two realms. As Xu Liying's account suggests, earthly manifestations—nation-states, psychiatric disorders, revolutions—do not abide by secular divisions of the this-worldly and otherworldly, religious and nonreligious.

For those who engage in mediumship in Hexian—and I elaborate on what I mean by *mediumship* later—the world is often spoken of through several sets of relations and contrasts. Here I simplify to offer a general sketch—a cosmography for the sake of orientation. There are the yin and yang realms: *yinjian* and *yangjian*. The yin realm is the world of spirits usually imperceptible to humans, including ghosts of deceased humans, deities, animal spirits, and others (but since the yin can connote the negative, true deities are often evoked through other terms). The yang realm—often used interchangeably with the "human realm" *(renjian)*—is the world of the living and visible. When humans pass from the living world to the world of the dead, for instance, they are said to move from their yang house *(yangzhai)* to their yin house *(yinzhai)* of the grave. While living humans in the yang realm are present through their own material bodies, invisible personae in the yin realm often need to occupy material presences in the yang realm to produce material effects—possess a human person to verbally convey a message or physically harm another, for instance. Conversely, certain manifest phenomena and materials afford techniques for living humans to affect the invisible yin realm—the burning of a paper body as a substitute for a human body at risk for harm, the burying of scissors to "cut" the lives of passersby, or, most commonly, the burning of paper money and goods as gifts and payments to those in the yin world.

Then there is the division between heaven *(tian)* and earth *(di)*, at times articulated in terms of a tripartite heavenly plate *(tianpan)*, earthly plate *(dipan)*, and human plate *(renpan)*. The heavenly is often simply referred to as "the above" *(shangmiande)*—the site from which divine commands are issued and deities, Buddhas, and bodhisattvas descend and watch over the human realm. While those from the heavenly realm can be included in the broader category of the yin world, ghosts and other more negative yin entities are less likely to be evoked by the "heavenly." Like other entities of the yin realm, those from the heavens need to deploy material means to produce effects in the visible world. They may, for instance, "borrow" human bodies, be "invited" into statues, and infuse symbolic words and things to transmit their signals. In the heaven-earth distinction, the "earthly" can refer to the world of the materially manifest, and, especially in the tripartite division of heavenly, earthly, and humanly, it can also speak to the underworld of the courts of hell. Meanwhile, the human stands between heaven and earth, where the world unfolds.

The notions of yin and yang and the heavenly, earthly, and humanly have been broadly used concepts across various Chinese contexts. There are therefore many shared terms between the conceptual and experiential vocabulary of contemporary mediumship and intellectual, medical, and religious traditions across time and space, although the semantic, contextual, argumentative, and efficacious fields they have operated in vary widely. The early Chinese compilation *Huainanzi*, for instance, describes the separation of heaven and earth from the ascending and descending of qi—which has been translated as pneuma, vital energy, material force, or simply air—paired with the splitting of yin and yang. The yin and yang then gave rise to the four seasons, and the four seasons gave rise to seasonal time and the "ten thousand things" *(wanwu)*. This characterization of the cosmos was evoked across the centuries for various aims and was itself a response to debates in its own time (Puett 2004). In such early texts as the *Yijing* (commonly known in the West as the *I Ching* or the *Book of Changes*), the threefold division of heaven, earth, and human map onto celestial and earthly calculation and divination systems, linking constellations and elements to spatiotemporal coordinates of human birth to bodily parts. Such concepts were taken up across Confucian, Buddhist, and Daoist thinking across time, often as mutually intertwined traditions, not always as fully distinct schools (Csikszentmihalyi 2006; Major 1993). The continuous, dynamic interplay between yin and yang, heaven and earth, would be elaborated in texts on Chinese medicine, statecraft, aesthetics, and beyond, and would find many contemporary articulations (Farquhar and Zhang 2012; Jullien 1995; Zhan 2016), including those that do not dwell on or that explicitly reject the world of ghosts and spirits.

In Hexian personae and forces from heavenly and yin worlds—deities, ghosts, and other spirits—are together described as that which "cannot be seen or felt" *(kanbujian mobuzhao)*. While they at times reside in distinct spatial realms, they also share the manifest geography of living humans, variously inhabiting the visible world. I thus use *doubling* as shorthand across these multiple sets of divisions, referring to the potentiality for any seen and felt person, place, thing, or action to simultaneously host that which cannot be seen or felt. Throughout the chapters, when not using the original Chinese terms, I use *cosmic* and occasionally *divine* when evoking the more heavenly and benevolent aspects of the unseen world; *spectral* and occasionally *demonic* when attending to the more ghostly, withdrawn, or harmful dimensions; and *otherworldly* to refer to the unseen, intangible world at large. These are used descriptively to convey rather than categorically to define, as these aspects grow slippery in the cosmic accounts of the times.

While I use these terms to render ideas and scenes more easily imaginable to those unfamiliar with such worlds, it is important to recall the risks of such ease, as the lived conceptual world they are used to describe here differs from their English connotations. In spite of apparent similarities in the contrasts between the higher and lower, visible and invisible, divine and demonic, and material and immaterial—and unlike the stronger divide connoted by the this-worldly and oth-erworldly in, for instance, Protestant and Protestant-inflected strands of thought—the yin and yang, heavenly and earthly, cosmic and technic are not so ontologically split and morally divided (Hall and Ames 1995; Hui 2016). They are in constant flux, one mirroring the other, one transforming through and into the other, in myriad ways.

On the smaller scale of time, the benevolent and the corrupt, the godly and the ghostly, have become dangerously blurred after Chairman Mao's death in the con-temporary cosmology. On a lengthier scale gods have been corruptible and ghosts relatable far beyond the modern political era, and boundaries between the so-called natural and supernatural throughout Chinese mythical and medical tradi-tions have been famously debatable. These and related differences have been vari-ously marked in studies of China and Chinese worlds through such terms as *acosmotic, correlative cosmology, holistic, dialectical,* and *analogical.*[5] I try to attend to relevant distinctions as they arise, and I pay the price, so to speak, of associative slippage for the sake of building a momentary shared imaginary.

With a similar risk, I use the word *cosmology* as a bridge between questions raised through China and recent debates raised through scenes elsewhere and to convey that which has its own account of the visible and invisible world. But, given the precarious, disorderly status of the cosmos as described by mediums in He-xian, I do not assume the connoted opposition between cosmos and chaos, which, in this instance as well as in others, are very much copresent (Puett 2014).[6]

Alongside the crossing of visible and invisible realms, cosmic or spectral dou-bling also creates links across scales of time. Through the copresence of yin and yang realms on a shared geographic plane, the temporal limits posed to the living—what may be thought of as lifespan—meet with operations grafted onto longer temporal stretches, some reaching asymptotically toward spans so long they are nearly indistinguishable from eternity. In the language of ghosts, gods, and immortals more resonant with Daoist repertoires, human souls *(hun)* are said to continue their existence after death.[7] But lacking proper cultivation or other destination, the unbodied soul continues to dwell on earth among the living as a ghost, carrying its decades or centuries of invisible existence with it. With proper cultivation the unbodied soul might gradually reach the status of a god, over a course of hundreds or thousands of years. Gods, who see human history from a much higher and longer vantage point, may look on and live a life of ease from a distance or choose to get involved in the plight of earthly affairs.

Intertwined and partially fused with these are also concepts more resonant with Chinese Buddhism. Veering from yet overlapping with Daoist forms of immortal-ity, these ideas turn toward the cycling of lives through reincarnation and karmic notions of merit accumulation, which combine with Daoist and Confucian notions of virtue and self-cultivation. Moreover, through such historically combinatory traditions as those surrounding the Eternal Mother (Wusheng Laomu) and the future Buddha Maitreya, discussed later, the temporal question of Chairman Mao as a figure of virtue and cosmic sovereignty is drawn into Chinese Buddhist kalpic and eschatological time. To evoke the cosmic doubling of Mao and the socialist state, then, is to indicate travels not only between present human and ghostly worlds but also between immense scales of time. Earthly political imaginaries of "five-year plans" and the "postreform era" are swallowed into *kalpas* stretching forward and back, to upward of tens of thousands of years. The revolution to come, as anticipated by mediums such as Xu Liying, may thus arrive tomorrow, next month, next year, or far beyond one's earthly lifetime.

CULTURE, AFTERMATH

While I evoke various sources of what might be called Chinese tradition, the centrality of Mao in the contemporary cosmology and the not-quite-legal status of mediumship also point to predicaments of sovereignty and symbolic elaboration in encounters with what might be called modernity. At the turn of the twentieth century, following the Opium Wars with the British, China, as a political and cultural entity, seemed to be gasping for survival. Faced with escalating military threats and peppered with foreign-occupied concessions—among them British, Japanese, French, Portuguese, Russian, German, Austro-Hungarian, Belgian, and Italian—what it would take to claim a place in world history, rather than be demolished by it, came to be an inescapable question. While the result of this historical moment was not full formal colonization, the status of culture and tradition came to be haunted by what early twentieth-century intellectuals, including Mao, termed China's semicolonialism or hypocolonialism.[8]

Sun Yat-sen, founder of the Republic of China, writes, "China is the colony of every nation that has made treaties with her, and the treaty-making nations are her masters. China is not the colony of one nation, but of all; she is not a semicolony, but a hypocolony" (cited in E. Lee 1930). Following Lenin's usage of semicolonialism as a passage either to full colonization or revolutionary independence through national sovereignty, Chinese Communist thinkers of the 1930s often characterized semicolonialism as a transitional state of partial autonomy, limited by unequal treaties and territorial concessions. Building on these, Mao deployed semicolonialism as a call for revolutionary tactics against imperialist powers, aimed at conflicts of shifting spatial and temporal scales (Karl 2017).

Entrapped by unequal treaties and tormented by a sense of national and cultural humiliation, a range of exasperated answers emerged in China—iconoclastic denouncements of tradition as superstition, chauvinistic defenses of nationalism, and urgent assertions of cultural essence. Maoism itself, some have suggested, also arose as one response, at once of and against semicolonial conditions. Through its incomplete and fragmentary forms, such conditions "sanctioned a degree of cultural colonization that was self-imposed," after which "culture . . . was neither readily established nor available as an untainted and untroubled sanctuary" (Shih 2001, 36–37).

Given the reverberations of this sense of interruption and reorientation, I consider the contemporary cosmology in Hexian not through rubrics of tradition and modernity but through what Stefania Pandolfo (2018) calls the "aftermath of culture," in which culture after colonial encounter comes, as Frantz Fanon (2008) puts it, to testify against its members. Yet this very site of devastation, Pandolfo suggests, offers potential grounds for transformation and spiritual encounter, and such transformation is at times reactivated precisely through imaginations of the beyond of human time.

To evoke themes of invasion and humiliation is not to presume the cultural as previously apolitical or unchanging or to sit contented with a so-called impact-response model of Chinese history. The very claim to the unity of China and of a Han ethnic majority by the Chinese state—before, during, and after Maoism—has been (and continues to be) produced through often violent demands for submission and varying degrees of assimilation, as well as civilizational discourses against barbaric others. And, as some have suggested, excessive gravity needs not be given to the role of the West when Chinese debates are centered elsewhere.[9]

Rather, to approach culture in and as aftermath helps elucidate the significance of a Maoism-inflected cosmology beyond more predictable responses of paradox, amusement, and surprise, produced through the conceptual tension provided by the bifurcation of religion and secularity, tradition and modernity. If classic anthropological accounts of symbolic efficacy relied in part on notions of a coherent wholeness of a symbolic system, the rupture and fragmentation of a "traditional" symbolic system by modern interruption would presumably rob the symbol of its efficacy, given its dislocation. In this, the symbol would no longer be able to act as a pivot between visible and invisible worlds. Yet cosmic doubling here points in part to the capacity of such pivotal operations to be activated by persons and things, words and images, beyond limits imposed by categories of tradition and modernity, religion and secularity. If the efficacy of such pivots is not assumed to rely on the wholeness or closedness of the system within which it is situated, then what could constitute an efficacious operator reaches far beyond what would customarily be located within a given tradition.

Recognizing a painful rupture to traditions of thought, in this sense, is not antithetical to taking seriously ongoing engagements with a cultural repertoire, as the cultural is loosened from assumptions of its qualities as an immobile, unbroken, closed system, and fragmentation is no longer assumed to be characteristic only of the modern or postmodern. Instead, attention to the aftermath of culture allows us to address how "culture" in the historical present is not simply an anachronistic concept but seethes in its simultaneous transmission of efficacious potential and tormenting attacks—from within and without. Here it is from these very pained sites and languages that the pivot between visible and invisible worlds might be foreclosed but also activated.

This precarious sense of possibility and impossibility is seen in the present yet withdrawn status of Mao in the contemporary cosmology. The mediums' accounts of the partial yet deferred possibility of fully exorcising harmful spirits in his absence point to a sense of incompletion with relation to efficaciousness. The cosmology thus gestures at once to openings and closures experienced in the present, tied to historical figures and movements of emancipation and domination. To attend to questions of aftermath, then, is to traverse the vicissitudes of aggression, which give force to renewed productions of internal exile—including the repeated exclusions of such figures as the spirit medium and the rural inhabitant. Those I met in Hexian inherit and offer their own responses to the stakes of this ongoing history, but not in any simple sense.

While this text is often elaborated in terms of conversations and debates on China, the questions it raises are concerns of the contemporary, of disparate worlds that nonetheless share certain dilemmas in their myriad manifestations, each pointing to a *here-else* beyond what can be grasped solely in terms of locality (Collu 2019). They are reverberations across concentric circles of violence, the resulting timbre of which carries both staid and surprising qualities. They are the enigmas of madness, which mark at once the impossibility of being and its very condition. They are dealings with the tired yet nagging problem of modernity, against whose image the (mis)recognition of many continue to be posited, the only grid through which many can appear, through their very disappearance. They are the oddities of representation, of the structuring forces of language and other mediums, and the ways things fall into and out of them. They are disappointments and horrors toward grand plans of the twentieth century and hopes that linger nevertheless.

In attempting to address these concerns through themes of mediumship, madness, and haunting, I have come to approach the person in part as a psychic-corporeal host to a meeting of temporalities—an individuation premised on cosmohistorical movements and collisions. To say this is not to define the person external to other terms, but to articulate the sensibility that allows me to hear resonances across disparate registers—the human body occupied by or dislodged of gods, ghosts, and souls in mediumship; parents and children caught amid intergenerational impasses in the clinic; and formulations of the subject in anthropology, philosophy, psychoanalysis, and China studies.

Such cosmohistorical encounters are mediated at various scales of personhood and collectivity. In this text they range from the singularity of symptoms to tales across families and villages, rural and urban, Hexian, Henan Province, China, the world historical, and beyond. And, in the case of Chairman Mao and the contemporary cosmology, the very movement between scales, figural positions, and symbolic orders seems to gather and intensify a certain potency. It is with this in mind that I turn to these figures and stories, both grand and minute.

THE STATUE

In December 2015 a 120-foot-tall golden statue of Mao was built in a village in Henan's Tongxu County. Its appearance led to a wave of amusement and ridicule across Chinese social media, regarding the poor degree of resemblance to the Chairman and the splurge of financial resources—reportedly around Chinese RMB 3 million (more than USD 450,000)—resources that, it was said, could have been better spent for social purposes such as local education. Chinese online commentators also offered angry reminders that Henan Province was among the hardest hit during the Great Leap famine in the late 1950s, considered an effect of catastrophic Maoist policies.

While the statue also received some bemused international media attention to the curious juxtaposition of the figurehead of Chinese Communism funded mainly by what they called "private entrepreneurs," it was what occurred next that propelled its full circulation: the statue was demolished at the instruction of local government soon after it was built, in a visually violent manner reminiscent of the destruction of religious icons during the Cultural Revolution. The Chairman's hands, legs, and feet were severed, and black fabric was draped over his head by a crane. State officials cited the lack of compliance with formal approval processes as reason for removal. Bemusement quickly turned to implicit critiques of government suppression and overreaction.

The subtexts undergirding the range of responses rang familiar. On the Anglophone front, they homed in on the ever-befuddling paradox of what the Chinese state calls socialism with Chinese characteristics, alongside easily renewed curiosities toward an "oriental despotism" (Wittfogel 1957). Chinese media and social media invoked modern antisuperstition as well as classic Confucian exhortations against the excesses of ritual expenditure. Their distaste echoed the Chinese intellectual discourse of the 1980s, which accused the peasantry of proneness to mob action and the blind following of a cult of personality, culminating in their blame for the violence of the Cultural Revolution. They also posited a certain irony, of a rural oblivion to the origin of the very historical catastrophes that struck them.

Less frequently mentioned across these accounts, perhaps owing to its dissonance with the paired motifs of rural irrationality and authoritarian terror, as well as the seemingly constitutive opposition of the Communist and the (properly) religious (Ngo and Quijada 2015), was the potential moral—not to mention cosmological—significance of the statue that may have brought it into existence and led indirectly to its desecration. A partial exception came from Liu Jianwu, dean of the Mao Zedong Research Center, who commented to the *Guardian,* "In the hearts of ordinary people, Mao represents fairness and justice." Careful to bracket further implications, Liu denied any political significance to the statue: "This doesn't exist." No possible ritual-religious dimension was touched on. But a degree of unease and forewarning was appended: "There is no need to build such a big statue, and I do not suggest people imitate this" (T. Phillips 2016).

The incident brings to surface a set of tensions undergirding the contemporary cosmology in Hexian. Since the economic reform era, Mao and Maoist policies had undergone waves of official denouncement, and the state today no longer relies as strongly on Mao's image for legitimacy. At the same time it seems that Mao had come to stand in for a certain difference and excess, prompting the nervous system of the party-state to erase an unauthorized monument to its own founding figure (Taussig 1991).

In partial continuation of more overtly violent destructions of local temples and icons during the Maoist era, the postreform state wavers between support of popular religious renewal and intermittent sweeps against so-called feudal superstition. It is a "politics of ritual displacement" through which the state repeatedly enacts its self-representation in a struggle of symbolic orders, while attempting to usurp a certain surplus value produced in community ritual practice (Anagnost 1994, 222). Yet in this instance the displaced symbolic order could not so easily be considered a localized externality to the state, as the state engulfed its own founding image in its demonstration of power. And although the precise reasoning and chain of events that led to the dismantling of the statue have yet to surface in full form, the enigma of the incident and the commentaries proliferating around it spoke to the ambivalence clustering around the figure of the Chairman.

Unlike the towering, if short-lived, presence of Mao's statue in Tongxu County, no major icon is dedicated to Mao at or near Fuxi Temple in Hexian at the time of my visit. Instead, the absent presence of the Chairman is manifest through recirculations of his words and images on the expansive temple square—pins and badges, drawings and posters, People's Liberation Army uniforms, poems, slogans. The passing appearances of such unofficial monuments raise questions of memory, mourning, and desire, as well as the never-quite-dead times of the gods amid secular historical time (Chakrabarty 1997; Winter 2014).

By many academic and media accounts, the Maoist era had been an age of religious repression and the post-Mao economic reform era a time of religious revival. In such accounts the Maoist years mark an apex of modern secularizing efforts, intensifying the antisuperstition campaigns of its Republican-era predecessors, culminating in the banning of religion during the Cultural Revolution (1966–76). Yet spirit mediums like Xu Liying offer a different account of the historical present. For the mediums the end of Mao's reign and the advent of market reforms did not mark a return of *religion* but a return of *spirits*—corrupt, duplicitous spirits by and large. Conversely, Maoist campaigns against religion, as Xu Liying puts it, were a matter of righteous, heavenly command, and the appearance of Mao on earth itself marks a reincarnation determined by otherworldly forces. The purportedly antireligious campaigns of the socialist state, for the mediums, constitute cryptic acts of divine intervention—acts inaugurated by otherworldly forces that allowed the earthly state to misrecognize itself as secular.

While many have pointed to the quasi-religious quality of the so-called Mao cult during his lifetime, it has often been distinguished from religion proper due in part to Maoism's explicit antireligious stance and policies. Posthumous circulations of Maoist iconography have also been said by some to be devoid of truly religious dimensions, even if ritualistic (Barmé 1996; Feuchtwang 2001; Leese 2011). While such distinctions may hold in some contexts of circulation, it seems that Mao's spirited presence in post-Mao ritual worlds might also be more widespread than previously thought, if perhaps scattered. Diane Dorfman (1996) relays similar accounts as the ones I write of here, regarding the banishment of (especially animal) spirits under Mao and their resurfacing after Deng by those in a rural county near Beijing. As in Hexian, the role of Mao there was articulated at the conjunction of peasantry and morality, against Deng as a figure of corruption. Koen Wellens describes a Premi interlocutor in Yunnan who responded to the question of ritual during the Cultural Revolution: "They told us there were no evil ghosts, so performing [this ritual] was not necessary, and, anyway, we thought that if there were evil ghosts, Chairman Mao would protect us" (2010, 11). Daniel Overmyer mentions hearing of possession by Mao in passing, among a list of other deities, in Henan (2009, 116). Liu Yongsi describes finding older women in rural Guangdong dressed in Red Guard uniforms performing revolutionary songs at temple festivals (qtd. in Goossaert and Palmer 2011).

There are also those who find Mao's presence in ritual contexts without a sense of his spiritual potency. Adam Yuet Chau notes the presence of temple-like structures dedicated to Mao, Zhou Enlai, and Zhu De in Shaanbei but writes that he "did not get the feeling that these were established and popular cults, but rather an effort to lend legitimacy to other popular religious temples" (2003, 50–51). Emily Chao (1999) describes a failed attempt to incorporate Mao and other Communist Party leaders in a post-Mao ritual in Yunnan, with its dismissal by the community signifying the incapacity of Mao to occupy a religious position. There are thus multiple ways of engaging figures and icons of Mao and the Party in ritual contexts.

In Hexian I had set out with a general wish to learn about mediumship and came to understand Mao's centrality in the cosmological accounts there after I arrived. This book is an attempt to sound out his significance to those I met, at times directly and at times through detours. In contrast to the irreverence toward Mao that Chao (1999) found in Yunnan, in Hexian the Chairman is central to the spirit mediums' accounts. The contemporary cosmos is elaborated around a mournful relation to the lost Chairman, who looks on from afar, watching over the dissolution of the world. Yet his absent presence also animates the "now" in the wake of loss, reinaugurating Henan and Hexian as a cosmopolitical center.

As Katherine Verdery suggests of Eastern Europe and the former Soviet Union, postsocialist politics move beyond novel forms of rationalistic government toward matters of "cosmic" concern, insofar as they involve a profound reordering of universes (1999, 125). Such cosmic reordering can be seen in transformations of ritual in the wake of violence across Vietnam, Mongolia, Siberia, and non-Han communities in southwest China (Bernstein 2013; Buyandelger 2013; Kwon 2008; Mueggler 2001; Pedersen 2011). Of peculiar force as well in socialist and postsocialist worlds is the "corpse-qua-symbol" of dead bodies (Verdery 1999, 52), including figures of sovereignty who continue to occupy a position of exception in the wake of their passing—Lenin (Yurchak 2015), Kim Il Sung (Ryang 2012), Ho Chi Minh (Ngo 2019), and, as I suggest of Hexian, Mao.

Between spatial claims to sovereignty modeled on the nation-state and temporal claims to sovereignty through class struggle across dreamworlds and catastrophes of the twentieth century (Buck-Morss 2002), the impossible presence and promise of the sovereign have made way for new horizons of anticipation in their collapse, both driven and afflicted by the very sense of impossibility. While Mao's theory of sovereignty might be fraught with contradictions alongside other articulations of the Chinese socialist state (Howland 2010), what interests me here is less the validity of such formulations than the spectral reappearance of the Chairman, which might be thought of on the order of the sovereign presence as miracle—"impossible, yet there it is" (Bataille 1993, 206; Song 2013, 316).

In this I am thinking alongside several works on North Korea: Sonia Ryang's (2012) on the "sovereign self," in which the leader is a direct manifestation of one's own higher self, and Hoon Song's (2016) on a "sovereign faciality" that lends its own embodied presence to the historical gap and promise of a (Marxist) knowledge to come. While the contexts and precise manifestations are distinct, these dimensions of sovereignty resonate here. In China the intensification of a sovereign selfhood and presence was enacted in part through Maoist storytelling practices and campaigns, in which a *cosmocratic mythologic* "telescoped" across scales big and small, fusing and mutually intensifying individual suffering, national history, and world history, "until Mao virtually fills the entire field of vision" (Apter and Saich 1998, 71).

I turn to the notion of sovereignty and its filling of vision to consider not the illegitimacy of autocratic rule as portrayed from the stance of liberalist (or nonliberalist) critique but the curious position of the sovereign, who stands at once outside and within the normative order, awakening under *exceptional* conditions of urgent necessity—here, threats and imaginations of China's very demise—in a secularized theological rendition of the miracle (Schmitt 2006), which, in this case, is redoubled cosmologically. Beyond a political theology at play in secular statecraft, slogans and iconography of the Chinese Communist Party provided dwelling for spectral power, redoubled as operators of cosmic force. If the souls of the dead in China have been said to be "transitional" by some, from what Philippe Descola (2013) calls an "analogist ontology" to an increasingly modern "naturalist" one (Kipnis 2017, 218), I consider instead how the living are deployed by a spectral polity sharing a symbolic repertoire with the earthly modern state. Socialist images and slogans come to make way for redistributions of the sensible (Rancière 2004), presencing an otherwise imperceptible world in the naturalist ontology of the secular party-state.

THE SOVEREIGN, THE GHOST, AND THE MEDIUM

Rather than the triad of gods, ghosts, and ancestors more common in approaches to Chinese popular religion (e.g., Jordan 1972; A. Wolf 1974), my thinking on the cosmology in Hexian pivots more often around the cast of the sovereign (the Chairman), the ghost, and the medium. This is not to say that the classic triad holds no relevance there but to reset the characters and shift the field of vision toward the present. I turn to the figure of the sovereign in part because Maoist articulations of revolution through an anti-imperialist principle of territorial sovereignty figure centrally in the cosmological accounts of the mediums. Alongside the acute sensitivity and knack for tactical evasions cultivated in the violent legacy of sovereign power (Farquhar and Zhang 2005), there also prevail ritual enunciations of longing for the return of the sovereign as a cosmopolitical figure. For mediums like Xu Liying, the Communist Revolution is not simply a worldly affair, and the desire to occupy that drives the imperialist enterprise cannot be understood without the demonic dimension of evil. In his descent into earthly form, the mediums say, Mao's revolution was an act of salvation in the face of crisis, in a moment when China was under threat of foreign occupation.

Moreover, accounts of the momentary vanishing of all spirits (gods included) during Mao's reign, the incapacity of post-Mao gods to similarly suppress dangerous spirits after his death, and longings for Mao's return together point to the Chairman's exceptional sovereign status in the contemporary cosmology. Although himself an instrument of larger heavenly schemes and although situated in cosmic alliance with other Buddhist, Daoist, and regional figures, in Hexian Mao's role in recent cosmic history seems beyond just one god among others. If the Chairman was once the sovereign guarantor of the existence of China and its People, keeping demonic spirits at bay, the death of the Chairman brought with it a time of ghosts.

Historically, the figure of the ghost has sat uneasy across writings of the Chinese elite and ruling classes. While the ghost, as the continued presence of the soul of the dead, implicitly forms the very basis of ancestor worship at the core of orthodox paternal filiation, the heterodox dimensions potentiated by engagements with the supernatural and the proliferation of ritual forms have provoked a range of responses: the abstraction of spirits into intangibility, the suggestion of respectful distance from ghosts and spirits, and official disapproval of excess in popular practices of mortuary ritual (Poo 1998). Beyond the ruler's realm, ghosts and spirits of various strains abound in Daoist, Buddhist, medical, and historical texts, as well as genres of the ghost story and anomaly tale; these will be addressed throughout the book. Moreover, works on spectrality, deferral, and intergenerational transmission are ongoing sites of dialogue.

Whereas classic ethnographic distinctions often emphasize the benevolence of one's own deceased ancestors from the often malevolent ghosts of strangers, and the higher position of power and virtue of gods from both ancestors and ghosts (toward which the latter two could eventually cultivate), in a time experienced as devoid of divine sovereign guarantee, gods and ancestors seem to become dangerously ghostlike, in their duplicity and corruptibility. Indeed, old, powerful ghosts and false, corrupt gods share the same name in Hexian: *xian*. The risk of encountering *xian* includes precisely their capacity to masquerade as true, virtuous gods.

Between the (lost) sovereign and the ghostlike spirits that swarmed back upon his death sits the spirit medium, the third figure. Spirit mediums, in both their own accounts and in my rendering, are receptacles and receivers, mediums and mediators of forces and entities across time and space. Crossing the threshold between yin and yang worlds, they mediate histories long and short colliding in the present, and in the case of those who "walk Chairman Mao's path," they work to bring forth a forestalled future to come—what Xu Liying and others have called a "true socialism."

In Hexian there are several terms for those I am translating under the more generic name of *spirit medium*. For those who provide consultation to supplicants regularly at their altars through possession and other forms of guidance by their tutelary spirit(s), the most common term is "those who see (or observe) incense" *(kanxiangde)*.[10] In contrast to the translated term *spirit medium*, the otherworldly entities being engaged with (spirits) go unnamed. In conversation, when a visit to an incense seer is suggested, the object "incense" is also dropped, and one is simply advised to "go find one who knows how to see" *(qu zhao ge huikande)* or, simply, "go see" *(qu kankan)*, softening the "see" *(kan)* with a linguistic reduplication, truncating both the subject and object and leaving only the acts of visitation and viewing, leaving unsaid just what is to be seen and who is doing the seeing. The unseen world is thus also marked by the unspoken.

Another category of those in Hexian who I am including in the term *spirit medium* are "those who walk (or run) for spiritual power/duty/merit" *(zougongde* or *paogongde)* and "those who stand guard for spiritual power/duty/merit" *(shougongde)*—those who might be translated conventionally as temple pilgrims and do not necessarily offer regular consultation to supplicants. Yet walking, running, and guarding, when used in Hexian, often imply not simply a reverence for sacred sites but direct guidance from deities and spirits through possession or other forms of otherworldly communication. Walking and running involve heading to spaces according to the wishes and commands of one's tutelary spirit(s); guarding involves similar otherworldly commands to tend to deities and spirits present at a temple or elsewhere. One's speech, songs, and actions are often said to belong not to oneself but to the spirit(s) being channeled.

These engagements—seeing, walking, running, and guarding—are not mutually exclusive and often overlap, and the latter three in particular are used more in their verb forms indicating action than in noun forms indicating social positions. Moreover, these forms of spiritual work are often seen as linked—many incense seers perform the work of walking and running on behalf of their tutelar deities prior to inaugurating their altar, and many walkers at the temple square have altars at home and may have the capacity to decipher incense but do not regularly receive supplicants. The categories are thus fluid, referring more to one's cosmic task at a given point in life than fixed roles. Relatedly, *yougong* (to have spiritual power/ duty/merit) suggests a spiritual capacity that can potentially be cultivated through such engagements, because of a preexisting relationship with at least one tutelary spirit, a relationship that might remain unknown to oneself until the time is ripe.

In contrast to these more sustained and allocated engagements (one is chosen by deities for these spiritual tasks), the common phrases describing those who become temporarily possessed by ghosts or other risky entities are *zhuangdao dongxi* (to collide into something), *you dongxi* (to have something), and *you dongxi pudao shenshang* (to have something pounce/thrown on one's body). To engage with temple visitation and the consultation of mediums, without necessarily involving the experience of possession, are referred to respectively as burning incense *(shaoxiang)* and going to get one's incense seen *(qu kanxiang)*.

Throughout this text I use *spirit medium* to refer to the first set of engagements—those who regularly receive supplicants at an altar and those who regularly undergo possession at temples and elsewhere without necessarily receiving supplicants, rather than those who are temporarily possessed or those who visit temples and mediums without their own specified cosmic role. This is a loose descriptive distinction rather than a categorical one, as one might shift into more sustained engagements following initial bouts of possession or distance oneself from (or retire entirely from) more continual engagements. The potential of the human body to act as medium to otherworldly forces is pertinent beyond any particular typology, as the extent of engagement remains an open question across one's life (or across one's multiple lives), and even those who think themselves untouched may be affected without their own knowing.

The power of perception, according to mediums, is gifted or borrowed from one's tutelary spirit(s), and the power to affect a given situation, including the power to heal, emanates from the possessing spirit(s), not from the medium. The medium lends *(jie)* a material body through which nonbodied entities can more easily create effects in the material world—they borrow your body *(jie ni shenti)* to act and borrow your mouth *(jie ni zui)* to speak.

Beyond issues of local conceptual mapping, I use the aggregate term *spirit medium* throughout this text for a few reasons. First and most simply, it is the term most often employed in the literature on parallel figures, such as the *tang-ki* of south and southeast China, Taiwan, and Southeast Asia (M. Chan 2006; Jordan 1972; Kleinman 1980) and, variously, the *xiangdao, xiangtou, wupo, shenhan, mapi,* and other figures in North China (Chau 2006; T. DuBois 2005; Overmyer 2009); though there are also others who use *shaman*, at times interchangeably with *spirit medium* (Chao 1999; M. Wolf 1990).

Second, in the now-classic accounts and debates of Mircea Eliade (1964) and I. M. Lewis (1971), the contended distinction between the shaman and the medium pivot around the theme of mastery over the spirits. The shaman, for Eliade, ascends in a movement of pride to join the ranks of the gods in the celestial journey, whereas the medium receives the descent and incarnation of gods upon the human. Lewis considers this typological bifurcation untenable, suggesting that the shaman can also act as a receptacle for possessing spirits. The contrast, for him, is not categorical but one of a degree of mastery—the shaman is a medium who has mastered the capacity for *controlled* spirit possession, whereas a medium is one who might be regularly possessed but does not always control their possessions. Thus, for Lewis, "all shamans are thus mediums. . . . It does not follow, of course, that all mediums are necessarily shamans. . . . Not all such mediums are likely to graduate in time to become controllers of spirits" (1971, 49–50).

In Hexian it is rare for mediums to suggest a mastery over their possessing spirits. Moreover, to claim equality with or identity as the deity is seen as a danger- ous sign of falsity, in the sense of feigned possession or of possession by demonic entities masquerading as deities. This is not to say that mediumship, particularly in the case of those who receive supplicants, does not require some command over the timing and conditions of possession—there is a "shamanistic" dimension of mastery involved, so to speak. But since the language for the capacity to contain possession comes in the form of lending on the part of the deity, the human gift of otherworldly perception and action is considered temporarily granted and may always be revoked at the displeasure of the deity or the breaching of the pact. Thus, I use *spirit medium* to connote the sense and language of nonmastery central to those I encountered in Hexian, in which the human does not reign *(bu dangjia)*.

Third, spirit mediumship is distinguished here from fortune-telling and divining, even though there are some mediums who also partake in them. Fortune-tellers and diviners I met in Hexian, particularly those who "calculate hexagrams" *(suangua),* do not usually engage in possession and tend to accuse spirit mediumship of being a false and baseless form, in contrast to trigram reading and divination techniques (such as *qian* oracle slips), which ground their authority on textual traditions drawing on the *Book of Changes*. Conversely, many spirit mediums dismiss fortune-tellers as those who merely memorize passages from a text they do not have the capacity to understand, particularly without direct relationship with and assistance from the spirit world. Perhaps not incidentally, spirit mediums in Hexian are more varied in gender distribution, while fortune-tellers are more likely to be men, marking a gendered tendency (but not absolute division) between oral and textual traditions.

Finally, the translated term *mediumship* evokes the question of mediation and what it might mean to be medium and mediator to inherited histories. Stigmatized for their nonscholarly professionalism and feared for their potential threat to imperial legitimacy throughout much of Chinese dynastic history, spirit mediums nonetheless shared much of the "orthodox" imperial cosmology and were consulted by elites even while at times being decried by them. Prior to their full modern denunciation, such figures mediated between Confucian, Buddhist, and Daoist versions of reality and between humans and the cosmos (R. Smith 1993). Written out of official state-sanctioned versions of Chinese religion and medicine under the modern governance of Republican and Maoist regimes, such practices as mediumship were marked as superstition across the twentieth century. Its practitioners came to represent not only a rural, premodern backwardness but also the quintessential charlatan (Unschuld 1985). Together with the ejected figure of the Henanese, described later, it is precisely from this position of being again and again written out of an already-turbulent history that I take the medium's gaze as a potent one from which to revisit the present.

While many of the engagements I describe might seem to fall squarely into what is often termed Chinese popular religion, the insufficiency of such designations must be reiterated. Despite repeated insistence of absolute self-distinction from "popular" practices by more orthodox, institutionalized strands of the "three teachings" of Confucianism, Daoism, and Buddhism—and state reinforcement of such distinctions across various purges—much more blurring and overlap have existed historically between the official and unofficial, the literati and illiterati, than such gestures of denial admit (Lopez 1996). Against assumptions of a localized provincialism that may be implicitly appended to the "popular," I approach contemporary rituals and cosmological accounts in Hexian as engagements with world historical conundrums, just as any metropolitan claims to time, space, and universality are, conversely, locally emplaced.

LANGUAGES OF MADNESS

My research in Hexian was, in a sense, a departure from and a sequel to an earlier project I undertook in the central psychiatric hospital of Shenzhen—the first major Special Economic Zone under Deng Xiaoping's economic reforms, emblematic of the coastal South, where I would be told to go by the elderly man in Hexian. That work focused on intergenerational shifts in experiences of mania and depression in patients diagnosed with bipolar disorder, in which the post-Mao generation increasingly individualized and psychologized their illness, with a heavy sense of self-blame, in contrast to the political, sociomoral, and situational accounts from those who came of age in the Maoist era (Ng 2009).

In Shenzhen I also spent time with a group of young artists and musicians. They felt lost, caught between the burden of tradition in what they perceived to be their parents' world (ironic, given the iconoclasm of the Maoist generation) and the world they were thrown into. The question of tradition often seemed uncanny, to be posed as if from without or from a sense of displacement, while questions of possible healing for their own exasperations were often posed to Western psychology and psychiatry.

As I considered their struggles, I found myself caught by the conundrum posed by Michel Foucault (2006) in *History of Madness,* wherein the discourse of scientific psychology and psychiatry marks a certain incapacity to engage with madness as experience and madness as a question of truth seeking beyond the service of reason. Between the urban hospital and the community of youth, it felt as if international mental health was unfurling with determination, and my imagination failed me as to what an attempt to approach madness otherwise would look like.[11] In spite of the histories of exclusion, governance, and philosophical closure archived in and reenacted by the psy-disciplines, they still seemed among the more intimate sites for engaging with profound concerns of the times. Western psychology—even if embedded in highly atomized conceptions of the self in their particular enunciations by the youth—seemed an increasingly central language for addressing the sense of despair and urgency of a generation, even in its alienated quality.[12] Or, precisely in their alienated quality, these imported genres posited a structure of feeling (Williams 1961) resonant with the present as experienced by the youth. Nonetheless, the conundrum of listening to madness beyond the languages of mental health, in a time when other languages may have been foreclosed by modern encounter, would not release me from its paradoxical provocation.

The possibility of learning from other grammars of madness, amid dilemmas of transmission, was, in part, what brought me to consider spirit mediumship in Hexian, since prior to campaigns to modernize medicine in China, spirit mediums would have been among the most common healers visited, particularly in rural regions. And while others have juxtaposed Western-style psychiatric practice with spirit mediumship as traditional healing (e.g., Kleinman 1980, in Taiwan), I approach the same theme holding in mind the problematic of healers in the aftermath of culture, in which the symbolic order could no longer be taken for granted in the wake of historical wounds.

I also sensed from my work in Shenzhen that I was missing half the story in a bifurcated symbolic cartography, as many of the young hospital patients had come from rural areas near and far for work, and I wanted to get a sense of that other side of migration. But before heading to Henan, several other encounters in China began conveying a sense of impasse arresting the present, between questions of mental health and mediumship. These would come to inform the way I approached, experienced, and thought about Hexian, not only in its local particularities but as one site of a broader dilemma of "China" as a geopolitical and conceptual entity, distributed and coconstituted through multiple sites and languages of difference.

. . .

It is 2010. A large conference hall in Pudong, the glistening New Area on the eastern edge of Shanghai, faces the Old City and former foreign concessions across the Huangpu River. It hosts one of the first major international conferences held in China dedicated explicitly to addressing cultural change and mental health since the reform era. I sit amid hundreds of Chinese mental health professionals, academics, and students, as well as a handful of foreign clinicians and scholars, mainly those invited as presenters. The workshops and panels pivot around a central question: what would it mean to offer a Chinese approach to Western mental health theories and methods in an ever-changing China?

In a set of opening remarks, a Chinese psychiatrist known domestically and internationally for his work on cultural psychiatry speaks of living through Nationalist, Communist, and reform eras across the eighty-some years of his life, across the pains and mistakes of the nation. Now, he declares, it is time at last for the Chinese people to live in dignity and happiness and to reclaim some Confucian values. Despite the overwhelming majority of Chinese attendees, he insists on speaking in English—it is an address intended for an international audience, to be heard by the world, not just the Chinese world, he says. Much of the audience thus listens through wireless headsets that broadcast his speech in real-time translation.

Next another prominent figure in the field of cultural psychiatry, who spent much of his career in Taiwan and the United States, insists in English that he will be conducting his speech in Mandarin and notes his enthusiasm for hearing discussions on Chinese mental health, for once, in the Chinese language, allowing for what could not be expressed in foreign terms. Last, a Chinese American cultural psychiatrist born in the United States, an expert in the field of cultural competency, expresses regret for not offering his presentation in Mandarin. It is a conundrum of tongues and histories, a question of the very language in which such problems could or should be articulated and in what language they could or should be received.

Throughout the conference, formulations of a mental health befitting of contemporary China are many. There is the employment of the Confucian Doctrine of the

Mean as the foundation for a Chinese psychological model. There are family-systems approaches to the shifting configurations of the Chinese family, vis-à-vis the one-child policy, as well as internal and transnational migration. Daoism is put into dialogue with cognitive therapy and the treatment of obsessive-compulsive disorder. Methods are sought for operationalizing Chinese medicine for mental health practitioners. Biopsychosocial approaches are evoked in the provision of postearthquake trauma recovery. Infrastructure for mental health care through social work is discussed as a new site for intervention. There are self-assured propositions for new approaches; there are pensive reflections on the complexity of changes taking place.

One moment in particular, though, stays with me. In a workshop on the implications of Chinese medicine for mental health, the presenter—a professor and practitioner at a major school of Traditional Chinese Medicine, offers a provocation: "There is nothing I can teach you in these twenty minutes. If you wish to learn something that can immediately be applied, you'd better leave now and find another workshop." Several, in fact, do.

Any such learning, he suggests, would require the effort of years, not minutes. He expresses his lack of optimism toward the notion of reconciling mental health and Chinese medicine, and whether Chinese medicine could be "applied" to mental health, standing as they do on divergent epistemological and ontological grounds. The only lesson he can offer given the setting, he suggests, is a basic qigong breathing technique, as an attempt to convey what it is that Chinese medicine "teaches," in mode rather than in content, if only to rouse curiosity in a few of us to pursue further learning.

Having been inculcated in the contemporary mode and rhythm of knowledge seeking, he ventures, even this small taste might prove difficult—the group may be incapable of a mere five minutes of silence, ravaged as we are for knowledge in the form of informational output. "Five minutes," he repeats, "is all I ask." The roomful of attendees grows quiet, following instructions for a technique known as reverse breathing. Inhalation, exhalation. Inhalation, exhalation.

No more than a minute later, an unease begins filling the room—eyes glancing, bodies shifting. At last, a middle-aged man bursts out, "What is the purpose of this?" He challenges the presenter's critique of attempts to combine technological innovation with Chinese medicine and begins listing evidence of successful projects. Soon factions of the audience break into heated debate.

The presenter's prediction prevails. Five minutes, an infinitesimal portion of the time it would take simply to begin considering the differential mode of knowledge posited by Chinese medicine, is an unbearable stretch for the crowd, attesting to the impasse faced by what it would mean to translate such teachings today. Beyond efforts toward indigenization more commonly advocated at adjacent conference workshops, this moment reveals a disjuncture of worlds and temporalities, one that points to a breach in the possibility of transmission.

This breach in transmission applies not only to Traditional Chinese Medicine, the state-sanctioned version of Chinese medicine that includes such modalities as qigong, acupuncture, massage, and herbal remedies. Indeed, the very effort to formally compartmentalize healing practices in China follows the felt need to contend with the perceived modernity of Western medicine.

While Western medicine was seen in modernizing campaigns as further along in the progression of science, official Traditional Chinese Medicine was deemed to possess theoretical knowledge and thus be open to potential modern transformations. By contrast, medicines excluded by official recognition, such as spirit mediumship, were cast out as feudal superstitions lacking in theory and thus incapable of progress (Scheid 2002). At the conference the only times such practices as mediumship are mentioned are in the few anthropological panels centered on ethnic minorities, more as objects of study than even techniques to be "applied" to mental health in China today.

DIVIDED SELF

Between antisuperstition campaigns triggered by the "century of humiliation," transmutations in kinship accompanying the search for a "new culture," and the influx of global pharmaceutical influence found at "the end of history," the question of madness sits at the brink of what anthropologists have called the "divided self" in China today (Kleinman et al. 2011). While North American media has become increasingly engrossed with the export of the Western psyche via the adoption of psychotherapeutic techniques in China (Osnos 2011; Watters 2010), the recent urban "psycho-boom" must be considered in context (H. Huang 2015).

A nineteenth-century import of missionizing and modernizing efforts, the psy-disciplines (Rose 1996) have long occupied a foreign yet intimate space in China, not only displacing spirit mediumship and ritual as modes of healing for possession and madness, but offering concepts for reimagining personhood in the aftermath of cultural devastation. From the influence of psychoanalytic texts on twentieth-century craftings of cosmopolitan revolutionary subjects (Larson 2009), to attempts in cross-cultural psychiatry to articulate culturally appropriate treatment modalities (Tseng and Wu 1985), through contemporary movements to indigenize psychotherapy (Zhang 2014), the psy-disciplines are home to uneasy projects of translation (L. Liu 1995). As with other nations wrought by dilemmas of revolution and postrevolutionary medicine, the struggle for health is poised at the junction of national and international politics, shifting tensely across ideals of political neutrality and calls for a politicized medicine (Adams 1998).

In China medical anthropology as a field has not only investigated such political tensions surrounding medicine but, through its very investigative efforts, has been a participant to the translations and transformations of the mental health scene. In his well-known work on depression and neurasthenia, Arthur Kleinman (1986) suggests that during the Cultural Revolution, neurasthenia provided a somatized, medically legitimized, and politically tolerable idiom through which to articulate otherwise punishable laments. Meanwhile, the publication of Kleinman's (1982) related finding that a large majority of patients diagnosed with neurasthenia in fact qualified for *Diagnostic and Statistical Manual of Mental Disorders–III* criteria for major depressive disorder and were responsive to antidepressant pharmacotherapy led to a scramble in the Chinese psychiatric world to account for their "misdiagnosis." Despite ongoing contention regarding its relevance for Chinese patients (see, e.g., Young 1989), neurasthenia was soon marked as controversial, while the findings were in turn utilized in pharmaceutical marketing (S. Lee 1999).[13]

Alongside the politics of diagnostic translation and pharmaceuticalization, the psy-disciplines also raise questions of modern governance with more explicit ties to the Chinese state. At the most overt level, the political deployment of psychiatry as a means to suppress political dissidence highlights the potential judicial deployment of the psychiatric apparatus across Maoist and post-Mao eras (Munro 2002a).[14] In the 1990s psychiatry entered the state's search for order, in response to the widespread practice of qigong in public space, which at times was accompanied by the loss of control of bodily and perceptual functions or by the heights of ecstatic mania. Qigong-induced psychosis thus emerged as a diagnostic category between attempts by the state to parse "scientific" (officially sanctioned) and "pseudoscientific" qigong and by anticult campaigns to quell potential disorder (N. Chen 2003).

State-sponsored psychotherapy programs in urban areas have also been implemented in the form of employment counseling, in an attempt to encourage an entrepreneurial spirit and to mitigate potential threats of unrest accompanying mass unemployment among the new working class. Jie Yang calls this a "political (mis)use of psychology," combining personal desire with state interest (2015, 17). Yet, even considering the potential power of the asylum as a total institution (Goffman 1961), nonbiomedical terms are deployed by patients and family members, in what Zhiying Ma terms a "cultural resistance" to psychiatry (2012, 223).

Rather than focusing on diagnosis and clinical efficacy, the critique of or resistance to psychiatry and psychology as practiced in China, or the urban proliferation of psychotherapeutic practices, I approach the psychiatrist, the patient, and the family in Hexian as figures caught in a shared dilemma—that of life in a symbolic field of death amid outmigration (H. Yan 2003). This is not to suggest that rural psychiatry is without its disciplinary dimensions but rather to take seriously the predicaments and ethical impasse being grappled within the fraught space of the clinic, in which an elsewhere is at times sought in the form of a hospital bed (Pandolfo 2018; see also Garcia 2010 on the sense of impossibility of an elsewhere). Moreover, psychiatric symptoms, like Maoist slogans, appear as cosmic operators opening up multiple worlds. At the hospital stories of madness spin out from a sense of intergenerational impasse and a suspicion that the grounds for intimacy could not be taken for granted. As my interlocutors put it, and as I will discuss later, it is a time when "the *qin* is no longer *qin*" (the familial is no longer familiar or intimate). This sense of the uncanny— or the *unheimlich* in its German rendering—lived out through divided selves, would also appear beyond the clinic, pointing to broader dislocations of culture.

CULTURE PETRIFIED

Prior to departing for Henan Province, I am told by many urban friends and colleagues that such characters as "spirit ladies" *(shenpo)* and "witchdoctors" *(wuyi)* were no longer present in today's China. I had arrived, they would say, too late. Moreover, even if there remained traces of such "superstitions" and "folk customs," they would not be found in Henan or among the Han majority—I would be better off in Yunnan Province and the southwest. Whereas Yunnan evokes culturalized images of China's "ethnic minorities" advanced by state discourse and a robust tourism industry, Henan evokes an unsightly manifestation of rural poverty—no place to seek any semblance of what one might call cultural.[15]

While I was conversing at an arts district in Shenzhen one evening with Wu Dongliang, a middle-aged artist and entrepreneur, after an open lecture on European improvisational jazz, he asks about the fieldwork I am about to undertake. Part of a foreign-educated returnee generation of the early reform years, he often speaks with pride and nostalgia of his years as a student in Europe. Upon hearing my plans, he nods with concern. To study this, he replies with graveness, I must relocate my project to Germany. He knows of a German library with a collection of Chinese shamanistic costumes and implements. No such thing remains in China.

Not unlike others of the intellectual classes in China, Wu Dongliang relays the sense that much of the Chinese cultural tradition, both in the form of knowledge and material artifacts, exists only in shambles on the mainland after the Maoist era. They are to be found instead in the repositories of Taiwan and Hong Kong or, in this case, Europe. In the case of "folk" traditions in the vein of shamanism and mediumship, he, like many others, points to the southwest. He himself encountered some old ritualistic animal hides at a small shop in Yunnan Province in the 1990s, he says, and even at that time such items were already scarce. It is, again, too late. "You might as well treat this visit to China as a vacation and purchase a flight to Germany for your research instead," he concludes. An orbit of impossibility forms around my anticipatory imaginations of the journey—impossibilities that begin sketching the shape of a hollow.

. . .

Since the 1990s anthropologists rethinking China and Chinese transnationalism have pointed to the need to unground essentialist notions of Chinese culture.

Writing in part against neo-Confucian returns to purportedly timeless features of Chinese culture, Aihwa Ong and Donald Nonini (1997) call for an approach to such invocations of culture as chronotopes situated amid alternative modernities and strategies of late capitalist accumulation. Taking up the time lag of cultural differ- ence posited by colonialism, Lisa Rofel (1999) suggests approaching "other moder- nities" as formative outsides of universalizing approaches to modernity, existing through a sense of repeated deferral from the reaching of parity with the West. And, as Mei Zhan points out, even as discourses of modernity and movements of trans- nationality might create a sense of delay and displacement, they also constitute worldings—of "multiple and effervescent worlds in the making" (2009, 24).

Meanwhile, ethnographies of postreform China in the first decade of the 2000s convey a sense of moral collapse, accompanied by a shifting moral landscape. In his work on rural Shaanxi, Xin Liu finds the lack of a coherent moral economy, a common ground on which social action or cultural meaning could take place. In the midst of this absence, between state retreat from local affairs and the rise of marketization, came an "immoral politics" of arbitrary punishment (2000, 168). In rural Heilongjiang, Yunxiang Yan finds a "moral and ideological vacuum" follow- ing decollectivization, across the rise of youth autonomy and the decline of filial piety, leading in some cases to the suicide of elders, shamed by unfilial children (2003, 234). More than a shift in material relations of care, the rise of the individual throughout and after collectivization also marks the collapse of the symbolic world, a sense that previous modes of organizing life are "once again (and probably forever this time) dying out" (186).

I draw on the former set of works on rethinking modernity and locality in con- sidering the sense of contingency, externality, and emergence conditioning any reference to the cultural with relation to China, both my interlocutors' and my own. I brood on the latter accounts of moral-symbolic collapse because they arrest me. They at once speak to the sense of evacuation accompanying profound reform- era transformations and evoke a sense of differential repetition—of a new return of a sense of interruption and decay from earlier times.[16]

It's helpful here to consider shifts in the Chinese intellectual world across two previous moments of encounter: engagements with Jesuits in the seventeenth cen- tury and those with Protestant missions at the end of the nineteenth century. Earlier Jesuits approached the Confucian literati in the manner of civilizational encounter, an exchange of intellectual magnitude. By the late nineteenth century, with the rise of Western military and economic power and the onslaught of foreign intrusion, Chinese intellectuals were forced instead to face west, and with this turn claims to Chinese tradition came to mark an agonized rupture despite apparent continuity.

If earlier references to Confucian classics were primary and "philosophical" in status, meant to approach questions of knowledge and truth with universal impli- cations, later invocations came to be secondary and "romantic," a clinging to a tradition no longer vital and operational, but what historian Joseph Levenson calls a "petrifaction of tradition by traditionalists" (1968, 1:xxx): "The Confucian Classics were the repositories of value in the abstract, absolute for everyone, not just Chinese values relevant to China alone. When the Classics make China particular instead of universal, it is a China *in* the world—still China, but really new, even as it invokes (indeed, precisely as it invokes) what connects it to the old" (1:xvii). The grounds for claims—whether iconoclastic or traditionalistic in guise—could no longer rest on Chinese thought as *thought* but rather on Chinese thought only insofar as equivalence could be drawn with the Western corpus, or otherwise on Chinese thought as *Chinese*. To put it in the phrasing of more recent critiques of naturalist multiculturalism, it became fraught to take indigenous thought seriously, to take indigenous thought as philosophy rather than mere empirical exemplifications of cultural instances (de Castro 2014; Skafish 2016). In contexts of colonial threat, this culturalization appears from within, as the national-cultural phantasm emerges through repeated inscriptions of external difference from the West, accompanied by disavowals of internal difference (Ivy 1995). Assertions of *a* Chinese tradition intensify, rendering tradition paralyzed through these very pronouncements, after previously dynamic intramural debates were "shocked into a semblance of unity" (Levenson 1968, 1:50).

Levenson's (1968) account has faced critiques of the dichotomization of tradition and modernity and a tendency toward the so-called impact-response approach to Chinese history, in which the West and the "initial collision" are afforded excessive attention and explanatory priority (P. Cohen 2010, 55; Hart 1999). While I take heed of such critiques, what Levenson's text importantly registers, in my reading, moves beyond historiographical debates on periodization and causality. As Lydia Liu notes, despite Levenson's (1968) tendency toward totalizing statements, "the question of how to explain the 'traumatic choices' made by the Chinese since their violent encounters with Western imperialism does not easily go away" (1995, 30).

Thus, in spite of important critiques, I return to Levenson as an effort to render visible what Fanon (2008) describes as the agonized state of culture following colonial legacy, in which the colonial system does not result in the disappearance of the preexisting culture but rather transforms it into a tormenting caricature of its former manifestation. In the same vein, to dwell on a sense of rupture facing evocations of Chinese tradition is not to posit a static cultural beginning and a modern acultural end but to attend to the devastation carried within the cultural after what Chinese intellectuals called semicolonialism, even if the formal political outcome is not that of full colonialization in the case of China.

Yet such an acknowledgment of fracture also summons its attendants to the task of reimagining and reactivating the work of culture, precisely from its ruins. In the case of spiritual traditions, acknowledgment of the impasse facing the reception of the divine message is perhaps a "necessary shock, towards the reanimation of the soul" (Pandolfo 2018, 8). In times of cosmic and political crisis, it may be from the very site of agony that an encounter with the otherworldly dimensions may be recapacitated. In the chapters to follow, I thus approach evocations of culture—including rituals and repertoires of spirit mediumship—not as a straightforward continuation but as painful enunciations and wounded reworkings after the cultural as such has been rendered petrified and petrifying. Moreover, it is from this very geography of hollowing and position of petrification that spirit mediums in Hexian inaugurate a new cosmic geography.

ORBITING THE HOLLOW

It is a week or two before I take off for Henan. I am at a midsize grocery store in Shenzhen near the apartment complex of Zhao Yun, an artist in his twenties whom I had been discussing the project with, as he grew up in Henan before moving to Shenzhen. We stop in the rice aisle. He reaches out for a sack. With an expert twist of the wrist, Zhao Yun turns the bag around to locate its place of origin. "Zhengzhou City, Henan Province," it reads—the provincial capital of his hometown. A slight shadow passes across his face. He thrusts the sack back on the shelf, in a swift movement that resembles the immediacy of a disgust reaction, a learned automaticity of bodily habituation.

He picks up another sack, twisting it around. It reads, "Shenzhen"—the place he has called home since he left Henan as a child. The shadow returns, the sack thrust once again back on the shelf. Lifting and turning a third sack, he is starting to get flustered. "Guizhou." Guizhou, as we see in a moment, is the first among the "poorest" provinces mentioned by Ma Shuo (2002). Zhao Yun pauses for a moment. It's another no-go: back on the shelf.

With a sigh this time, he goes back to the second option—Shenzhen. Furrowing his brow at the back of the bag, now more stilted and deliberate in his movements than the smooth, optimistic gestures before, he seems to hope that something new might appear, offering some reassurance. He doesn't seem to find what he is looking for but tosses the sack into his shopping basket regardless and heads toward the checkout stand.

I ask Zhao Yun later about this series of rejections and the significance of the places involved. Laughing, he says he does not recall that moment and does not know why he proceeded the way he did. But, he says, he has indeed been worried about food safety, following numerous scandals over toxic and "fake" foods in China, from the melamine in milk and infant formula to rumors of artificial eggs he recently heard about. More than concerns over food safety in any simple sense, Zhao Yun's hope and hesitation, disgust and disappointment, strike me as a small manifestation, habituated in a flick of the wrist, of the ambivalence and distrust toward various places of origin in China today. The very capacity for "home" to sustain oneself, to offer a site of life, seems to be deeply compromised, whether imparted through the thrusting of rice back on the shelf or through the well-intended counsel to "hurry up and leave." Whether an urban coastal periphery flung out from the edges of the pot, as Xu Liying put it, or a landlocked center sticking to the pot bottom, questions of home and habitability remain fraught. Where is there to go, if every source of suste-nance seems, somehow, tainted?

. . .

Zhao Yun's habituated sensibility speaks to the various potential affective rever-berations of culture as aftermath, which can also be heard in other moments and forms across twentieth-century China. In the literature of New Culture and May Fourth Movements of the early twentieth century, the petrifying dimension of the imagined origin can be seen in the cannibalistic visions of Lu Xun's 1922 "Diary of a Madman": "I have reason for my fear" (Lu 1977, 8). Murderous gazes from those in the old hometown. The neighbors. The landlord. "All those green-faced, long-toothed people began to laugh derisively." The tenant. The brother. "Only today have I realized that they had exactly the same look in their eyes as those people outside. Just to think of it sets me shivering from the crown of my head to the soles of my feet. They eat human beings, so they may eat me" (9). One by one civiliza-tional claims of history and intimate claims of kinship are ravaged from within: "My history has no chronology, and scrawled all over each page are the words: 'Virtue and Morality' . . . until I began to see words between the lines, the whole book being filled with the two words—'Eat people'" (10). The protagonist is not exempt. The "I" of the story is unwittingly fed the flesh of his dead sister at the hands of his elder brother. "Now it is my turn" (18).

Amid the cohort of those who fled the mainland to Taiwan in the 1940s, this sense of petrified origin can be seen in Bo Yang's 1985 *The Ugly Chinaman.* "Chinese culture is infected with a virus which has been transmitted from generation to generation and which today still resists cure. . . . Can an entire nation of moral degenerates be saved?" (1991). It can be seen differently in Tu Wei-ming's exhorta-tions to a "cultural China" beyond national boundaries, in which the affordance of dignity to diasporic identity ("the peripheries as the center") takes distance from a *declining, humiliated* center—a homeland that is not lost, but, precisely in its per-sistent, *impotent* presence, haunts the émigré as an *abyss of misery* (1991; 1995). It can be seen in recent calls for "post-Confucianism," returning to Confucian classics in search of the origins of corruption, debating whether and how to extract poison-ous roots, to reformulate a tainted corpus that failed to lay claim to a universal ethics.[17] In the language itself, it is also the difficulty of discerning indigenous and exogenous elements in modern Chinese. In the scramble for neologisms with which to counter defeat and occupation, translational circuits *interrupted* classical etymons, transforming their meaning and world of reference despite appearances and despite usage of the same characters (L. Liu 1995).

To attend to the sense of rupture and humiliation, of corruption and petrifica-tion, is not to deny a tie between a *now* and a *then* or the concurrent existence of more vitalistic or optimistic accounts. It is rather to acknowledge a violent cut and an unshakable sense of infestation, out of which new enunciations and worlds emerge, bearing its traces. Repudiations of tradition inherited from missionary and colonial discourses continue to torment new forms. This is not to say that such forms are immobile or carry no force. On the contrary, they carry what might be pondered as a spectral force—akin to the spectral nationality of postcolonial libera-tion literature (Cheah 2003) or the shamanic redeployment of colonial violence that draws its healing power from a space of death (Taussig 1987). Yet even as such spec-trality carries within it transformative potential, it also haunts the postcolonial sub-ject and manifests through disorders both social and subjective (Good et al. 2008). They are symptoms of history that mark its intolerable weight, as well as the truth of existing within it. They sit "between the story of the unbearable nature of an event and the story of the unbearable nature of its survival" (Caruth 1996, 7).

My impetus for walking through these writings, which together coconstitute contemporary visions of China, grows from a felt need to reckon with the many-faced (and faceless) inheritances of traumatic rupture that, in my work in Hexian, also bespeaks the creation of new, if haunted, worlds. In the case of Hexian and Henan Province, to consider history and culture is to dwell on what it means to allegorically embody a humiliated and humiliating center, a petrified and petrify-ing core—what writer Ma Shuo calls "the China of China," a China that scares itself in its intimate exteriority, in its very imagined provincial intensification of its Chinese characteristics (2002, 75).[18]

In my encounters, mention of Henan did not only evoke the sense of cultural evacuation facing China at large; a profound sense of revulsion and fear tainted more philanthropic images of rural dispossession. It was a "bad" place, my urban and transnational Chinese friends, colleagues, and interlocutors would divulge after some moments of discomfort, thinking they were the first to break news of its infamous reputation. I was offered cautionary tales of fraud and swindling and gory tales of abduction, poisoning, and murder, detailing the many ways in which I may not make it back out in one piece. Despite a trained skepticism toward such tropes, I grew more petrified by the day—I was starting to scare myself. These stories carried force.

. . .

In an analysis of what he calls the demonization of Henan, Ma Shuo tellingly names Henan "the China of China," and the Henanese "the Chinese of the Chinese" (2002, 75). Home to capitals dynasty after dynasty and the birthplace of ancient philosophers, present-day Henan once constituted a powerful political, geographic, and cosmological center—"the center of the world"—and has contended with Shaanxi Province for the title of the "cradle of Chinese civilization" (73). Yet, while its spatial centrality remains in the contemporary cartographic imagination, Henan has come to epitomize China in another sense. With the burgeoning of international trade since Deng Xiaoping's post-Mao economic reforms, the coastal metropolis has come to the fore in a geography of value, rendering the inland—*neidi* (lit. "interior land")—a conceptual periphery and symbolic space of stagnation.

Whereas classical dynastic histories depicted the Henanese, variously, as "gentlemanlike, elegant, luxury loving, and ceremonially extravagant" (Eberhard 1965, 604), reread through developmentalist and postreform discourses, it was rather the tropes of rurality, poverty, backwardness, and overpopulation that came to mark Henan's Chinese characteristics. Now neither the poorest nor the wealthiest province, Henan, like China, appears trapped in the inertia of an ever-developing stage. Not east or west, not north or south, it seems to have lost itself; yet, Ma (2002) writes, if anything is left, it is that Henan, like China, remains doggedly agricultural, doggedly from the soil, to borrow Fei Xiaotong's (1992) notorious characterization.

Ma relays a joke heard in Beijing labor recruitment markets: "A high-end hotel is recruiting service staff but declares that they don't accept Henanese applicants. A labor migrant from Henan who doesn't know what's good for him approaches to inquire, and the boss replies, 'If a Henanese bellboy stands in the hotel lobby, then this place will become impossible to keep clean—dirt never stops dropping from Henanese bodies'" (2002, 26). It is not surprising that the joke appears in a space for the selling and purchasing of labor, staging the fraught encounter between urban and rural, poverty and wealth, and between the allures and devastations of marketization's promises. Such imaginations of rural filth and urban hygiene, as Lili Lai (2016) writes, also infuse self-conscious languages of distinction in rural Henan, amid the state promotion of rural consumption and lack of waste management infrastructure. Paralleling the intensified circulation of jokes and rumors during reform-era labor migration—rumors that also incorporated themes of a clannish rural tendency toward horde violence—businesses across Shenzhen, Guangzhou, Shanghai, and Beijing were known to adopt in their hiring policy, and at times in explicit signage at the factory entrance: "Henanese may not enter" (Ma 2002, 54).

Beyond rurality, which might otherwise conjure a notion of naiveté, there was another motif borne by the figure of the Henanese: that of the imposter and deceiver. Before I left for Henan, a friend relayed another joke: when the train approaches Henan, the sound that emerges is *piansini . . . piansini . . . piansini* (cheat you to death . . . cheat you to death . . . cheat you to death).[19]

Ma considers three levels of analysis for the vilification of the Henanese. The first is one that hinges on notions of population, which he calls a "surface-level explication": as Henan was the most populous province in China, yet one with underdeveloped industry and insufficient employment opportunities, there was an increased chance of encounter with rural Henanese migrant laborers and thus an increased chance of negative incidents (2002, 171). With the additional impact of media attention, such incidents come to flood the popular imagination. The second, what Ma terms an "inner-level explication," involves Henan's intermediary status in developmental narratives (174). No longer evoking abjection so strongly as in the decades of famine and warfare, postreform Henan—"poor but not hungry," as Ma puts it—is newly potentiated as an object of humor, while the poorest provinces (Ma lists Guizhou, Gansu, and Yunnan) tend to remain off-limits to the violence of mass ridicule (178). Finally, Ma offers what he deems a "deeper-level explication" (189). Under conditions of radical transformation and economic growth, those in contemporary China know only that from whence they came and that it is a past to which they must never return. Yet in the flash of transition, they know not where they are headed.

With a smattering of Western concepts at hand, the Chinese have yet to resolve the gap between the tradition to which they cannot seem to return and the foreign that has yet to be assimilated. In the words of Fanon, "Not yet white, no longer completely black, I was damned" (2008, 117). Under such conditions, Ma writes, the Chinese have entered a state of absolute negation of the self and the past. Yet, along with the depth of entry of Western thought, there came the sense that there is something "un-Christian" about the manner in which the Chinese insult their own at every turn; hence they eventually found a substitute: the Henanese (2002, 190).

From the intimate affinities between the figure of Henan and the figure of China, both historical and contemporary, favorable and deplorable—a fallen cradle of civilization—a certain satisfaction arises from the attack of the externalized self. By critiquing, vilifying, and discriminating against the figure of the Henanese, an abreaction of the deep resentment toward Chinese tradition is made possible— a resentment too painful if directed toward the figure of China itself, as it is impossible for one to dodge its effects while residing in a Chinese body.

Much of Ma's rendering rings true to my encounters, particularly in major cities, where practices of regional distinction heighten in new forms with the exigencies of labor migration (see Zhang 2002). This is not to say that the Henanese is the sole figure of regional ridicule—provincial caricatures abound in China, recent and historical. Yet during my visits to Shenzhen and other Chinese cities in the first decade of the 2000s, mentions of Henan did seem to provoke a notably strong reaction. And what interests me in Ma's reading is the sense of civilizational fall and the rise of a despicable figure in its place. Henan provides one site for an intensified self-othering and self-substitution, through a procedure of geographic-imaginary circumscription. To journey to Henan, then, is to enter this imagined embodiment of a petrified and petrifying Chinese past, through such figures as the peasant, the charlatan, and the unruly masses. And, it is to consider how those inhabiting such a space transform this rendering from within, rewriting this history cosmologically.

THE CHAPTERS

In the next chapter, "After the Storm," I pair my train ride to Hexian with a reflection on language, violence, and trauma, followed by a historical overview of the figure of the peasant in China as a means of providing a setting by detour. I consider several ways in which the May Fourth Movement and Maoism have been described as traumatic ruptures in Chinese history, culminating in the violence of the Cultural Revolution. Then, proceeding from the ethnographic sense that the Cultural Revolution did not constitute the main signifier of historical violence for my interlocutors in Hexian, the chapter shifts its gaze toward the rises and falls of the figure of the peasantry across twentieth-century writings and campaigns. It traces renderings of the "voiceless" peasantry as both a symbolic lack and a site of transformative realness in early modern Chinese realist fiction, as radical futurity in Maoist writings and campaigns, and as an outmoded persona drained of its previous revolutionary horizons after the reform era. These chronotropic thrashings of the peasantry—from voiceless to central to peripheral, from realistic to futuristic to backward—come to give force, I suggest, to the cosmic-symbolic position of the peasant in the contemporary cosmology.

Chapter 2, "Ten Thousand Years," explores the centrality of Mao in the contemporary cosmology and the sense of spectral sovereignty haunting the present. For spirit mediums in Hexian, Mao's reign marks not only an earthly rule but an interval of cosmic protection. Through rituals and encounters on the expansive square of Fuxi Temple, I consider spirit mediums' accounts of Mao, the Communist party-state, and state slogans and campaigns. Like the spirited presences in other postsocialist and atheist secular worlds, the this-worldly and otherworldly in Hexian are by no means clear-cut. For spirit mediums who "walk the Chairman's path," Maoist campaigns against religion marked an act of divine violence and rectification, while the post-Mao boom of temple visitors paradoxically marks a cosmic disarray with the return of dangerously corrupt, duplicitous, madness-inducing spirits.

The following chapter, "Spectral Collision," turns to the reemergence of specters following the symbolic and economic evacuation of the rural after the reform era. The chapter traces the aftereffects of a collision between my host, Li Hanwei, a truck driver who spends much of the year away from home, and a ghost from a Republican and Maoist-era mass grave. It follows a series of visits to a spirit medium by Li Hanwei's wife, Cai Huiqing, in attempt to appease the ghosts that begin to multiply. Through Cai Huiqing's ritual engagements and dreams, the chapter considers contemporary mediumship as a form of distant intimacy amid outmigration. And, through notions of afterwardsness and phantomatic passage, I approach spectral collision as a (quasi-)event and mode of transmission, in which temporalities near and far bump and barrel into the present, across geographies cohabited by the human and nonhuman. In this case wandering ghosts from the time of the Second Sino-Japanese War put the present at risk, threatening the lives of an entire family and its future generations.

Continuing the themes of generationality and collision but through the site of the psychiatric ward, chapter 4, "A Soul Adrift," dwells on how it feels to be a rural "problem" in China today, from the county People's Hospital. Drawing from time spent with those who have fallen ill and the family members accompanying them, I consider the devastation wrought by a crisis of filial piety in face of intergenerational and urban-rural fracturings of worlds. Here madness spins out from fissures of kinship and economy, at the disjointed confluence of geography, class, and history. A grandmother and former leader of a Maoist brigade has been diagnosed with schizophrenia since the dawn of the reform era and feels uncared for by her daughters. A village high schooler, diagnosed with depression amid college entry exams, feels her father, whom she considers a textbook peasant, is to blame. Pasts and presents stack up to a sense of failed reciprocation, in which the hospital offers but a site of transient respite.

Staying in the hospital but turning again to the contemporary cosmology, the final chapter, "Vertiginous Abbreviation," centers on Xu Liying, the spirit medium and hospital patient at the opening of this introduction. Through paradoxical descriptions in her hospital file of simultaneous madness and lucidity, I take her diagnosis—"psychiatric disorder intimately related to culture"—as an inroad to contemporary and historical crossovers between mediumship and psychiatry. Inheriting Western concepts of religion and superstition, mediumship and possession came to be defined in psychiatric terms as a culturally peculiar form of psychosis. But Xu Liying herself offers an inverse diagnosis: it is through today's chaotic cosmos that psychiatric symptoms can be understood. Only through the continuation of an otherworldly Maoist revolution and the arrival of a socialist end time would the world be rid of madness-inducing spirits. I put Xu Liying's cosmological accounts in conversation with the Maitreyan Buddhist eschatological thought of so-called White Lotus groups and European philosophical reflections on messianism and chronological time. Through an apocalyptic recentering, spirit mediums like Xu Liying upend accounts of "the China of China" as a stagnant periphery, reinaugurating Hexian as the center of a new world to come.

After the Storm

"Would you like to know how a person of my era feels when riding on this train?" Yang Shaoliu's eyes spark with no uncertain mischief. His wife, Fan Jie, gazes past us, out the window. We are hours in on a day-long train ride, northward from the coast, away from the sprawl of factory dorms, through deep-green fields of rice paddies and banana trees, past hillsides peppered with homes and tombs. Traversing the thousand miles between the rolling landscape of South China and the vast expanses of the Central Plain, the K1040 links my departure point in Shenzhen, the booming "factory of the world" in Guangdong Province, to one among the more emblematic sources of its floating population *(piaoliu renkou)* of migrant laborers, Henan Province. A native of Henan who has resided in Shenzhen for several decades, Yang Shaoliu is heading to his hometown for a visit and agreed to introduce me to the province.

Aboard the train carts, migrant workers and families return to the old home *(laojia)* from the South. Young mothers bring grandchildren to their grandparents "left behind" in the hometown, and grandparents bring grandchildren to their parents "floating" in the city. Entrepreneurs navigate potential markets in so-called second- and third-tier cities across central China, although those who have the means often prefer the plane or bullet train. Older passengers chat in local dialects, and younger riders swap stories and advice, often in standard Mandarin—the language of the nation, the language of cities and strangers. Children run up and down the aisle, finding new playmates. There is the rolling sound of the train, the murmur of voices, and the crackle of sunflower seeds. There are no empty seats or bunks.

"Let me tell you how a person of my era, a person of the sixties and seventies, feels when riding on this train," Yang Shaoliu repeats emphatically, after I answered his initial question with a smirk. Yang Shaoliu was born in the 1950s, so the 1960s and 1970s mark the time of his youth across the Maoist era, which he spent in his hometown, when not traveling with the People's Liberation Army. He begins slowly, with a theatrical grandiosity:

Aboard the train of *soaring* speed	*Zuozai* feikuai *de lieche shang*
Through the *brilliant* windows of the cart	*Touguo* mingliang *de chechuang*

"Is this a poem?" I interrupt.

He laughs and turns to his wife. "She thinks I'm reciting a poem!"

Fan Jie gives a slight nod but continues busying herself cracking sunflower seeds, showing little interest in endorsing his antics. A loyal and jaded public administrator, Yang Shaoliu rarely misses an opportunity for lessons in jest. Mouthing his words with sardonic deliberateness, he retorts, "No, it's not a *poem*. I'm just telling you my *feelings* about riding this train. Did you get those two lines down?"

"Memorize it or document it?"

"Either." He starts over.

Aboard the train of *soaring* speed	*Zuozai* feikuai *de lieche shang*
Through the *brilliant* windows of the cart	*Touguo* mingliang *de chechuang*
See the *great, grand* rivers and mountains of the homeland	*Kankan zuguo de* dahao *heshan*
All around are scenes filled with *flourishing* vitality	*Daochu chongman le* shengqibobo *de yingxiang*

He bursts into laughter. "That's what a person of my generation feels riding on a train." He glances over at Fan Jie, who is now listening. He continues, "In fact, trains of that era weren't fast at all, to say nothing of 'soaring' speed. The windows weren't clear either—there was a metal frame barring the view. Since there was no heat or air-conditioning like there is now, the windows had to be opened, so the view was never 'clear,' always disrupted by a window frame. Perhaps the rivers and mountains were truly more decent though."

"There was no pollution or environmental destruction back then!" A neighboring passenger pitches in, a young migrant worker who shifted his attention from his cell phone to join our conversation for a moment. Yang Shaoliu ignores him. It is a stage, not a forum.

I raise an eyebrow. "Those verses—that's how people in fact *felt* about the train back then?"

"People of that era didn't really *feel* much at all. They weren't very internal; everything was external. But they did *say* this a lot. Everyone said this. If you were going to say anything at all while sitting on the train, it'd better be this. If you wanted to say something else—for instance, that the train was *not* soaringly speedy—then you're better off keeping your mouth shut. In that era people were very good at speaking. They spoke very precisely, very carefully. Because if you didn't speak carefully, you'd never get to your stop on the train, understand?"

Fan Jie pitches in, in disagreement. "The verses simply express how joyous we are while riding the train, looking at the pretty scenery." She breaks into a wide smile, tilting her head side to side, a gesture associated with the singing of children's songs. Yang Shaoliu and I sneak each other a sidelong glance.

Thinking back, I realize that our moment of jest and collusion against Fan Jie's more seemingly straightforward reading of Maoist-era language and affect missed something she was reminding us of—that unlike retroactive caricatures from within China and abroad, the powerful vocabularies and grammars of the Maoist era were polysemic and carried multiple simultaneous potentials for engagement and detachment, feeling and nonfeeling. In this chapter I first reflect on accounts of language, trauma, and history in China. Then, following the ethnographic sensibility I would later come to in the months after this train ride, I reconsider the affective power infused in language and speech before, during, and after Maoism, with relation to the figure of the rural and the peasantry, to register the historical forces infusing cosmological accounts in Hexian.

MAKING HISTORY SPEAK

In *Illuminations from the Past* (2004), Ban Wang writes that the trauma encountered by China, first manifest through the 1919 May Fourth Movement—a modern political and intellectual movement after the collapse of the dynastic system—as response to imperial and colonial threats following the Opium Wars, then in escalations of the Maoist era culminating in the Cultural Revolution, instituted a shift from history to memory. History, for Wang in this sense, refers to the possibility of generating meaningful narrative linkage between past and present—a present capable of making sense of the past through available symbolic resources.[1] While modern historiography came to the fore as a challenge and an aim during the May Fourth era, what finally rendered the coherence of historical narrative an impossibility (albeit an impossibility that in turn occasioned a proliferation of new genres—what he terms *memory*), for Wang, were the decades of Maoist revolutionary campaigns.

The campaigns' traumatic disruption of historical narrativity stemmed from their infliction of world-shattering experiences on the one hand, from public humiliation to corporeal violence, and the political aesthetics of Maoist newspeak on the other hand, which pushed language to its limits—to a codedness so heightened that language could no longer operate as a means of expression. In Yang Shaoliu's words, if you were going to say anything at all while sitting on the train, it'd better be this. One had best remain within the authorized genre of coded speech, in a regime of language reinforced by the threat of violence that rendered its usage *precise*—an external precision marking the split between feeling and say-ing, a precision that required the delinking of speech from interiority.

If the violence encountered across the May Fourth and Maoist eras inflicted a rupture of narrative coherence for Ban Wang, Ann Anagnost provides another reading of these two moments: narrativity—realist narrativity, specifically—itself constituted a genre imported during May Fourth, one that provided the very con-ditions for the later manifestation of corporeal violence in the Maoist era. Drawing on Marston Anderson's (1990) work on Chinese literary realism of the 1920s and 1930s, Anagnost writes that the figure of the subaltern shifted in this period from a passive object of pity *(tongqing)* to a subject of speech.[2] This "'coming into voice' of the subaltern subject" in literature, for Anagnost, was then "eerily doubled" in later Maoist campaigns—realism moved from the text of intellectuals to the body of the peasant, as villagers were *made to speak* the truth of history through the public practice of "speaking bitterness," or *suku* (1997, 19).

Moreover, the corporeal emphasis of this realist "myth of presence," Anagnost suggests, eventually led to the physical violence of the Cultural Revolution and still echoes in post-Mao narrative practices (1997, 17). Through an enacted "localiza-tion of the sign," abstract notions of world historical forces—imperialism and capitalism—were transposed onto a "highly embodied form identifiable within a local cast of characters," resulting in bursts of mass violence (35).[3] In short, literary realism provided the discursive precondition for the corporeal literalization of a politics of representation. Narrativity acquired a style that claimed direct access to the real, and hence a particular political valence could subsequently be assigned to spoken narration, predicated on the realist claim.

Across Wang and Anagnost are two approaches to narrativity and the Maoist era. In Wang, narrativity constitutes the precondition for what he calls *history,* grounded in the coherent temporalization of experience (linking the past and present meaningfully) and interrupted by the traumatic rupture of corporeal vio-lence and the rigidification of language: an official newspeak.[4] In Anagnost, narra-tivity constitutes a party-state apparatus that offered the basis for both subjectiva-tion and the apparent (but in fact discursively consistent) excess of corporeal violence. The formation of the national subject was thus continuous with the for-mation of violence; both were premised on a realist conception of language. Draw-ing on trauma studies, particular the work of Cathy Caruth (1996), Wang's concern pivots around the state-impinged threat to the possibility of a narrative-based sub-jectivity, in which the state is to some extent distinct from and external to the subject.[5] Taking up Michel Foucault's (1995) notion of the semiotechnique as dis-tinguished from disciplinary power, Anagnost tasks the Chinese state with the former's play of signs "on the surface of subjects, reordering their outward practice rather than their inner psyches," addressing subject-making operations at the site of the social body rather than subjective interiority (1997, 116).

To these two accounts, let us add a third: Arthur Kleinman's work on depression and neurasthenia. Addressing the Cultural Revolution through the accounts and symptoms of psychiatric patients he encountered in the clinic, Kleinman suggests that the risk of complaints about depression and mental illness would have been dangerous in China in the 1960s and 1970s, taken as a sign of skewed political thinking. In contrast, neurasthenia *(shenjing shuairuo)* was exempt from such politically fraught associations at the time and thus provided a bodily, medically legitimized, and politically tolerable idiom through which to articulate otherwise punishable laments.[6] In light of the discussion here, Kleinman's account thus adds another dimension: during the Cultural Revolution, in the case of some patients diagnosed with neurasthenia, the body became a shelter for speech and a sheltered object of speech, in a time when certain narrativizations of suffering might have been subject to persecution. Neurasthenia offered a "hard exoskeleton congealing key meanings," an indirect reference to potential disaffection and dissent, with historical antecedents in the deployment of chronic illness by Confucian literati as a mode of withdrawal from dangerous political circumstances (1986, 159–60).

Across Wang's, Anagnost's, and Kleinman's writings and Yang Shaoliu's staging on the train arise variations on a theme: *something* happened to narrativity during the Maoist era and during the Cultural Revolution in particular. Between May Fourth and Maoism, the function of language and the possible sites of enunciation were interrupted or altered. While such alterations may inflict aphasia at one site, it could also produce—in simultaneity or in deferral—other forms of ciphered, shattered, or proliferating signification: the codification of speech and delinking of interiority in Yang Shaoliu, the literalization of historical truth through bodily violence in Anagnost, the somatization of lament in Kleinman, and the fragmentation of historical coherence and proliferation of new genres in Wang.

In these post-Mao reflections, various disfigurations of language are ascribed to Maoism as distilled and encapsulated in the language-shattering violence of the Cultural Revolution. Yet what of a scene in which Maoism and the Cultural Revolution reappeared differently? By turning to spirit mediumship and accounts of madness in Hexian in the chapters to come, I consider another dimension of language and Maoism: the sense of cosmic-symbolic guarantee during Mao's rule and hollowing after his death and the spectral reanimation of Maoist vocabularies in the contemporary cosmology. But first, to carve out a setting for what would come to be experienced as hollowed and reanimated in contemporary rural China, I trace a series of moments, approaching accounts of history and speech, violence and aphasia, through the figure of the peasant in literary and political writings and campaigns.

My attempt is inspired in part by Anagnost, in following the emergence of the peasant as a world historical figure of speech across May Fourth, Maoist, and post-Mao eras. But here, I consider the position of the "actually speaking peasant" not in terms of a reproduction of official language but also as a subject, to borrow from Jacques Lacan (2007), who falls out of the signifying chain of language and has no place in it, yet is constituted through its delimitations. Like Wang, I am interested in questions of trauma and narrativity. Yet parts of Wang's text take narrativity and sense making to be the preferential mode of experiential transmission. By turning to Kleinman, albeit somewhat sideways, I also consider the significance of other modes of transmission that depart from coherent narrativization, from the symptomatic to the haunted. The detour across the twentieth century, I hope, offers equipment for registering the affectivities of the present, as the present is always-already historical, at times through surprising rehabituations (Berlant 2008).

WHERE IS THE NOW

Perhaps it is not entirely incidental that the rhythmic shuttling of the train evoked Yang Shaoliu's theatrics. Once an emblem of a modernity just out of reach, the figure of the train now seems caught between its ever-deferred arrival and its bittersweet nostalgia, a reminder of the very process of modern time making. By the time of my visit in 2012, the honorific *K* in the K-series train—*K* for *kuai* (fast)— had come to be teased for its anachronism in the ever-accelerating race for more speed. Since their introduction in 2007, the new Harmony Line bullet trains had become darlings of the Chinese transportation world, overshadowing the K series' once-revolutionary seventy-five miles per hour with more than double the speed.[7] Yet, during the time of my visit, the now comparatively sluggish "fast" train remains the most popular mode of long-distance transportation for labor migrants, given the sense of its relative economy, reliability, and geographic reach.

Besides speed and its postponed perfectibility, the shuttling of the train also offers a blurring passage between landscapes at once manifest and ethereal, retracing a spatialization of time that maps a here and there to a then and now. While linking geographies through infrastructural networks, the movements between city and country can also reactivate a sense of distance between an imagined past tethered to the rural hometown and an imagined future reaching toward the urban metropolis—a denial of coevalness, to use Johannes Fabian's (1983) words. Between the purportedly forward-looking metropolis and apparently backward glance toward the home village, the back-and-forth of the train provides a moving glimpse into the conundrum of the "now." To consider Yang Shaoliu's didactic oratory, alongside the writings of those of Wang, Anagnost, and Kleinman, is to dwell on the juxtaposition of language and experience on a moving stage of time and space. The to-and-fro of the train can stir up the worlds produced by this very movement, including rural worlds amid labor outmigration after economic reform.

Prior to my visit to Henan, in conversations among urban friends and scholars in China, the notion of the Maoist revolutionary peasant, and to some extent that of the Maoist People *(renmin)*, often seemed a distant, outmoded past. They seemed to ring of ideology, impossibly lofty ideals, political opportunism, and satire and kitsch. Images of propaganda posters, slogans, and relentless campaigns came to mind at their mention. Their significance was colored scornfully by the "ten-year calamity" of the Cultural Revolution, now seen as an ineluctable outcome of the Maoist project. Such figures seemed, by many urban and intellectual accounts, of a bygone era and, as such, a bygone question to the now of China—just as spirit mediums are no longer supposed to exist in today's Han majority, as Wu Dongliang suggested that one night in Shenzhen.

I am forced to rethink this when I arrive in Hexian. For those old enough to recall, Mao and the People seem indeed of the past, but of a past at once near and far—irrevocable yet still palpable, as if they had come and gone just yesterday, despite more than three decades having passed in between. For the younger generations there, this past is encountered in the form of stories and images, but ones that inherit an air of admiration, if also enigma and ambivalence.

For many I met in Hexian, some of whom self-referentially adopt the term *peasant* even if agriculture was no longer their main source of economic sustenance, Mao signifies a time in which contemplations of rural revolutionary virtue was still possible and still had a point of symbolic reference—a mode of virtue that carries not only local moral significance but world-historical significance. Groups of middle-aged men and retired cadres gather in their morning exercises and noontime drinking, chatting about local, national, and international politics, lamenting woes of the present with a swift phrase: "If Chairman Mao were still alive."

In such conversations the Cultural Revolution rarely comes up spontaneously, even in discussions of the Maoist era. Instead, *wubanian*, '58, referring to the Great Leap famine of 1958–59, is more often evoked than any other punctuated Maoist moment. In some sense this is unsurprising, as the former targeted intellectuals and urban elites and has been said to be a mere "sideshow" in some rural regions, whereas the latter had much broader and deeper impacts on the countryside than the cities (P. Huang 1995; J. Watson 2010). Nonetheless, the distinction is worth noting, as it gives reminder of a bifurcation of history, in which intellectuals and writers who tended to draft post-Mao texts of remembrance and adjudication likely lived a Maoism overlapping yet distinct from those I met in Hexian.

In the urban academic settings I have encountered across Shenzhen, Shanghai, and Beijing, as well as those in the United States, the Cultural Revolution not only constituted a particularly piercing moment of Maoism but often appeared as a condensed image of the Maoist era in its entirety. As Rebecca Karl (2006) suggests, in popular imagination and in much of academic discourse, the Cultural Revolution often comes to be conflated with the much longer history of the Chinese Communist Revolution. It seems that by using the Cultural Revolution as a shorthand for the many painful and ambivalent scenarios arising from revolution-ary experiments, Maoism comes to conjure first and foremost the horrors experi-enced by those falling on the wrong side of the Cultural Revolution, an image so potent that it begins eclipsing other moments and dimensions of the Maoist years. Moreover, the implicit necessity of qualifying any positive sentiment toward Mao-ism with a reiteration of its violence—particularly through the reiteration of num-bers of deaths—is linked in part to an anti-Communist bifurcation and imperative to stand for or against Communism as such (Sorace, Franceschini, and Loubere 2019). To rethink Maoism, then, requires attention to its reverberations beyond more familiar images produced through Cold War bifurcations.

In contrast to its centrality in academic and media portrayals, many I met in Hexian spoke of the Cultural Revolution as but another instance amid the longer ebb and flow of state campaigns. In one occasion, as a group of neighbors gathered to discuss a gray area in a new local state compensation program, one woman notes, "It's just like the Cultural Revolution; you have to snatch the opportunity when you see it, or it's gone." It was a curiously breezy, entrepreneurial image of the "ten-year calamity." This is not to say that the Cultural Revolution did not take a toll on Hexian. Many I spoke to agree that it was a chaotic *(luan)* period, and reform-era county gazetteers employed a similar language. Rather, the divergent remembrances at two ends of a train route, between city and country, between the coastal South and the landlocked inland, together form a question: what might it be to recall the Maoist era from a post-Mao time, without fixing the deplorable effects of the Cultural Revolution as the presumed dénouement?

Given the significance of the urban-rural divide animating this question, I turn to a series of portrayals of the peasant across the twentieth century, the same period through which Wang and Anagnost track the violence leading up to the Cultural Revolution. But rather than ending at the Cultural Revolution, I consider a different sense of rupture that struck the figure of the peasant in the reform era.

Peasant speech and the peasant body became central in May Fourth–era litera-ture, when realism came to be seen as the most viable genre for self-diagnosis and self-determination amid foreign imperial threat. There the peasant came into liter-ary view, albeit chiefly as a figure of concern and pity. Extending this attention to the peasantry, early Chinese Communist and Maoist-era rearticulations inaugu-rated the peasant as a revolutionary political subject, imbuing the rural with national and world-historical significance, albeit not without ambivalence. The end of the Maoist era and the dawn of reform, with some exceptions, reversed these terms once again, devaluing rural space and rendering abject the peasant body as an impediment to national progress amid a world of transnational capital. I turn to these three moments as they illuminate the sense of hollowing hosted by the contemporary cosmology and offer a tentative setting—a spatiotemporal imaginary—for the chapters to follow.

WRITING ABOUT OTHERS

In *The Limits of Realism* (1990), Marston Anderson ponders Lu Xun's satirization of the Chinese revolutionary literature debate in his 1928 essay "The Tablet": "The fearful thing about the Chinese literary scene is that everyone keeps introducing new terms without defining them. . . . And everyone interprets these terms as he pleases. To write a good deal about yourself is expressionism. To write largely about others *(bieren)* is realism. To write poems on a girl's leg is romanticism. To ban poems on a girl's leg is classicism" (1990, 3). Although placed here on an equal satirical platform, realism more than any other genre came to carry the burden of hope in China, writes Anderson, after a "frankly traumatic" series of shocks to the very possibility of national sovereignty (3). Generating the largest body of literary works since Lu Xun's remark (although not without detractors), realism was credited with a powerful social efficacy by Chinese reformers. The notion of social efficacy through literature was not new; what was new was the turn to Western models rather than extending well-established Chinese approaches. Rather than an origin in the realm of literary discourse as such, those who promulgated realism attempted to reach toward that which is "intimately connected with life," of a fiction that would "speak with the voice of living individuals"—that is, individuals aside from the writer, whose intellectual class status was now taken as an index of a distance from "real" life (39).

In contrast to those considered romanticists in the literary debate, the realists deemed the voice of the author and of the intellectual literate class an insufficient ground for claims. Instead, the moral and emotional force of writing must "first be mediated through concern for others" by means of pity *(tongqing)* and sincerity *(cheng)*. These "others" through whom writers were now to mediate their concern included a new range of figures—among them women and peasants—who tended to be passed over historically in literature and politics. Such previously peripheral figures came to center stage in modern debates on social reform. It would be, through those like Zheng Zhenduo, Mao Dun, and others, a "literature of blood and tears," which would give voice to "silent China" (Anderson 1990, 44, 90).

More than attending to a new cast of characters as literary subjects, realism imported a new wedge between the world and the work in Chinese aesthetics and literature. Noting the deployment of authorial disavowals in early realist fiction, in which authors opened their texts with claims to their origin in documentary or journalistic reports, Anderson points to the ambivalence fundamental to any notion of a "realist fiction." Whereas much has been made of the problem of mimesis and imitation in Western aesthetic debates, in which the arts held an imperfect representational relationship to the world, Chinese discussions of literature and the arts had rested on different epistemological and ontological assumptions: "For the Chinese a work of literature was not a copy of the natural world but one of the many manifestations of the fundamental patterns that underlie both the natural and social worlds. . . . The writer, instead of 're-presenting' the outer world, is in fact only the medium for this last phase of the world's coming-to-be" (1990, 12–13). What is it to be medium to the world's coming-to-be in China today? What is it to engage in mediumship while occupying the position of the peasant, a position that has differentially—at times in contradictory ways—stood in for the very embodiment of the figurative real?

Before we move forward, it's important to bear in mind that the reception of realism and its associated epistemology and ontology was by no means total. As Anderson notes, most major Chinese writers who experimented with realism concocted their own "deformations" of the genre, eluding its perceived determinism by employing "elaborate parodic or ironical contrivances to make the work its own self-criticism" (1990, 180). Thus, heterogeneity emerged from within the genre, marking a dissonance that was never fully absorbed. But here what is significant in the rise of realism is the merging of the figure of the peasant and the figure of reality in a moment of perceived crisis, a threat to sovereignty in which the speech of an other previously marginal to literature not only came to occupy a central place but became the very mediator between reality and representation, seen as requisite for the rescuing of the nation.

A MIGHTY STORM

While literary realists of the 1920s pursued a nearness to nonelite life, this very scrutiny and effort to rewrite social relations began to make apparent the distance between the literate authors and their subjects, "the now visible but still mute *bieren* [other]" (Anderson 1990, 26). By the early 1930s, alongside the establishment of the League of Left-Wing Writers, Chinese intellectuals began raising the question of audience and how literature was to affect the lives of its readers. Beyond the educated elites, the imagined audience began shifting to proletarian and peasant classes. Moreover, the protagonist of realist literature shifted from the object of humanist concern to a freshly awakened, heroic subject, and the persecutory crowds characterizing earlier realist fiction came to be replaced by unified, purposive masses. In 1933 the notion of socialist realism was introduced to China by literary theorist Zhou Yang, following the officially sanctioned Soviet model, in which literature was to "constitute the author's objective observation of and research into reality but only from the perspective of a correct worldview, specifically that of the workers and peasants" (Anderson 1990, 57).

Meanwhile, the figure of the peasant was coming to the fore in early Chinese Communist articulations of revolutionary class, as one strand in the literary debates. With the formation of the Chinese Communist Party (CCP) in 1921, a problem soon presented itself: Marxist texts rendered the revolution in terms of

the overthrow of capitalist relations and a seizing of state power by the urban proletariat. Yet at that time China was largely agrarian, with a much smaller urban
industrial sector, and rule was divided among warlords and Western and Japanese
powers, amid the relative lack of a fully centralized state.[8] On what front would the
revolution take place and against whom?

Several tentative responses were posited, including a 1920 articulation by Li
Dazhao, cofounder of the CCP and mentor to Mao. First, given the exploitative
relations of foreign imperialism, China as a whole could be considered a "proletarian nation," as "the whole country has gradually been transformed into part of the
world proletariat" (cited in Spence 1990, 308). Second, in what Spence terms a "bold
intellectual leap," Li Dazhao in 1921 suggested, "Our China is a rural nation and
most of the laboring class is made up of peasants. If they are not liberated, then our
whole nation will not be liberated; their sufferings are the sufferings of our whole
nation; their ignorance is the ignorance of our whole nation; the advantages and
defects of their lives are the advantages and defects of all of our politics. Go out and
develop them and cause them to know [that they should] demand liberation, speak
out about their sufferings, throw off their ignorance and be people who will themselves plan their own lives" (cited in Spence 1990, 308). Here and in the moments to
follow, the rural would become metonymic of the nation, and the nation metonymic of the world proletariat as a global class. Inspired by his writings, a group of
Li's students from Peking University established a "Mass Education Speech Corps,"
traveling to nearby villages to examine rural living conditions. Moreover, a series of
peasant movements soon lent palpable links between the rural and the revolution.

In 1925, when Mao Zedong was spending time in his hometown in Hunan
Province, spontaneous peasant unions were springing up there and in nearby
provinces. Without much explicit interest in the peasantry previously, Mao began
to turn his attention toward its revolutionary potential, departing from the largely
urban emphasis of both the Communists and Nationalists at the time. Writing
against then CCP chair Chen Duxiu and others, who still advocated an urban-
centered revolution in line with orthodox Marxism and the Moscow-directed
Comintern agents in China, Mao increasingly advocated the radicalization and
mobilization of peasants (Karl 2010).[9]

In his March 1926 essay, "Analysis of the Classes in Chinese Society," Mao (1967)
attempts to rearticulate the Chinese social along the lines of revolutionary alliance
and enmity. Here the peasantry is subsumed under the question of class yet begins
to emerge as a significant figure in the incitement of revolution. Mao deemed a
small portion of "owner peasants" (those who for the most part needn't rent land
from others to provide for their own subsistence yet are not big landlords) "suspi-
cious" and "a little afraid" of revolution, as their "mouths water copiously" upon
seeing the small fortunes amassed by the middle bourgeoisie. But he designated the
vast majority of peasants as supporters or potential supporters of the revolution:

"The overwhelming majority of the semi-owner peasants together with the poor peasants constitute a very large part of the rural masses. The peasant problem is essentially their problem. The semi-owner peasants are . . . more revolutionary than the owner-peasants, but less revolutionary than the poor peasants" (16–17).[10]

If the peasantry became a site for the other of attentive pity in May Fourth realist literature—a simultaneous disdain and concern as representation of a stagnant, hapless old China—the peasant in this well-known essay begins gathering revolutionary potential, partly in an effort to render the sign of the proletariat in Marxist and Soviet writings locally salient to the Chinese scene (Barlow 1991). Nonetheless, in these earlier writings by Mao, the figure of the peasant remained one to be led, an ally to the revolution rather than its propelling force. Following Soviet lines, the industrial proletariat constituted the core and force of the revolution: "The modern industrial proletariat numbers about two million. It is not large because China is economically backward. . . . Though not very numerous, the industrial proletariat . . . is the most progressive class in modern China and has become the leading force in the revolutionary movement. . . . Our closest friends are the entire semi-proletariat [including semi-owner and poor peasants] and petty bourgeoisie [including the owner peasants]" (Mao 1967, 18–19).

Similarly, in his September 1, 1926, "National Revolution and the Peasant Movement," Mao (1967) opens the essay, "The peasant problem is the central problem of the national revolution, if the peasants don't rise up to participate and assist in the national revolution, the national revolution will not succeed." He then urges comrades to "ask them whence their bitterness . . . [and] from their bitterness and need, lead them to organize, lead them to struggle/battle the gentry." Even as they became the rhetorical center of the revolutionary problem, the figure of the peasant remained a relatively passive one, an embittered other from whom complaints must be elicited and who would be led by their urban comrades.

Yet Mao's rendering would soon shift after a month-long investigatory visit to a series of rural sites in Hunan Province, said to be an epicenter of the peasant movement at the time, then debated and critiqued by the Left. In his 1927 "Report on an Investigation of the Peasant Movement in Hunan," Mao states,

> All talk directed against the peasant movement must be speedily set right . . . for the present upsurge of the peasant movement is a colossal event. In a very short time, in China's central, southern and northern provinces, several hundred million peasants will rise like a mighty storm, like a hurricane, a force so swift and violent that no power, however great, will be able to hold it back. They will smash all the trammels that bind them and rush forward along the road to liberation.
>
> They will sweep all the imperialists, warlords, corrupt officials, local tyrants and evil gentry into their graves. Every revolutionary party and every revolutionary comrade will be put to the test, to be accepted or rejected as they decide. There are three

alternatives. To march at their head and lead them? To trail behind them, gesticulat-ing and criticizing? Or to stand in their way and oppose them? Every Chinese is free to choose, but events will force you to make the choice quickly.

In a few months the peasants have accomplished what Dr. Sun Yat-sen wanted, but failed, to accomplish in the forty years he devoted to the national revolution. This is a marvelous feat never before achieved, not just in forty, but in thousands of years. (1967, 23–24)

In contrast to Mao's earlier essays, not to mention existing Communist and Nationalist literature, the peasant rushes to the forefront of the revolution, threaten-ing at last to leave the Communist Party and the nation behind, reversing the terms of their previous condemnation as the quintessential backward hindrance to a pro-gressive history. While the "peasant problem" elicited concern across political and literary writings of the time, Mao's radical reformulation and subsequent campaigns (land reform in particular) would transform the figure of the peasant from a loath-some Chinese problem to a revolutionary force to be reckoned with. Even if subse-quent Maoist writings and campaigns may not have lived up to this upholding of the peasantry, a new vision of the peasant had been inaugurated, one that I would find reverberations and reanimations of decades later in Hexian. The Chinese peasant would become a world-historical subject of an international Communism to come.

COSMOCRATIC MYTHOLOGIC

In "Cultural and Political Inventions in Modern China: The Case of the Chinese 'Peasant,'" Myron Cohen traces the history of the peasant *(nongmin)* as vocabulary and as political-administrative category in late nineteenth- and twentieth-century China. Cohen suggests that the Chinese Communist state imposed a deeply inac-curate term for what he calls China's economic culture, as subsistence farming was rarely the sole livelihood of rural inhabitants, both before and after the Maoist era. Rather than a descriptive term, he writes, the notion of the peasant made way for the legitimation of administrative acts, alongside inventions of an "old" society against a "new" liberated one—a New China. While the category held "staying power" due partly to the labeling of poor, middle, and rich peasants and landlords during land reform campaigns, Cohen argues that such an approach proved "cul-turally impotent" and foreclosed "viable cultural expression," as the "economic liberation of the peasantry required its cultural destruction" (1993, 152–57).

Rather than entering the debate on what a more accurate description of Chi-nese economic culture might look like, Cohen's stance points to several significant dimensions of Maoist world making: Maoist language as a speech act that had the capacity to move autonomously from material economic worlds and the role of land reform campaigns in concretizing this new notion of the peasant.

The categories congealed through land reform and the narrative techniques that helped establish them were first formulated in Communist bases in Yan'an in the 1930s and 1940s, where early Communist Party members gathered. Drawing on their 1986–89 interviews with surviving participants and local residents of the Yan'an period, David Apter and Tony Saich (1998) describe the centrality of spoken word and text in the creation of what they call a cosmology of power, with a *cosmocratic center* condensed and intensified in the image of Mao. Through the establishment of a "special discourse community," they suggest, Mao drew from Chinese traditions and Marxist lineages to transform stories of world history, Chinese history, and individual histories into a *mythologic*: "Indeed, word and text themselves came to have iconographic significance. They not only embodied the new meaning but also represented it as artifacts, as things in themselves, with the same force as the portrait of Buddha imprinted on a tanka" (35–36). Historical sequences of various scalar proportions "telescoped" into one another until the particularities of each began to vanish with repetition: "There is a long story of the decline and fall of China and the loss of the patrimony; an intermediate one, the struggle with the GMD [Nationalist Party]; and a short one, which covers the bitter internecine conflicts between lines and factions within the CCP. The shorter the story, the more closed down the optic, the bigger the image, and the smaller the field until Mao virtually fills the entire field of vision" (71).

Through the craft of oral storytelling, they suggest, Mao reenacted and unified history and experience. Drawing on the life stories of those who traveled to join Yan'an, Mao came to articulate prototypes that would be turned into text (Apter and Saich 1998, 144). These texts brought together the immediacies of life histories with the history of China, and the history of China with the history of the world— "China *as* history becoming China *in* history" (172). Stories of poverty, debt, avaricious landlords, the rupturing of lineages, betrayal, and natural catastrophe were linked to larger forces of foreign imperialism and complicities of Chinese comprador capitalism.

While Apter and Saich write with an air of cynicism toward the Maoist project, they nonetheless find that, for many of the survivors they interviewed, the submission to an authority of interpretation was regarded as an act of *realization*: "for them word and text, far from being oppressive, became a form of unique knowledge and understanding" (Apter and Saich 1998, 21). Such texts were then read collectively in study groups, and this practice of reading "produced a certain *jouissance,* what Roland Barthes has referred to as the pleasure in the text" (114). In the interviews participants recalled the journey to Yan'an as a "going home"—a psychic and physical crossing that first required a severing from one's previous family and community. In a time when the very existence of China had been put into question, a sense of going home was no doubt profound and hints at the reanimating force of Mao that would return in Hexian amid a broader sense of evacuation.

Maoist narratives reached across a divide marking previous Chinese tales—between the orality of storytelling and literacy of texts and between the largely illiterate and powerless populace and the literate elite. Combining elements from myths, folktales, and literary texts, alongside a Communist line of descent, "punctuated with barnyard humor and classical allusion," Mao deployed techniques as well as existing tales that transgressed hierarchies or turned them upside down, including the figure of the peasant—the peasant warrior who became emperor, the Taiping rebellion as exemplary for peasant revolution (Apter and Saich 1998, 88).

Through Apter and Saich's focus on Yan'an, the question of violence takes on a different appearance than that of the authors earlier in this chapter, who had linked the theme of violence with the Cultural Revolution—which ended in effect with the death of Mao, thus marking the culmination and demise of Maoism. Apter and Saich also discuss the violence of the Cultural Revolution as recounted by Yan'an survivors, many of whom were later targeted. Yet, in their rendering, violence also constituted a *genesis* of revolutionary storytelling, not only its tragic ending. Tales arose from a war-torn China already filled with scenes of despair and yearning, and in such a moment "Mao's storytelling became an act in itself, an assertion of control over violence" amid the sense of loss and chaos (1998, 73). Violence was ever-present and storied the generalized condition all around; the storied victims would in turn use violence to reestablish order. Encounters with ongoing violence within the vicinity of Yan'an provided a "constant testing ground" of ideas, whether it be against the Japanese, the Nationalists, or factions within the Communist Party (35). Here violence is thus placed in formative and recursive relation to narrative—that against and through which Maoist storytelling emerged and continuously transformed. It was amid these redeployments of aggression, their account suggests, that Maoism came to create its own symbolic order, through which a revolutionary subjectivity would be articulated.

AN EXISTENTIAL POLITICS OF LAND REFORM

If Yan'an constituted a "miniature" of the broader Maoist project, as Apter and Saich (1998) put it, it provided a microcosm for experiments in language and praxis, in language *as* praxis. This language, arguably, gained macrocosmic reach through the processes and practices of Liberation and land reform, as well as the many campaigns that came after. In a call to account for and distinguish between what he calls representational realities and objective realities of rural class struggle, Philip Huang (1995) cautions against taking 1949 as the decisive marker of the Communist Revolution's arrival. Rather, he turns to the full-scale land revolution, which abolished rent and redistributed 43 percent of cultivated land to around three hundred million poor peasants—over half of China's population at the time (see also Cheng 1982, 66).

Paralleling Cohen's comment, though in the spirit of observation rather than rectification, Huang suggests that in the process of effectively ending landlords and rich peasants as *material* classes, land reform simultaneously produced *class* as a symbolic and moral category: "By the end of Land Reform, millions of intellectuals had participated in actions and thoughts that turned *class* from its material meaning in Marxist-Leninist theory into a symbolic-moral meaning in the dramatic struggle of good against evil within every village. It was in the Land Revolution that the practice of manufacturing class struggle where there was no material basis for such became widespread. . . . Class took over not only the material but the symbolic realm" (1995, 125). Huang outlines three stages of land reform, each marking a distinct relation between what he calls *representation* and *reality*. In the old liberated areas (1937–45), he suggests, techniques were less drastic, and theory and action were often most congruent. Rents were decreased, taxes were increased, and "poor peasant" landholdings rose, bringing them into a "new middle." During the Civil War period (1946–49), class struggle became a weapon in the clashes between the Communists and Nationalists and became increasingly arbitrary and violent. After Liberation (1949–52), the intensity of arbitrariness and violence decreased overall, yet conundrums still arose. Many of the most highly propertied rural landlords in North China were in fact absentee landlords and thus escaped class struggle. Many villages lacked any person who met the criteria for landlord or even rich peasant. Yet cadres were at times pressed to identify class enemies, thus middle peasants who allegedly concealed property were targeted for struggle.

Extending the question of representation to the Cultural Revolution, Huang suggests that these earlier moments of disjuncture between land and class widened the gap between the material and the representational. While class labels were still linked (even if thinly) to material property during land reform, by the time of the Cultural Revolution, "connections between representation and objective realities were severed," and "class [became] almost exclusively a matter of political attitude . . . a matter of representation alone" (1995, 133–34).

The notion of class was thus first produced as linguistic and lived praxis through its tie to the material redistribution of land. Subsequently, the mapping of class onto materiality grew increasingly distanced, until the language of class grew autonomous from questions of land ownership and took on a force of its own as a moral-symbolic order. As in Claude Lévi-Strauss's (1963) rendering of symbolic efficacy in shamanism, a parallel map was created through language and ritual that doubled the physical landscape, eventually severing from the physical to produce effects.

Linked with the production of class as a moral-symbolic order, such campaigns as land reform also generated a new relationality between the one and the collective: the suffering of each and every poor peasant came to be linked to a national whole and, beyond that, to world history. Reflecting on Fang Huirong's (1997) sociological work with the Oral History Project on rural remembrances of the Maoist years, Xin Liu writes that the performative repetition of narratives of suffering amplified the particular into the general and brought the general into the particular, through what Fang calls a "narrative transfer" between the two. Not unlike the "telescoping" of Yan'an narratives described earlier, the "I" was fastened to the "we"; the pain of each Chinese peasant was rendered a "symptom of a *universal illness,* diagnosed by Marx as the capitalistic-imperialistic oppression of the working-class people of the world" (2009, 144). But this time, rather than a small, select group as in Yan'an, such practices became forms of life across Chinese villages, guided and habituated by the political technologies of the work team.

Through the "interiorization" of a "phantasmal unity" of the People, Liu suggests, a powerful *existential politics* was created through waves of campaigns, through which peasants, as Maoist ethical subjects, "saw themselves for the first time as a *living force*" in history (2009, 168). In day-to-day praxis this involved mass campaigns of pouring out grievances or "speaking bitterness," through which discrete memories were condensed into "impressionistic images," conjoined by the repeated induction of particular narrative plots (149–53).

Rather than chains of causal relation mapped onto linear time, memory became "anti-calendrical," reorganizing the interior experience of time to a nationalist time (X. Liu 2009, 151). Decades later Fang's interviewees could not seem to recall the years of particular occurrences but rather placed occurrences in relation to national temporal markers—before or after collectivization, for instance. This temporality was also pointed toward a future of perpetual struggle and of a "promised utopian tomorrow that would perhaps never arrive" (161). Liu calls the intense mythical power and energy generated by such practices a "Maoist shamanism" (144)—a term that resonates beyond the bounds of official campaigns in the context of this book.

I turn to Huang and Liu, as well as Cohen and Apter and Saich, for their considerations of the shifting linkages and ruptures between language and world, which simultaneously produced a new symbolic order, wherein the peasant figures centrally in the question of the moral, by way of class. Through distinctions broad and minute, instantiated through localized practice, notions of the peasant as world historical subject articulated in earlier Maoist and Communist writings became part of daily life, the basis on which material relations were reorganized and where recognition was sought.

Through the very campaigns that were later seen to have ruptured the function of language, a new language was born, centered in part on the revolutionary, moral-political position of the peasant. This new language, needless to say, did not go uncontested. Nonetheless, as I show in the chapters that follow, what Apter and Saich (1998) termed Mao's cosmocratic mythologic and Xin Liu (2009) termed

Maoist shamanism, and what I consider here as a new, if deeply fraught, symbolic order, regains cosmological significance in spectral form in contemporary mediumship. Specifically, Hexian and Henan Province, which would experience an inversion of valence postreform through the very figure of the peasant and of the rural, would return to Maoism as a foregone world, a language that returns in fragments of speech, ritual, and psychiatric symptoms to illuminate the conundrum of the "now." To grasp this inversion of valence between the Maoist and post-Mao eras, I end with the radical reformulations of the peasantry postreform.

AGRARIAN ANACHRONISM

If the peasant was in part figured as a force of heroic revolutionary potential during the Maoist era, with the death of Mao in 1976, this vision was quickly dismantled by intellectuals and officials in the search for a new technocratic and purportedly apolitical approach to modernization. By the Third Plenum of the Eleventh Central Committee in December 1978, the refutation of Maoism gained strength with the start of Deng Xiaoping's rise. The intellectual class targeted during the Cultural Revolution relegated Maoism to an anachronism alongside the feudalism it was once posited against, and with it the focus on history and class struggle. The future, instead, was to be found in the concepts of rights and democracy, against what came to be framed as a feudal totalitarianism. Although intellectuals first relied on early Maoist notions of economic determination in peasant class consciousness, the peasantry's relationship to time and history were soon reversed:

> Contrary to the stress on the revolutionary nature of the peasantry in the 1960s and 1970s, intellectuals stressed the conservative nature of the peasantry's egalitarian tendencies during the early reform era. This conservative peasantry, in turn, was seen as the social foundation for an autocratic state, for dictatorship, and the cult of personality. . . . As the reform era developed, peasant historical and political agency was increasingly denied, and the two poles of the peasantry's dual nature were reversed: egalitarian and revolutionary tendencies were redefined as conservative, while the petty-bourgeois tendencies of the small property owner were now seen as progressive and entrepreneurial. (Day 2013, 28–29)

The forward-moving potential of the peasantry as a rebellious, exploited class was replaced by the image of a dispersed, unruly mass in need of an autocratic ruler, thus linking the peasantry with the political errors of the Maoist era. As the deputy editor in chief of the *People's Daily* put it during a speech at a Communist Party conference, "Due to their [small farmers'] dispersed, self-sufficient and mutually isolated nature, they were unable to form a 'national bond.' . . . This kind of socioeconomic condition nurtures monarchical thinking and produces the personality cult" (cited in Brugger and Kelly 1990, 143).

Mao and the peasants were together sent back in time, in a periodization of monarchy and feudalism set against democracy and modernization. Peasant populism entered discussions of the so-called Asiatic mode of production, in which an agrarian society with a dominant state would hinder any possibility of historical dynamism. The peasantry came to stand in as the root cause of stagnation. Amid discursive efforts to delink the peasantry from the state and relink the peasant question with those of entrepreneurship, a language of peasant "quality" *(suzhi)* came to the fore. Paralleling notions of population quality accompanying the one-child policy, the notion of labor quality came to explain and justify the "differential value produced by equal quantities of labor power," reinstating the difference between mental and manual labor that Maoist-era policies attempted to eliminate (Day 2013, 37). The difference of value coded in the language of *suzhi,* in which the rural populace and rural labor are seen as excessive in quantity while lacking in quality, at once facilitates the extraction of surplus value from rural migrant labor and renders invisible this very process of difference production (H. Yan 2003).

This new coding of value was elaborated in particular through the paired contrast between the body of the rural migrant, a corporeal sign of the absence of quality, and that of the urban, middle-class only child, "fetishized as a site for the accumulation of the very dimensions of *suzhi* wanting in its 'other' . . . a play of plentitude and lack" (Anagnost 2004, 190). In such discourses "quality" was defined by a sense of entrepreneurial spirit, openness to ideas, efficiency, initiative, drive, and risk taking in contrast to the defensive, inward-looking, despotic, and authoritarian tendencies imputed to agrarian society (Day 2013).

The status of the peasantry as an embodiment of the revolutionary People was reversed into signs of dependency and backwardness, ever in lack of urban bourgeois "quality." In such postreform recodings, the sense of rural historical and political agency articulated in the Maoist era faded into a realm of impossibility—the peasantry that would smash the trammels and rush forward on the road to liberation would instead come to be condemned for holding back the very future of China.

FUTURES PAST

"Every revolution creates new words," William Hinton writes in *Fanshen,* his 1966 firsthand account of early land reform in rural Shanxi Province in the late 1940s. "The Chinese Revolution created a whole new vocabulary" (2008, vii). By the time of its sequel, *Shenfan,* based on observations from 1966 to 1971, Hinton had grown deeply disturbed and dismayed by the unfolding of Maoist campaigns, the Cultural Revolution in particular. What began as radical, well-intended political efforts, in the eyes of Hinton and other former supporters of Maoism, ended in disaster. Some blamed local implementation. Some blamed Mao and those around

him, particularly toward the end of his rule. The knotted complexities of the Maoist era, like any other era, are more than any single account can capture.

By tracing the rise and demise of the figure of the heroic revolutionary peasant,
I am not suggesting that rural inhabitants in the Maoist era simply experienced
their lives as such. Instead, I conjure the grandeur of what was pronounced—call
it propaganda, revolution, or utopian intention—in effort to trace the contours of
what would come to be felt as a hollow thereafter, to follow the shape of what
would be emptied out. This sense of virtuous revolutionary grandeur—more than
attempted scoresheets of Mao's rights and wrongs, more than the most nuanced
assessment of any given campaign—spoke to and animated the potent visions of
loss and transformative potential among spirit mediums I met in Hexian.

While the devastations occasioned by Maoist-era campaigns may indeed have
shattered language and speech across many scenes in China and beyond, the new
vocabulary inaugurated by Maoism was also taken up and merged with other languages in the contemporary cosmology. Together these would lend a grammar for
cosmopolitical reconfigurations of the present, carving out horizons of a powerful
rural futurity, in a time and place where the rural and the future seemed to otherwise resound in dissonance. To consider the figure of the revolutionary peasant in
the now, then, is to encounter a future past, to borrow from Reinhart Koselleck
(2004).[11] Such formerly anticipated futures may find ways of reappearing in the
present, even as they come to be overshadowed by other formulations. Indeed, the
very disjuncture of time produced amid the eclipsing of past horizons by present
ones may intensify the former's potency in new ways.

. . .

"See, isn't it backward? [Luohou bu luohou?]," Yang Shaoliu muses as we peer out
the window at the vast expanses of wheat fields. We are nearing the end of our
train ride to Henan.

"What's backward about it? It's just the countryside," I try.

"Yes, but not all countrysides are the same." His flippant tone begins to fade. "In the
United States, agriculture is industrialized. Here you still have families of farmers,
with just a few people farming on the small scale without much mechanization by
comparison. There are still people fertilizing the fields by hand, for instance, or using
very simple equipment. Some larger farms have more advanced machinery, but not
everyone. It's still backward." He shakes his head slightly. For the first time on the trip,
I sense a certain disappointment from Yang Shaoliu, a sense that things could or
should be otherwise—more advanced, more industrialized, more something.

Like Zhao Yun's thrusting of the rice sack back onto the shelf, there seems to be
something amiss about the hometown as we neared it. Yang Shaoliu will later tell
me about how he had grown averse to the taste of sweet potatoes, served locally in
gruel and other dishes as a staple, after years of insufficient food supplies during

his childhood, when "big-pot" meals *(daguofan)* under Maoist collectivization consisted day after day of sweet potatoes in various guises. He will also speak of his relatives, who died of starvation during the Great Leap famine years.

But, in spite of these harrowing memories, like those I would soon meet in Hexian, Yang Shaoliu does not simply denounce Mao in the style that some urbanites and scholars I met did. He says that the most difficult of Maoist years was a painful but necessary process that China had to undergo, to reach where it is today. After all, he says in a phrasing I would also come to hear from others, if there was little to eat in the years of big-pot meals, at least there was *something* to eat, unlike the times before.

Perhaps this might be called a remnant of coded speech from the Maoist years that Yang Shaoliu himself made jest of, in which statist projects must be verbally valorized regardless of one's discontents. Perhaps this was the very stylized recollection of time shaped by the condensation of individual and national narratives, in which Yang Shaoliu's childhood hunger was strategically linked to China's growing pains. But to simply deem them as such and end thinking there would miss the point. The campaigns and struggles of the Maoist years were experienced differently across geographies, and not without profound ambivalence of various forms. As oral histories with those who lived through various Maoist-era campaigns have shown, remembrances range from a sense of a devastating loss of one's best years to the most inspiring time one could recall, and sometimes both at once.

That life is complicated, as Avery Gordon puts it, may seem a banal expression but also constitutes a theoretical guide; power relations and dire circumstances that might appear obvious at first glance are never quite so simple. And, in attending to such complications, we may be amid hauntings—in her words, "How that which appears to be not there is often a seething presence" (1997, 8). The absent presence of the Maoist years in Yang Shaoliu's didactic stagings, and in the various retrospective attempts at deciphering them, would appear in another form once I reached Hexian. As our conversation comes to a close, the train comes to a rolling stop. We have arrived.

Ten Thousand Years

An older man stands in the shadows of the temple gate, reciting Mao Zedong's poem "Snow" in a bellowing oratory to no one in particular. Several passersby gather around, myself included. They say his recitation is verbatim and his delivery resembles Chairman Mao's.

> North country scene:
> A hundred leagues locked in ice,
> A thousand leagues of whirling snow.
> Both sides of the Great Wall
> One single white immensity.
> The Yellow River's swift current
> Is stilled from end to end.
> The mountains dance like silver snakes
> And the highlands charge like wax-hued elephants,
> Vying with heaven in stature.
> On a fine day, the land,
> Clad in white, adorned in red,
> Grows more enchanting.
>
> This land so rich in beauty
> Has made countless heroes bow in homage.
> But alas! Qin Shihuang and Han Wudi
> Were lacking in literary grace,
> And Tang Taizong and Song Taizu
> Had little poetry in their souls;

And Genghis Khan,
Proud Son of Heaven for a day,
Knew only shooting eagles, bow outstretched
All are past and gone!
For truly great men
Look to this age alone. (Cited in Terrill 1999, 170)

The voice, those around me whisper, is not his own. It is, they said with a quick nod upward, "from above" *(shangmiande)*—from the heavens.

Oft-cited as Mao's most well-known poem, "Snow" was composed in 1936, after the end of the Long March, amid revamped efforts at a united front against Japanese forces, and was published in 1945, after the Japanese defeat in World War II. At the time of its publication, Mao had been seen as a revolutionary persona, but not yet the central political figure he would later become. The poem's evocation of emperors known for the unification and territorial expansion of China, deployment of classical Chinese poetic form, and circulation in modern mass media were together taken as a grandiose gesture of his intent to rule, causing a stir in the intellectual and political scene at the time (Z. Yang 2013).

Under the dim glow of street lamps outside of Fuxi Temple in Hexian, "Snow" takes on a new life, causing a new stir. That the poem's voicing comes "from above" signaled the unseen presence of Mao, channeled through the "borrowed" mouth of the orator. The language of borrowing, in Hexian, indicates various degrees of possession, in which the human is deployed, in part or in whole, by a persona from the heavens or from the yin realm.

Three stout elderly women in cotton coats *(mian'ao)* deliberate the recitation in murmurs. A middle-aged man, showing only his eyes through a black scarf, peers at the orator, pupils dark as fire. A pale bookish businessman, perhaps in his twenties—glasses, small briefcase, button-up shirt—is seemingly an outsider to the temple scene, like myself, judging by his comportment and manner of listening. Then again, the out and the in, the affected and unaffected, are hard to distinguish on the temple square, particularly when night falls. While some humans are considered more porous to invisible forces than others and may take up recognized roles in the mediation of spirits, any human body can be borrowed or collided into by deities and ghosts with or without its own knowing. Such spaces as the temple square are known to draw in a multitude of unseen entities, bringing both spiritual powers and risks.

"December 26, 1893, [Mao was] born to a family of farmers. After the Xinhai Revolution erupted, [he was] a soldier for half a year, in service to the new military of the uprising. . . . He encountered and accepted Marxism around the time of the May Fourth Movement, and in 1920 founded a Communist organization." The orator is now reading from a tattered red booklet he pulled from his satchel—an unofficial biography of Mao.

"Do you understand what he's saying?" the bookish man, my companion in alien status, asks under his breath.

"Half." I don't know quite how to answer.

He shakes his head. "I don't understand. I feel *mi*—disoriented, confused, lost. The more I listen, the more disoriented I feel." Indeed, from the slight tremble of disturbance on his face, I worry that the scene might take him too far. In early medieval Chinese Buddhist scripture, *mi* was often employed in the form of *midao*, to stray, deviate, or "lose one's way" from the proper path (Campany 2003, 304–5). In Hexian the sensation of *mi* can be used as a general term for confusion arising from being overly caught up by someone or something, confusion and delusion arising from illness or senility, or confusion and delusion accompanying spirit possession and other encounters with the ghostly realm.

"I don't understand," he repeats. He had spent some time as a student here in Hexian, he says, but now lives in the South—the coastal magnet for young rural labor migrants since Deng Xiaoping's economic reform era—and has not been back here for years. Now on a business trip nearby, he decided to stop through the temple after work and found himself seized by the recitation, caught in a moment of bewilderment. In this chapter I turn to the place of Mao at Fuxi Temple and in the contemporary cosmology in Hexian. The orator, as it turns out, is just one among many who transmitted the words and absent presence of the Chairman.

THE TEMPLE SQUARE

Fuxi Temple is considered by many in Hexian to be the primary temple in the county, both in terms of scale and spiritual potency. Known in Chinese mythology as the first among the Three Sovereigns, Fuxi is referred to colloquially in Hexian as the Deity of Human Ancestry (Renzuye). Numerous renderings of the Fuxi mythology have circulated historically and regionally, but most have pivoted around his role in the rebirth of humanity some thousands of years ago (Birrell 1993). Following a great deluge, Fuxi and his sister, Nüwa—depicted as intertwining half-human, half-serpent entities in some Han and Tang dynasty murals—wished to marry each other to repopulate the earth. The two were uncertain whether marriage was proper among siblings and sought divine authorization atop Kunlun Mountain. Upon receiving heavenly sanction, they created what we now know as humanity. In Hexian Nüwa is often said to have kneaded human figurines out of mud, from which new human life sprang.

Unlike creation myths that begin ex nihilo, Nüwa was said to have repaired the four pillars that held up the sky before their damage amid calamity, and Fuxi marked the founding of humanity as a civilizational entity, not the birth of humanity as such. Credited variously with the invention of animal domestication, fishing and hunting implements, culinary techniques, the eight trigrams, and the marriage system, Fuxi was said to have distanced humanity from conditions of chaos and matriarchy:

> In the beginning there was as yet no moral or social order. Men knew their mothers only, not their fathers. When hungry, they searched for food; when satisfied, they threw away the remnants. They devoured their food hide and hair, drank the blood, and clad themselves in skins and rushes. Then came Fu Hsi [Fuxi,] [who] looked upward and contemplated the images in the heavens, and looked downward and contemplated the occurrences on earth. He united man and wife, regulated the five stages of change, and laid down the laws of humanity. He devised the eight trigrams, in order to gain mastery over the world.[1] (Cited in Wilhelm and Baynes 1967, 329)

In Hexian the presence of Fuxi Temple evokes a sense of regional protection. While Fuxi is known for presiding over the human realm at large, residents say that he watches over those in the vicinity of his temple in particular, preventing calamity in the region. The temple was built and rebuilt, from one dynasty to the next, before and since it came into ritual prominence in the Ming dynasty (1368–1644). Aside from mythologies of Fuxi, one of the more commonly circulated temple legends during my time in Hexian was that of Zhu Yuanzhang (1328–98), the first emperor of the Ming dynasty. Born to a destitute peasant family, Zhu was known for leading an intermittent life of a wandering beggar before joining the Red Turban Rebellion against the Mongol-led Yuan dynasty. The originators of the rebellion drew on the eschatology of so-called White Lotus groups, announcing the coming end of an empire in chaos, while anticipating the dawn of a new order following the reincarnation of the Maitreya Buddha (H. Chan 2008).[2] While the Maitreyan dimension of Zhu's own political history is not always elaborated in the oral accounts I encountered, its significance becomes apparent in chapter 5, as these eschatological horizons return in the contemporary cosmology.

According to local legend, prior to the overthrow of the Yuan dynasty and before his rise as emperor, Zhu once sought refuge in the Fuxi Temple while fleeing Yuan dynasty troops. Once inside the temple, layer upon layer of cobwebs miraculously formed, covering the temple gate. Fooled by the abandoned appearance of the temple, the soldiers rushed on, leaving Zhu unharmed. In gratitude for his life, once Zhu took reign as emperor, he rebuilt the temple. Thereafter the temple would reenter cycles of disrepair and renovation, across the dynasties.

In Hexian everyday accounts of Fuxi Temple's past often move between the time of Fuxi and Nüwa, the time of Zhu Yuanzhang, and the Maoist era. During the Cultural Revolution portions of the temple and its icons were desecrated. According to the county gazetteer, in August 1966, under the slogan "Destroy the Four Olds and Establish the Four News" *(Posijiu Lisixin)*, the Fuxi icon was destroyed, the temple was bombarded, the guardian lions were smashed, and numerous other historical sites were damaged by the Red Guards.[3] During my time there, rumors circulated that several of the Red Guards who initiated the destruction later fell prey to strange illnesses or died bad deaths. Simultaneously, cosmological accounts pointed to the divine sanctioning of such acts.

In the 1990s, following the advent of economic reforms and loosening of restrictions on religious sites, the county government began establishing the temple as a cultural and touristic site. Drawn to the consumptive potential of such temples, the state co-opted the ancestral fair historically held at the temple, transforming the fair into a matter of state management, with leadership selected by the county head and county-level Communist Party committee members. Given this state-sponsored platform, private entrepreneurs were also drawn in, in hopes of profit from the hundreds of thousands that attended the fair each year.

Moreover, in what many residents I met in Hexian see as stagings of political power as well as occasions for economic gain, the temple square was expanded once and again over the years by incoming county leadership, until it reached its now massive proportions by the first decade of the 2000s. Standing on the temple square on a sparse day, one gets the sense of an endless horizon, stretching north to south, east to west. Indeed, visits to Fuxi Temple are often referred to as "heading to the square" (shang guangchang).

The vast expanse of the square, or guangchang (lit. "broad space or site"), as an architectural element has been emblematic of modern Chinese state power particularly since Maoist years, with Tiananmen Square being the most politically and symbolically centralized instantiation (Hung 1991).[4] Prior to the twentieth century, the space just south of Tiananmen (lit. "the Gate of Heavenly Peace") had no name. When what would come to be known as Tiananmen Square was taken up for the first time as a space for a large-scale public rally during the 1919 May Fourth Movement, the press referred to it simply as the "empty space" outside of Tianan Gate (N. Lee 2009, 32).

Of prior political significance instead were the series of walls and gates themselves, which marked a nested set of contrasts between inner and outer in the cosmopolitical landscape of Beijing, between the outer, inner, imperial, and finally forbidden cities. From south to north each gate marked a successive hierarchy of exclusion. Tiananmen had acted as both entry and barrier between the inner and imperial cities, inaccessible to commoners until the fall of the dynastic system. The philosophy of power operated according to a logic of concealment, and what had to be hidden was precisely the body of the emperor. Even during rituals of exchange between the emperor and subjects, the imperial side was embodied by ritual objects rather than the body of the emperor itself, and the subjects by formal representatives (Meyer 1991).

With the victory of the Communist Party in 1949, the Maoist administration enacted a collapse and reversal of this political-symbolic geography: Mao appeared atop Tiananmen, with thousands of commoners and soldiers gathered beneath.

Power had become visible rather than hidden, and the People now had visual access of the Chairman, from the public space of the square.[5] The nested walls previously segmenting the city were gradually demolished, as the gate and the square were continually expanded, realigned to be the new symbolic center rather than the Forbidden City (Hung 1991). Conceptualized as a national space for the joining of Communist spectacle and mass mobilization, the square at once drew on and denied the previous sacred geography of the imperial complex (R. Watson 1995).

From its informal inauguration to its formal take-up as modern political space, the square has continued to stage various forms of official and unofficial power, in their distinction, simultaneity, and encounters. It has been a space of state proclamations, military parades, and protests—June 4, 1989, being the most well known—and forms of monumentalization and pilgrimage both encouraged and discouraged by the state, including pilgrimages to the Chairman Mao Memorial Hall (Wagner 1992).

Beyond Tiananmen, the square as a concept and architectural element was installed throughout the People's Republic, transporting its symbolic geography across cities, towns, and villages. The expansion of the square outside the front gate of Fuxi Temple in Hexian thus partakes in this history of public and political space making. Moreover, a copresence of powers is similarly hosted at the temple square, this time through a multiplication of the party-state itself—a spectral polity doubling the earthly state.

WALKING THE CHAIRMAN'S PATH

"Most here at the square are those who have undergone bitterness, those who have undergone hardship." It is the orator from the night prior, now speaking into a crackling clip-on microphone in the bright of day, from a short wooden stool (*mazha*) on the temple square. He introduces himself as Wang, a peasant from an adjacent county to the north. This morning, despite attempts to amplify his message with the small microphone, Wang's voice is drowned out by the song and drums reverberating from the proliferation of rituals across the temple square. It is the first day of the twelfth lunar month in the year of the dragon. Thousands of men, women, and children from nearby villages and towns gather both inside and outside the temple gates. "This society is chaotic. What I heed is not money, what I heed is the person. Gods are humans; humans are gods. Humans are living Buddhas, living immortals," Wang continues.

I inquire about the small red booklets by his side—the same kind he was reading from in the night, the unofficial biography of Mao. He hands me a copy. "The Great Thought of Mao Zedong Radiates Eternally," it reads in bold yellow, atop a portrait of Mao in a gray suit. Beneath the portrait: "The Heroically Sagacious Shakes All under Heaven; Mighty Feats Shall Be Lauded Generation after Generation."[6] Inside the front and back covers, iconic color photos show Mao greeting families and workers, addressing troops, fishing, reading the newspaper, or simply smiling warmly. At the end of the booklet is the name of a print shop, from a county a hundred miles or so from the temple, dated December 2011. Several county residents are listed as donors, four of whom donated fifty renminbi, two of whom donated one hundred. It thus seems a relatively local undertaking, yet one still marked by movement and circulation.

He once met a man, Wang says, who could tell that he had *língqì* (spiritual airs). The man handed him a book and told him to head to a certain temple. Upon reading the book, he immediately felt *líng* (spirit or soul; here, a sense of spiritual potency and efficacy). Upon visiting the temple, he discovered the deity who would guide him. He then decided to publish and spread this book. Whoever was meant to read it would experience *líng* upon reading it, but not everyone would feel *líng*—those who read a copy of the book and felt nothing would simply discard it. Someone else might then pluck it from the refuse, bring it home, read it, and experience *líng*. It's simply so. I would see him at the square regularly, speaking of social ills, reciting Mao's poetry and biography. As knowing onlookers at the square say, Chairman Mao's rays illuminate him.

Those like Wang who frequent the temple square often refer to their undertaking as *zougong, paogong,* and *shougong*—the work of walking, the work of running, and the work of guarding. Walking and running signify the movement toward temples—temple pilgrimage in formal terms; guarding is the act of tending to deities upon arrival.[7] While temple pilgrimage, more broadly speaking, often finds its aim in the central icon(s) present at a given temple—in this case, Fuxi—many of those who frequent the temple square describe their task as "walking Chairman Mao's path." Though the slogan is an ostensibly secular socialist one by conventional accounts, such "walking" takes on a double meaning here—an allotment of heavenly work in cosmopolitical alignment with the absent sovereign, entailing a mediation of spirits.

To be sure, participants in possession-centered temple pilgrimages are not necessarily spirit mediums, if *spirit medium* is taken in the more classic sense: those who regularly receive supplicants at an altar *(tangkou),* referred to in Hexian as "those who see incense" *(kanxiangde).* Nonetheless, those who frequent the temple square I speak of here do consider their spiritual task to involve the reception of otherworldly transmissions and hosting of spirits upon their bodies. They thus carry out a mediation of otherworldly entities and forces just as those who set up an altar. I use *spirit medium* as a translational term for those who regularly lend their bodies to spirits for various cosmic tasks, making distinctions when needed.[8]

Thousands visit Fuxi Temple from surrounding villages and counties every first and fifteenth of the lunar month—common ritual days—and even more on such ritually significant national holidays as the Chinese New Year. Many come to burn incense and make offerings to the deities, appealing to the gods for health and fortune. Others come to peruse the temple market for goods, from culturalized handicrafts to toys to discounted housewares. And still some, as is often joked, came to swindle and steal—as one man prays for promotion, another man prays to steal his wallet. Only some frequent the temple square for dedicated purposes of carrying out otherworldly tasks assigned by their guiding spirits, from ritual to possession and mediumship. Yet the lines are blurred. According to those who frequent Fuxi Temple, many arrive at the square unaware of their fated task. One's otherworldly participation thus cannot always be understood by what meets the eye, whether the other's or one's own. My own claim to a mere role of university researcher, for instance, is rarely taken at face value.

And, of those who engage in mediumship, not all center their practices on Mao. They might be chosen by a number of tutelary deities from Buddhist, Daoist, and local pantheons to join their spiritual family and work in their service, or they might simply be vulnerable to possession by ghosts and spirits without an allocation of a divine task. But those who walk Chairman Mao's path have a continual and notable presence at the temple square, on and beyond common ritual days, and even those who dedicate their ritual labor to other deities acknowledge Mao's position in the cosmology.

Many of those I met who walked the Chairman's path describe themselves, like Wang, simply as peasants *(nongmin)*. At the temple square and beyond, the terse self-designation of "peasant" provides a certain shielding of generic anonymity, while gesturing toward a virtuous, symbolic position in the contemporary cosmology. Most of those who frequent the square come from surrounding villages and nearby counties, and, while many know of one another to varying extents, the geographic range was also wide enough such that not everyone was certain of the other's social positionality. There is thus a simultaneous air of familiarity and mystery among those who frequent the temple square, creating a tension of proximity and distance that lends a charge to encounters. Direct inquiries about one's home village and earthly identity—not to mention otherworldly affiliations and cosmic tasks—are often met with suspicion and left unanswered, because of the still-present secular political risk of such "superstitious" *(mixin)* participation as well as the cosmic risk of clashing spiritual affiliations. Those at the temple square at times quip to those who inquire that they are "doing superstition" *(gao mixin),* performing a self-interpellation by the modern gaze that, in those instances, simultaneously enacts a tactical deflection of further questioning.[9]

Of those I met, some are farmers and small vendors, and some put behind previous earthly work when they took up spiritual work and received support from their families and intermittent remuneration for carrying out ritual and spiritual tasks on behalf of others. Laments at the temple square are often sounded against those with wealth and political power, though this does not exclude the possibility that some could be associated with moneyed families or official authority. A number of those I met were themselves or had family members who were local brigade leaders in the Maoist era, and some participated as Red Guards in their youth. One medium I met who operates her own home altar is married to a current village head and party member, and the copresence of spiritual and Communist roles in their marriage did not seem surprising or odd to supplicants who knew of this. Meanwhile, security guards hired by the local government to police the temple shoo away mediums who gather outside the temple gates from time to time, particularly when anticipating the visit of officially sanctioned festivals and Communist Party leader visits. Such practices, after all, remain under the formal if murky designation of illegal superstition and are considered unsightly in contrast to visits on officially sanctioned holidays and ritual days. The lines between earthly and cosmic party alliance are thus blurred—not mutually exclusive nor entirely coincident.

TEN THOUSAND YEARS

The air is dense with anticipation. Those who do not otherwise frequent the temple rush toward the gate, jostling their way through the crowds to burn the last batch of incense for the year. Making my way across the square, I am drawn toward a rumbling drum beat, steady and declarative, in sets of three. A large circle of onlookers gather around six women and two men, middle aged, as they prepare for ritual. They don matching and seemingly brand-new green Mao-era army coats, topped with brown Soviet-style fur hats, a single red star at the center. One woman at the inner edge of the crowd holds a tall pole, topped with a large yellow flag with the word *lìng* (lit. "command, order, or decree"; in this context meaning "divine command") etched in red.

"*Ayahao!*" Another woman, in a red parka and red embroidered dress reminiscent of old Shanghai, traces the edges of the encirclement with her steps, pausing at its northernmost point. Facing the heavens, hands outstretched, her arms slowly lift toward the sky. She is receiving not only *língqì* from above but also divine command for the opening of the ritual. "*Ayahao!*" she cries again—an interjection confirming an otherworldly presence or signal, often one's own possession or infusion by spiritual personae or airs. "*Ayahao! Ayahao! Ayahao!*" echo several spectators in the crowd—a signal that they too acknowledge and experience the presence and signal of the spirits. While some rituals on the square involve particular appeals to the powers above, rituals such as this are often considered a mode of acknowledgment and oblation for the gods as well as a means of gathering spiritual force.

Inside the circle eighteen sheets of yellow fabric—used commonly in local rituals and often considered, on the temple square, the color of the emperor—have been laid out in the shape of a fan, flanked by a head of cabbage and two large stalks of scallions. Agricultural goods are often incorporated into ritual spreads at the temple square, sealing within them symbolic meanings and forces both shared and esoteric. As common cultural referents, cabbage *(baicai)* often pointed to wealth *(bai* nearly homophonic of "hundred"; *cai* nearly homophonic of "wealth"), and scallion *(cong)* to intelligence *(congming).* North of this more yellow fabric, this time in a row of five, every other sheet topped with a bamboo platter—a regional kitchen implement used for drying grains and vegetables—is covered by paper cuttings of four concentric red stars, one embedded in another, the emblem of the Communist Party.

On the central bamboo platter, three cigarettes point northward, an offering to the gods, I am told. A common offering in Hexian in ritual and mediumship, cigarettes are often smoked by mediums and at times are burned in an upright position in place of or in conjunction with incense on the temple square. Some say the use of cigarettes as incense was a carryover from the Cultural Revolution, when incense sales were banned and visits to mediums were held covertly behind closed doors in the night. Above the cigarettes four sticks of incense burn in a golden urn—three for humans, four for ghosts, as the saying went—aside a row of plastic-wrapped sausages, "because gods like to eat too."

At the very top, farthest north, thus of highest position in the cosmic-symbolic geography, is a large poster of Mao in a red collared shirt, seated and flanked by his generals in blue uniform. Placed on the poster are three mandarin oranges and three slices of metallic-gold ritual paper—two covered in looping spirit writing, the third with the words, "Through virtue, one gains all under heaven" *(de de tianxia).*

Fifty or so onlookers have gathered around by now: men smoking, women bundled in scarves, several in their teens and twenties peering on, gawking, giggling. A man, perhaps in his late thirties, cigarette dangling from his lips, begins swinging a three-foot-long necklace of Buddhist beads above his head. After a minute or so, he meticulously lowers the necklace atop the poster of Mao and the generals. The two men in Maoist army coats begin striking a gong and cymbals, tracing deliberate steps across the spread of ritual offerings. Others—mostly those I have seen frequenting the square before—join to walk the perimeter of the encirclement, some singing, some dancing, some plucking offerings off the spread, brandishing them toward the heavens. The percussion gains speed. The cries intensify. *"Ayahao! Ayahao! Ayahao!"* A woman walks to the center of the circle and closes her eyes. Another twirls, palms up high to collect spiritual airs from above. A voice bellows amid the drum and song.

"*Wansui! Wansui! Mao Zhuxi wansui!* Ten thousand years! Ten thousand years! Ten thousand years for Chairman Mao!" A woman, standing beneath the yellow flag of divine command, howls at the top of her lungs. *"Wansui! Wansui!"* she calls out again and again, until her voice grows hoarse. In an adjacent ritual circle, the drumming also reaches its peak. "*Shenglile!* Victory! *Dajia shenglile!* Victory to all! *Shijie daping le!* The world has reached supreme peace! *Zhongguo shengli le!* China has reached victory!" "*Wansui! Wansui! Wanwansuiiiiii!* Ten thousand years! Ten thousand years! Tens of thousands of years!"

An address reserved for emperors for much of Chinese imperial history, *wansui* (lit. "ten thousand years of age" and commonly translated as "long live") exploded in usage during the Cultural Revolution, after Mao's public mass reception on August 18, 1966. He took the crowd—as well as his security guards—by surprise with an early morning appearance on Tiananmen Square. As described in the *People's Daily,*

> This morning at 5 a.m., as the sun had just spread its first beams of light from the Eastern horizon, Chairman Mao informally appeared on Tiananmen Square.... Chairman Mao wore a grass-green army uniform. On the Chairman's military cap glistened a single red star. Chairman Mao ... walked directly among the masses.... At that moment, the Square boiled over, everyone raised their hands over their heads and jumped in the direction of the Chairman.... Many people clapped their palms until they turned red; many people shed tears of excitement.... On the Square, tens of thousands of people loudly called: "Long live Chairman Mao! Long live! Long, long live!" One wave of hurrahs surpassed the other, shaking the sky above the capital.

After this appearance and its press coverage, *wansui* and its variant, *wanshou,* were soon incorporated and codified into official Chinese Communist Party discourse. By 1968 texts, meetings, speeches, and phone calls often opened with a formal wishing of eternal life and eternal health for the Chairman, and badges and images of Mao—not unlike those now reappearing at the temple square—also came into mass production and circulation during this period. While Mao himself was said to have been cognizant of his iconic power and to have curbed the unofficial duplication and distribution of his words and images in initial post-Liberation years, by the late sixties, amid the Cultural Revolution, unauthorized media began multiplying at unprecedented speed, launching their circulation and signifying capacities far beyond the grip of the state (Leese 2011, 131).

With the death of Mao and the rise of Deng Xiaoping in the late 1970s, a series of official denouncements of Mao, particularly with regard to the violence of the Cultural Revolution, seemed momentarily to diminish the reproduction of such tokens. Yet another decade later, in the late 1980s, a new "search for Mao Zedong" began—one that would come to include the now familiar, often satirical renderings of the Chairman in (mostly urban) Chinese contemporary art and pop culture. Cultural historian Geremie Barmé notes that in contrast to the Cultural Revolution, the posthumous "Mao Cult" moved in inverse relation to official state promotion, documenting the drop of popular sentiment and paraphernalia sales during periods of government-orchestrated commemorations of the Chairman and the rise across other periods. Images of Mao thus not only continued to slip beyond their official usage but offered an implicit counterpoint to officialdom in their new circulations. Yet, while Barmé suggests that this "new Mao Cult" was "divested nearly entirely of its original class, ethical, and political dimensions," as well as any sense of "moral revival, sanctity, and the general religiosity and fervor that characterized the earlier Cult," invocations of Mao in Hexian, in ritual contexts and otherwise, pointed precisely to his status as an ethicopolitical and, for some, cosmological figure (1996, 5, 13).[10]

Not unlike metaphors of imperial bureaucracy in localized popular religion (Feuchtwang 2010), the ritual presence of Maoist imagery in Hexian marks both a repetition and difference from its use by the formal central state. In an inversion of the state's ritual displacement of popular religion (Anagnost 1994), the potency produced through Maoist-era political rituals is reactivated in post-Mao mediumship. Sharing a symbolic repertoire with the earthly state, the spectral polity speaks to the sense of a morally hollowed present and a revolution incomplete.

BLACK CAT, WHITE CAT

"When Chairman Mao was still alive," Li Hanwei points to the thick padlock on the wooden front gate of his house, "we didn't even need locks on the doors." Not an uncommon way of phrasing things, but it strikes me nonetheless—something about the weight in his voice, the distance in his gaze. Li Hanwei is my host in Hexian, along with his wife, Cai Huiqing, though he works away from home much of the year, driving long-distance trucks.

"These walls?" he gestures toward the tall brick enclosure that marks the boundary of their yard.[11] "These walls used to be dried sorghum stalks, barely a meter high." He lowers his hand waist high to approximate. "There was no 'wall.' Just a few stalks loosely strung together. You could see everything inside, and no one ever worried about it." Standard yard enclosures in Hexian have come to be built of brick, then concrete, and now stand at more than double their previous height, well over the sight line of passersby—an opaque barrier between the inside and outside of the home. As someone who prefers to keep a distance from village gossip, Li Hanwei normally seems far from nostalgic toward the visibility and engagement implied by sorghum fencing. Yet, even for him, it seems that something was amiss as the art of *chuanmen*—the informal and often unannounced visits to the homes of neighbors and kin—dampened with the rise of the brick wall, both producing and signifying a transformation in social life.

"It's the sense of *safety!*" Li Hanwei snaps. "Nowadays, there's no sense of safety anymore," no *anquangan*. "When Chairman Mao reigned, there was a sense of safety." Li Hanwei shakes his head and grimaces. Concerns with theft heightened with the advent of the reform era, when, he says, everyone had to find their own path. Privatization and labor migration intensified both the sense of opportunity and disparity and, with it, desire and envy of one's neighbors. Moreover, many I met in Hexian lament that with the death of Mao came the return of corruption. During the Maoist era, it is often said, if a single renminbi was gained by means of corruption, it would eventually be returned. Chairman Mao would not allow otherwise. But with the reform era, alongside Deng Xiaoping's exhortation, "It doesn't matter whether a cat is black or white; as long as it catches mice, it's a good cat," state officials began losing fear and gaining courage, siphoning increasing amounts in their dealings, to the injury of commoners. Put forth in the official political realm as a statement of Deng's pragmatic stance toward market versus planned economies, the phrase is usually evoked in Hexian for its moral implications in authorizing an era of greed.

What villagers call corruption, often involving *guanxi* (personalistic relations or connections) and trust cultivated through economies of gifts and bribes, became central to the then-tentative exchanges between the Communist bureaucracy and semi-illicit experiments of entrepreneurs in the early years of market reform (Chan, Madsen, and Unger 2009; Wank 2001). With the deepening of privatization since the 1990s, such "corrupt" forms of economy and sociality intensified, upping demands for meals, bribes, and sexual entertainment, producing what some have called a "hollow state" in rural regions as gains flowed upward, away from the "commoner" class, which Li Hanwei and others saw themselves as part of (G. Smith 2010; Sun 2004; M. Yang 2002). Although personal connections and favors were also at play in determining one's lot and potential subjection to violence under the Maoist era (Wemheuer 2014), those I met in Hexian tend to associate the notion of corruption with the intensification of the market economy. By the time of my visit, talk of corruption was further animated by announcements of pending anticorruption campaigns led by incoming president Xi Jinping, bringing a sense of official legitimacy to local laments alongside a cautious optimism.

Yet the so-called commoners are not external to the economy of corruption. Beyond formal politics, a deep sense of distrust permeates the most intimate and mundane dimensions of everyday life—the forgery of electricity bills by village collectors, the injection of water by butchers into their meat for weight inflation, the nonfulfillment of promised reciprocations after receiving a gift or bribe, the unpaid debt of once-trusted kin. It is a logic of practice too weary to bank on returns, yet which cannot afford the luxury of refraining from wagers. Greed *(tan)* and corruption *(tanwu, lit. "greed-filth")* saturate imaginations of the social, and there is a sense that most of those living in this era would exploit any opportunity that arose, whether black or white. This sense of distrust and collapse postreform is tethered to the loss of the Chairman, as a figure of former moral-political guarantee.

"This is why many people treat him as a deity," Li Hanwei posits. While Li Hanwei is staunchly against what he calls superstition and couches his laments in this-worldly terms, he acknowledges that there is another understanding of the Chairman in Hexian.

THE EARTHLY STATE AND ITS COSMIC DOUBLE

For those in Hexian who engage with the world of spirits, "the time when Chairman Mao reigned"—a common phrase for articulating contrasts with the present day—marks not only his earthly rule but a cosmic punctuation and rectification.[12] Echoing everyday evocations of post-Mao distrust and disintegration, spirit mediums' accounts of Mao center on a mythohistorical rise and fall of greed, corruption, and fakery across heaven and earth. Tracing yet upturning secular periodizations of the destruction and return of *religion,* the mediums suggest that the reign and death of the Chairman mark instead the departure and return of *spirits,* most of whom had grown corrupt.

Since the post-Mao reform era, a sweeping appearance of "religious revival" has come to the attention of China scholars and commentators. In conversation with the anthropology of the secular (Asad 2003), some China scholars have emphasized the irreversible effects of the violent and totalizing process of secularization, engineered to capacitate the birth and expansion of the modern state (M. Yang 2008). Others have suggested that precisely in their attempts to condemn "the religious"— which did not exist as an autonomous conceptual category prior to missionary encounter and the modernizing impetus—such secularizing efforts have in fact acted as foil for new forms of religiosity (Goossaert and Palmer 2011). In the past, debates on Chinese religion have sprung up around its (desirable) relationship to secularist rationality, its holism versus multiplicity, and its role in kinship and lineage organization.[13] In contradistinction, a central strand linking more recent approaches to Chinese popular religion is the question of its relationship to global capitalism and modern governance, whether in resistance, collusion, or otherwise.[14]

In approaching emergent forms of ritual and mediumship in the wake of modernizing campaigns, I engage both the irreversibility of violence and its production of new forms. In this I am inspired by Erik Mueggler's work on Lòlopò ritual in Yunnan Province as a subversive temporal strategy, in which poetic and material engagements with the living and the dead produced an alternative mode of history in the aftermath of violence. There the state was imagined not as external to daily or intimate life but as a "constitutive presence at the center of the social world with an intimate relation to loss," at once "abstract and uncanny" (2001, 6). When writing of Hexian, I similarly approach local rituals and cosmologies not as direct oppositions to or complicity with the state but as profound practices that incorporate and transform statist time.

Reference to the local here is inherently troubled. It is used to conjure the significance of place in grasping the particular histories giving weight to the cosmology, both from within and without—in this case the presence of the county Fuxi Temple, regional histories of famine, and contemporary tropes marring Henan Province, for instance. At the same time the cosmological engagements I encountered involve matters of national, world-historical, and cosmic proportions far beyond what "the local" tends to connote. Moreover, cosmologies travel—at times with smugglers—in an era of rural-urban and transnational migration (Chu 2010). Thus the question of place must be suspended to disturb assumptions of rural localization and urban cosmopolitanism that continually leave the former in their place.

For many spirit mediums I met in Hexian, Mao stands as a central, if withdrawn, figure in the contemporary pantheon, and the party-state itself is redoubled cosmologically—a spectral polity out of joint with the earthly postreform state. In these accounts, in spite of their self-designation, Mao and the Chinese Communist Party were never truly secular. Beyond a political theology at play in secular statecraft (Schmitt 2006), the slogans and iconography of the Party provide dwelling for spectral power, redoubled as operators of cosmic force.

Paralleling the problem of the king's two bodies, a tension grows between the question of the body natural and the body politic with the passing of Mao. In Ernst Hartwig Kantorowicz's readings of medieval European theology and political thought, the mortal time of the living king is accompanied by the timeless eternity of the crown and eventually a *persona mystica* of a plurality capable of constituting a collective across time rather than simply simultaneously across space: "Briefly, as opposed to the pure *physis* of the king and to the pure *physis* of the territory, the word 'Crown,' when added, indicated the political *metaphysis* in which both *rex* and *regnum* shared, or the body politic (to which both belonged) in its sovereign rights. . . . For the Crown, by its perpetuity, was superior to the physical *rex* as it was superior to the geographical *regnum* while, at the same time, it was on a par with the continuity of the dynasty and the sempiternity of the body politic" (1957, 341–42). The figure of the king "who never dies" thus proceeds in tandem with the People "which never dies," one moving the other into perpetuity, informing not only the unfoldings in medieval theology and law on which Kantorowicz draws, but—he notes in passing—the philosophies of unlimited progress in the generations leading up to the two world wars (1957, 274, 312–14). The king is dead; long live the king. Yet what of a figure who is considered not a mere ruler in a longer line of rulers but an exceptional ruler in exceptional times?

The title of Chairman *(zhuxi)*, some mediums in Hexian suggest, is more than a title among others; there was only one true Chairman. "Chairman" means more, they implied, than the formal titles of president of the People's Republic and general secretary of the party held by later successors, or even "Paramount Leader" as taken up by Deng Xiaoping.[15] For many mediums the title of Chairman is thus a barely veiled cue that Mao had received the mandate of heaven granted to emperors past.

"Otherwise," as one medium poses to me, "why would he be the only leader who dared name himself Chairman, and why has no other leader dared so since?"

The mandate of heaven, in early Chinese writings, referred to the divine granting of sagehood, an order that must be submitted to if the patterns of all under heaven were to continue—the foundational potentiality of the cosmos, human culture, and virtue. This was accompanied by the notion of a cyclical rise and fall of rightful dynasties, in accordance with moral-political timeliness. Across a wide range of contending Confucian, Daoist, Mohist, and Legalist dealings with *ming*—variously translated as mandate, fate, or lifespan—the mandate of heaven *(tianming)* was a central expression of morality, "link[ing] macro-destiny with virtue" (Raphals 2003, 543). In their descriptions of Mao's position as Chairman and covert emperor, the mediums echo the centrality of virtue to the divine guarantee of the cosmos. To return to the ritual writing from the temple square: "through virtue, one gains all under heaven."

According to spirit mediums at the temple square and those at their altars, given the Chairman's rightful heaven-sent status, ghosts and spirits did not dare appear during his reign. With his pronouncement, "Sweep away all cow-ghosts and snake-spirits," all the spirits vanished.[16] Some say they hid in remote mountain caves. Some say they disappeared altogether. An editorial title inaugurating the Cultural Revolution in 1966, this Maoist slogan, outside of the context of mediumship, has generally been considered a secular political call for heightened attacks against so-called reactionaries and class enemies. Moreover, it marked the beginnings of some of the most intense and thorough campaigns against religious infrastructure and practice, including the destruction of icons at the temple and arrests of spirit mediums in Hexian.

Yet, in its cosmological rendering, the slogan takes on a force of heavenly command beyond earthly statecraft—a call for the banishment of spirits in a moment of cosmic chaos, when nearly all spirits, deities included, had been tainted by greed and corruption. Mao's infamous temple-destruction campaigns, according to the mediums, were then not truly acts of an atheist state but cryptic acts of spiritual rectification. The figurehead of Chinese Communist sovereignty is inextricable from an otherworldly sovereignty—the spectral polity acts as a cosmic double of the earthly state, deploying its images, words, agents, and acts for purposes beyond its own knowing.

Despite its formal opposition to sovereign power feudal, traditional, or otherwise, something of an analogue to sovereignty is carried in Communist power, in part through its very origin in the abolition of sovereignty (Bataille 1993) and through the creation of its own cosmocratic mythologic (Apter and Saich 1998). Linked to this was a potential "theological" dimension, but one, Georges Bataille ventured in a footnote, "independent of monotheism . . . seeing in the sacred and in the gods, as well as in the principle of sovereignty" (1993, 453). In other words, it was a religiosity akin to what has been described as correlative or analogical in such contexts as China.

While the divine status of Mao and the coalescing of secular and nonsecular power might produce a sense of surprise for some, such surprise inherits post-Protestant conceptualizations of secularity, involving efforts to keep apart the sacred and mundane, nature and culture, creator and created (Descola 2013; Latour 1993). In many strands of Chinese thought, such ontological divides—between gods and humans, mind and matter—do not provide the central conceptual tension (Hall and Ames 1995; Jullien 1995). Traditions of human apotheosis have had a long history prior to secularization, and paths to becoming a god were various: Daoist and Buddhist arts of self-cultivation, the accumulation of sufficient merit during one's lifetime and through one's ancestors for appointment as a temple god after death, and becoming a historical personality with potency sufficient to remain after death (Puett 2004; Seaman 1974).[17]

The cosmological role of Mao in Hexian, given this lineage, is unsurprising and parallels other "atheist secular" worlds in Asia and elsewhere, in which such co-mingling of gods and politics is remarkable in their unremarkableness (Ngo and Quijada 2015). Grappling with religiosity in Communist and post-Communist worlds, as Tam Ngo and Justine Quijada suggest, involves moving beyond Cold War tropes of the Communist repression of religion and the quasi-religious irrationality of Communist ideology. Yet the sense of the expectable also does not saturate the arena of becoming-god, if one is to register the potency of the scene. In the case of Mao, effects and affects of the *incredible* continued to be produced on both sides of the former Iron Curtain, speaking to his peculiar position at the crossing of world-historical imaginaries, past and present.

In Hexian part of this sense of the incredible comes in the very ending of Maoist times, which in the mediums' accounts feel like but a glimpse in hindsight, truncated by a death come too soon. Such tensions surrounding the divine allocation of earthly rule and lifespan are by no means novel to the postdynastic era, when notions of modern sovereignty came to comingle with those of emperorship. Early Confucian and Mencian writings on the mandate of heaven also point to the sometimes punishing simultaneity of moral and arbitrary power.

Heavenly command stood, akin to formulations of the sovereign, at the limit of normative moral rule, constituting the very origin and potential continuation of the norm while reserving the absolute power to operate beyond it. To accept the mandate of heaven, then, was not only to live in accordance with moral rule and action as patterned by heaven but to accept also its destructive, transgressive dimension—the breaching of its own moral terms for purposes unavailable to human knowing. Cosmological alignment of the past and present requires the true sage to endure the seemingly amoral effects of heaven's acts—the reign of wrongful rulers, the exceeding of normative dynastic cycles, the premature arrival of one's own death—all the while carrying on in moral cultivation without resentment. In contrast to later accounts and interpretations of unity between moral heavenly ordination and its rightful earthly recipient in the sage-king, a constitutive ambivalence was thus central to early depictions of the ruler (Puett 2005).

The question of rightful rule by divine ordination and the call to virtuously remain and remain virtuous in its absence are central to the mediums' rendering of the contemporary cosmology. What was it that lived on in the wake of a ruler deemed exceptional in his rightfulness? What of the (covert) recipient of the heavenly mandate whose succession—and with it the survival of the body politic at large—might not be guaranteed in the *physis* of the world that follows? With the Chairman's death, the time of the People teetered with him, in a time of ghosts.

Tales of a more virtuous time under Mao in everyday village recollections are doubled in spirit mediums' accounts as a time of moral-cosmological alignment and divine protection—a protection lost with the loss of the Chairman. With Mao's death, ghosts and gods came swirling back upon the withdrawal of sovereign guarantee. The same reform-era slogan cited by Li Hanwei and others—"It doesn't matter whether a cat is black or white; as long as it catches mice, it's a good cat"—are cited by mediums I met as a declaration that lifted the cosmic ban against corrupt spirits placed by the Chairman, marking a new era of spiritual chaos.[18]

CORRUPTION AND MIRRORING

Back at the temple square, I hear rumors of a pantheon in disarray. According to some mediums, despite the thousands that visited the temple every lunar first and fifteenth, their pleas have gone unheard—Fuxi is no longer present at his own temple. Some say he left some time around the Cultural Revolution, when the Red Guards destroyed his icon. Some say he left when the local government raised the entrance fee after the market reform era—from mere change to five renminbi, from five to ten, from ten to twenty, and, since 2008, to a staggering sixty renminbi. Indeed, many who frequent Fuxi Temple for ritual and cultivation remain on the temple square, outside the temple gates, because of the ticket price.[19] According to some, Fuxi now drifts from place to place in an act of self-exile, assisting only those who truly deserve his care. According to others, he is simply in hiding in a mountain cave, furious with the moral failures of humans today. As the deity assigned to the realm of human affairs, as one medium puts it, how could he but be dismayed by what he saw?

Still others give a more alarming assessment: it was not that Fuxi departed in a spatial sense. Rather, Fuxi himself has grown corrupt (*fubai*) and can no longer be trusted. The rising ticket prices and the demands for increasing amounts of offerings in exchange for divine favors are signs that he is no longer acting in the capacity of a benevolent protector. The sense of moral-political dilemma thus comes to taint the very origin of human ancestry, as the progenitor is himself now moved by desire for gain. Moreover, some mediums contend, Fuxi is not the only one—almost all deities have grown corrupt, overcome with greed, mirroring politicians and other humans today. Among deities accused of corruption are those no less than the ranks of the Goddess of Mercy (Guanyin Pusa) and the God of the Heavens himself (Laotianye). Which gods remain virtuous it is difficult, if not impossible, to discern, hence the heightened danger of possession today. Yet across almost all variations of this tale, Mao remains an exception. Even those who dare accuse high-ranking figures in the Chinese pantheon still hold the Chairman in the highest esteem, as the supreme ethical exemplar, one who differs from the rest precisely in his incorruptibility.

In contrast to mediums I met at the temple square, those I met at their home altar (topped with the icons of deities) were more likely to downplay or reject this fraught claim of widespread divine corruption, maintaining a stronger distinction between the virtue of gods and the danger of ghosts. Yet even those who denied a generalized cosmic corruption acknowledge the place of Mao in the cosmology and the return of spirits upon his death. Moreover, although it occurred less frequently, some supplicants who visited mediums also mention Mao's role in the suppression of corruption and fakery.

"When Mao Zedong conquered all under heaven [datianxia], people did not have to worry about such things. But nowadays charlatans are everywhere," one woman laments while waiting for a session with a medium, speaking of a fraudulent medium she had once visited. Mao's death marked not only the return of ghosts but a crisis of discernment between the true and false, moral and immoral. Those who are capable of or vulnerable to possession must thus remain cautious, to distinguish between true, righteous deities (zhengshen) and fake deities (jiashen) that might usurp one's body and lead one to evil deeds.

Perhaps a sign of this dangerously hazy zone, the customarily positive term xian, commonly translated as immortal, transcendent, or celestial being, is often used in Hexian to describe powerful old ghosts, ghosts masquerading as gods, and deities who have grown corrupt—who are morally false, thus "fake." Those who claim possession by a particular deity—mediums who assist supplicants at their altars included—may thus in fact be working on behalf of a fake deity, whether they know it or not.

The alternating designations of "god" and "ghost" amid shifting moral relations has some historical precedent. In a collection of ghost stories and anomaly tales by Qing dynasty writer Pu Songling (1640–1715), the spirit who extorts sacrifices from humans was referred to as both god (shen) and ghost (gui) across the narrative: "This item's change in nomenclature, from shen to gui, reinforces the sense that this spirit-being has crossed the fine line dividing the 'normal' relationship of reciprocal exchange on which local cults are based from the making of excessive demands backed by threats. Other items document similarly greedy, excessive demands by local spirits for particular goods and services. . . . Some do so with impunity, [and] others are eventually punished for their violations of the implicit code of reciprocity" (Campany 1996, 374–75). In a postreform era filled with news of fakery and corruption, the interchangeability of ghosts and false gods through the shared term *xian* gestures toward—as Jeanne Favret-Saada (2015) writes of witchcraft—fissures at the very heart of the social order.

While the death of Mao is said to inaugurate this current moment of cosmo-moral crisis, causal operations of cross-realm corruption are not usually described as unilinear. When I ask those who frequent the temple square about the directionality of corruption between realms, the response is often murky. Whether the humans or the gods grew compromised first, it is hard to say. They act in tandem, one mirroring the other, one leading the other further astray. Although heaven and earth have been considered distinct in many Chinese cosmological writings historically, there is no radical ontological divide between them, no prime mover: "Heaven proceeds without causes, through its interaction with Earth, simply through their mutual dispositions. . . . Heaven is superior to Earth but could not exist without it" (Jullien 1995, 225). In contrast to foundational splits in Christian theology between human and divine, spirit and matter, what has often been termed a correlative or analogical modality infusing various schools of Chinese thought and religious traditions centers on correspondences—qualities and attributes traversing entities and substances, human and nonhuman (Descola 2013). Here, rather than a prime cause—this or otherworldly—the mediums describe the crossing of the human and nonhuman by the traveling attribute of corruption.

Aside from the more systematic Han dynasty charts of elements oft-cited as a template for the correlative, I am thinking here with David Hall and Roger Ames's broader notion of the analogical as a sensibility, aesthetic, and posture already present in pre–Han Confucian and Daoist writings—one that involves "mirroring the world" as a way of knowing and proceeding (1995, 67). But while mirroring may offer a path to sageliness in those texts, in Hexian it also marks the less desirable dimensions of resemblance and contagion, in which the immoral qualities of spirits and humans enter a zone of mutual attraction and escalation. According to the mediums, like attracts like. Angry or corrupt gods and ghosts are drawn to angry or corrupt humans, and the meeting of the two intensified the attribute, together moving the human to lie, cheat, steal, and kill. With the Chairman's withdrawal back to the heavens postreform, an epidemic of brazen charlatanism and greed was unleashed across human and spirit worlds.

COSMIC PRECARITY, SPECTRAL SOVEREIGNTY

In *Specters of Marx* Jacques Derrida raises questions of inheritance and mourning following the collapse of the Soviet Union. For Derrida, to consider place and time "since Marx," following pronouncements of the triumph of global capitalism, is to consider "what remains to be" in the "non-advent of an event" that carries on in forms secret and ghostly, that in its very deferral affirms a sense of "the coming of the event, its future-to-come itself" (1994, 19). This anticipation is accompanied by a today in which *time is out of joint*, at once out of order and mad—*haunted*, as it were (20). The links drawn between the ghost, the work of mourning, and the meaning of the "after" or "since" of Communism form a striking resonance with cosmological accounts in Hexian. Marx, in spite of himself—like Mao, in spite of himself—would be found, again and for the first time, in the living-on *(sur-vie)* of "more than one/no more one" *(plus d'un)* specters (2). Then there is the question of being an heir: "Inheritance is never a *given*, it is always a task. . . . We are heirs of Marxism, even before wanting or refusing to be, and, like all inheritors, we are in mourning" (67).

The ghosts and corrupt deities that have returned to Hexian, upon the loss of the Chairman, signal for the spirit mediums a time out of joint, a time of madness that also speaks to the cosmopolitical significance of psychiatric disorders. Ghosts thus mark a certain inheritance and mourning with relation to the absented sovereign. Yet the ghosts and spirits that swarmed in after Mao's death do not always map neatly onto earthly political times and positions. The space of the temple square brings together the mythical time of human (re)generation by Fuxi and Nüwa, the time of dynasties past, the time of China's near extinction, and the cyclical time of dynastic corruption, signaled in the present by the loss of Mao. In this sense, to think with Sigmund Freud's (2006) distinction between mourning and melancholia, in which melancholia points to a loss beyond that of a known object that can be consciously metabolized through the work of mourning, the ghost might also be said to contain a melancholic dimension. The return and proliferation of ghosts after the Chairman's death include ghosts known and unknown, those who died during, after, and long before Mao's time.

As an invitation for revisiting the question of Marx differently, the spectral in Derrida's elaboration is continuously marked by an openness toward otherness, in which ethics after the disappointments and horrors toward socialist states resides in a nonexpectant, future-facing stance. Yet, and as Derrida acknowledges but dwells less on, the spectral can also open up to radical risks of evil. Drawing on the works of Nigerian author Amos Tutuola, Achille Mbembe (2003) suggests that ghostly sovereignty, particularly amid death worlds of the postcolony, can violently sever any Western sense of self-mastery beyond appeals to otherness as potentiality. Such forms of the spectral rattle imaginations of heterogeneity that make way for possibility—a decapitated subject rendered a site of uncontrollable speech, the speech of an *arrivant* in its alterity indeed.

In Hexian those who walk the Chairman's path, along with the spirits they channel and discern, might indeed be thought of in terms of living on—as inheritors of Mao, himself an inheritor of Marx, inheritors in mourning, in the wake of what Mao and others termed China's semicoloniality. But while those who walk the Chairman's path see their reception of spirits as a moral task critical to the present, such work is undertaken under the assumption of a radical (if fluctuating) lack of self-mastery.

In contrast to religiosities centered on a sincerity of belief and initial pronouncements of faith, otherworldly calling in mediumship often begins with a sense of reluctance and coercion with relation to one's tutelary spirit(s). Mediums refer to the condition of their cosmic duty as *bu dangjia* (lit. "not heading one's own household"). It signals a lack of control over one's own body and psyche, action and desire, ranging from minor discomforts and small odd acts to life-threatening illnesses and florid madness.[20] Such symptoms are relieved only when one complies with the call to become a healer, though some negotiation is possible.

Indeed, this cycle of psychocorporeal torment, spiritual compliance and negotiation, and symptom relief is recapitulated across initiation and subsequent engagements. One cannot help but comply when called to task—walkers must travel to designated places; incense seers must receive supplicants—lest one is willing to suffer the consequences. Refusal may be met with unbearable torment to the point of death. Then again, compliance is not without its own risks—those who take up spiritual work are said to be "retrieved" back to the heavens early, as their bodies get used up, deployed, and exhausted as a device for spectral transmissions. Ethicospiritual acts are thus situated within this very loss of self-sovereignty, which concurrently marks one's utility to the invisible, nonhuman world.

Spirits borrow human bodies for work and human mouths for song and speech. Questions of debt and mourning are drawn into ongoing, if fraught, chains of lending and affliction. Those who are called to walk the Chairman's path are deployed by a spectral polity, their bodies host to ghostly forces of multiple histories. Given the ambivalent status of gods and spirits that populate the contemporary, the spectral remnants of Maoism are not beyond an economy of revenge as Derrida had hoped and can make way for terrifying closures of possibility as much as openings. In the wake of cosmo-moral collapse, a spectral sovereignty lives on, ever present and ever deferred.

Moving sideways (but not opposite) from articulations of spectral sovereignty as a latency of sovereign power within newer forms of governmentality amid precarious times (Butler 2004), I use spectral sovereignty here to describe the otherworldly doubling of the earthly state and the ghostly mirroring of earthly affairs, at once animated and devastated by foregone promises of Maoist and post-Mao regimes.[21] Like Derrida's rendering of specters that remain in spite of Marx's own attempts to exorcise them, spirited manifestations of sovereigns past are ever present in atheist secular worlds.

Through their embodied reception of divine and demonic forces, described at once as coerced and dignified—a conjunction hard to grasp through autonomy-centered approaches to the subject—spirit mediums in Hexian gesture toward the always-already nonsovereign status of the human and the state, as well as the not-yet-aligned status of heavenly and earthly sovereignty. Multiple latencies are at play, sounding out precarity across political, cosmological, and moral registers— the Maoist in the post-Mao, the otherworldly in the atheist secular, virtuous futures in the corrupt present, deadly pasts in the living body. It is in this sense that I refer to a cosmic precarity, in which forms of precarity occasioned by market reforms and labor migration signal a constitutive instability across visible and invisible realms. To navigate and inhabit a scene saturated by uncertainty, those in Hexian must take painstaking care to discern between the genuine and the disin-genuous, both human and nonhuman, even if absolute clarity is more than one could hope for.

Such subjection to the risks and operations of the nonhuman world pertains not only to more peripheral figures such as spirit mediums and rural residents. The sagely gentleman—classical exemplar for the righteous ruler—must also heed the caprice of heaven's commands; heaven acts from the very limit of moral and arbitrary rule, at once establishing the moral norm and reserving the right to exceed it. If Mao was said to hold sovereignty across realms during his transient incarnation, absolute sovereignty belonged still to the heavens, which remained, to some extent, beyond the particularities of human history and the passing corruption of deities. There was an unwitting dimension to Mao's divine role— many mediums say he did not know of his own otherworldly identity during his lifetime—which, together with what the mediums often describe as his premature death, point to the darker dimension of divine time. Heaven watched over history with a tormenting patience, in which the observant must endure stretches of chaos and precarity without resentment—spans that might outlast one's lifetime regard-less of one's devotion to moral cultivation. At the same time the unfolding of the cosmos does not occur without its earthly manifestation, and heaven still acts through and as the human bodies deployed for the tasks at hand.

As the rituals, images, and slogans show, the earthly regime might itself be haunted by its double. In Hexian this spectral sovereignty is set amid the spec-tralization of the rural in postreform China. The economic and symbolic evacua-tion of the village carves out a hollow, through which gods and ghosts have reemerged. The bodies of the rural inhabitants, rendered low "quality" by state discourse in an era of labor migration and surplus value extraction (Anagnost 2004), find themselves possessed by spirits that returned upon Mao's death. Mean-while, the withdrawn presence of the Chairman emitted his rays from above, speaking through the voicings of spirit mediums, at once registering and reactivat-ing lost promises of a peasant political subjectivity. Through their allotted tasks and what I later describe as their eschatological visions of a revolution yet to come, those who walk the Chairman's path conjure Mao in his ten thousand years, gesturing toward a divine socialist sovereignty of which he acts as a reminder and remainder.

FALLING, WAITING

As the sun moves past the bright of noon, and things wind down on the temple square, I wander here and there, peering at what remains. Pausing near a ritual spread, I begin chatting with a male medium. I ask for his thoughts on the problem of divine corruption. "These days, humans are gods, and gods are humans," he says, echoing the earlier words of Wang. "The gods are not 'up there' anymore. You see how the world is in chaos right now? That means the heavens are in chaos also." Amid this disarray, he explains, the gods have fallen from the sky and have lost track of one another. Although some have indeed grown corrupt, virtuous deities also descended and mingle among the false spirits. They borrow human mouths for song and speech, seeking one another through the bodies they occupy.

When I ask those who frequent the temple square about the nature of their being-there, two answers are common. Most often, they simply say, matters from above *(shangmiande shi)*—heavenly matters, as in the case of Wang's recitation of Mao's poetry. Then there is another response: waiting for someone *(dengren)*. This person, this *someone,* is not merely the human person but a proxy, a double or multiple presence, one deity seeking another. Your possessing spirit registers the utterance of mine, through our borrowed mouths, after they have long lost track of each other. The public presence of this mode of active waiting is itself an act of unfolding, revealing the ongoing movements of cosmic history in and through the history of the earthly present.

"Why do you think there are so many people here right now?" He continues, looking across the square. I follow his gaze. "It is a sign, a sign of incompletion. If the gods have all found one another, would there be so many people here still? That we see people here day after day is a sign of incompletion." We stand in silence, looking out at the square.

3

Spectral Collision

Cai Huiqing sits in the *tangwu,* the central room, picking up her cell phone, gazing at the screen, then putting it down again. "Sister should be calling soon. I haven't told her yet." Cai Huiqing and her husband, Li Hanwei, are my hosts in Hexian, and she is speaking of her daughter, the second of her three children and older sister to me in our fictive kinship, who lives and works in Shanghai. As many times before, despite her longing to speak with her daughter, she holds herself back, waiting instead for her daughter to initiate the call.

Several days prior, before the break of dawn, the demands of the yin world—the spectral world of spirits set in contrast to the yang world of the living—resounds in a loud pounding at my door. It is Cai Huiqing, yelling my name. I snap awake and leap out of bed, alarmed, and stumble to the southwest corner of the yard, the lowest cardinal direction in the cosmic geography of the house.[1] I see a pit around four feet deep in the soil. Cai Huiqing just spent hours in the night digging and is drenched in sweat. Beaming, she hands me a rusted metal semicircle, six or seven inches wide—an old defunct pipe clamp. The excavated object in question was named by the spirit medium we had visited earlier, and it posed no less than a threat to the lives of her family members.

This chapter follows the ghosts that entered Cai Huiqing's life and dreamscape and prompted this excavation, to consider the multiple registers of time that came together through spirit mediumship, as well as the distant intimacy mediumship capacitated in an era of labor migration. Not simply old or simply new, encounters with mediumship and with ghosts beckon those affected to wrestle with the status of the present. To begin with a homonymic pairing, a link was drawn in the Han dynasty between the words *guǐ* (ghost) and *guī* (to return), addressing the transformation and return of the human body into its essential spirit, into its ghostly form (Csikszentmihalyi 2006). Here I hold this link open to consider the ghost as a form of return, more broadly writ—not only the transformation from a fleshly human form to an unbodied form but also the return of histories through ghostly entities, prying open the meanings of the present and refiguring its potentiality.

. . .

"Let's go," Cai Huiqing announces abruptly, as we finish a quiet lunch of home-made sesame-leaf noodles. I ask her where to. "To see a *shenpo!*" she quips, deploying a term (meaning "spirit lady" or, in some English translations, "witch") that I had brought to the scene, one intelligible to her while marking my externality to local articulations. It was a phrasing more common to urban friends with less familiarity with such matters and carried a slight air of modern accusation. The term is rarely used in Hexian without either a note of disdain from those who denounce so-called superstitions or a knowing emphasis from those who do engage with such practices, as in the case of Cai Huiqing's bemused exclamation. In Hexian mediums who consult the unseen yin world at their altars on behalf of supplicants are most commonly known as "those who see or observe incense" *(kanxiangde)*. Cai Huiqing knew of my interest in mediumship but did not mention her own plans for a visit until that moment.

Boarding a county bus, Cai Huiqing tells me that the medium we were to visit, Zheng Yulan, warned her during a visit several months earlier that this lunar month would be of risk to her family, in particular to her husband. As the days wore on, Cai Huiqing grew increasingly anxious. Living at the edge of the rural county seat without formal employment, with Li Hanwei away from home for much of the year, Cai Huiqing might be considered one among the "left-behind women" *(liushou funü)* in rural regions, a position called forth by postreform discourses of progress. Two of Cai Huiqing's three children have moved away years ago to distant cities for employment, and the youngest is expected to soon follow suit. Li Hanwei, since diving into the seas of the newly privatized economy in the mid-1980s, works as a truck driver and spends much of the year on the road. Cai Huiqing remains at home in Hexian, with her elderly adoptive mother, an aunt to whom she was "given" at a young age, whom she continues to look after.

Since the first decade of the 2000s, the term *liushou* has been used commonly in Chinese academic and policy literature as the translational equivalent of "left behind." Yet this neologistic usage of *liushou* sits atop other meanings. Taken separately, *liu* may be defined as to stay, to remain, to concentrate on something, to keep, or to leave something behind for the next generation, and *shou* as to guard, to defend, or to observe. In classical Chinese *liushou* referred to an emperor's order to a minister to act on his behalf during his absence from the capital or, when a small number of troops remained at a garrison, to defend an area after the emperor and his entourage had departed (Luo 2001). As a translingual double to the left behind, what does it mean to *liushou*, if we also take a hint from its older usage? What is it to stay, to guard, to leave something behind for the next generation, to wait for a phone call, or to excavate for the remnants of a shadowed past? How might mediumship offer a site for engaging what remains?

THE TEN-THOUSAND-MAN PIT

The bus comes to a stop at an unmarked spot. We have arrived at a village ten miles or so from Cai Huiqing's home. Although there are several other spirit mediums Cai Huiqing knew of closer in distance, it is common to visit mediums away from one's immediate vicinity as a matter of inclination and perceived spiritual potency, as well as for a degree of removal from the intimate perils of village rumor, since details of one's earthly and otherworldly circumstances are often revealed during the visits. Once off the bus, Cai Huiqing navigates the dirt roads of Zheng Yulan's village with a swift familiarity. Zheng Yulan's house appears no different than those around it; no markings or architectural divergence tell of its cosmic significance. Across waves of state campaigns against institutions and practices designated as feudal superstition, more elaborate temples across China have been replaced by secret home altars and petite icons, long chants with bells and drums quieted to shortened muffled murmurs (T. Dubois 2005)—what Adam Yuet Chau (2006) calls a minimalist mode of religiosity. The only visible distinction of Zheng Yulan's house is that the tall metal front gate leading to the yard, unlike other front gates, is left slightly ajar, a sign for those in the know that her altar is open to supplicants.

Like many other home altars I visited in Hexian, Zheng Yulan's altar has its own dedicated wing in the house complex, with its own entrance. In this case it is a western wing directly adjacent to the central building of the house, where the family lived, both built of brick with curved gray clay-tile roofs. It is an architectural style common to rural houses in the region, particularly those constructed several decades prior. In the 1980s and 1990s, such brick houses (*zhuanfang*)—often single level with multiple wings and an enclosed yard—signaled an upward economic shift from smaller mud-based houses reinforced with hay (*tufang*). But by the time of my visit, brick houses are seen as a step or two behind the times, to be replaced by *yangfang* ("foreign"-style houses), usually a single two- or three-story cement-covered building, more imposing and blockish in stature, with higher ceilings, larger interiors, and smaller yards. Indeed, to the east of the older brick-based altar wing and central wing, a three-story *yangfang* towers above, casting a shadow on its neighbors. This is the home recently built for the medium's son—a sign, Cai Huiqing comments, that Zheng Yulan indeed draws in many supplicants and thus is economically well off, which in turn signals that she indeed knows how to see well *(hui kan, kan de hao)*, referring to her spiritual capacity and efficacy.

At the altar we take a seat across from Zheng Yulan on the west side of the square ritual table—the spiritually and symbolically less powerful side of the arrangement, in contrast to the east. In front of the altar, sitting between Zheng Yulan and us, is a large metal wash bin filled with incense ash from previous sessions. North of us all, thus at the top of the cosmic hierarchy, is the altar lined with several icons flanked by guardian lions, with Queen Mother of the West (Xiwangmu) at the center. Cai Huiqing places a five renminbi bill on the table as incense money (xiangqian)—a gesture that initiates the ritual exchange.[2] Zheng Yulan unwraps a new batch of rusty-gold incense, lighting it slowly, attentively, squinting to determine when the batch was properly lit before finally planting it into the large metal bin.[3]

The flaming incense, as I would learn through conversations with her and others, constitutes the beginning of an invitation (qing), an opening of a portal between the human world and the spirit world, between the living and the dead.[4] Session after session I would begin to sense the tension between presence and absence offered by the flame: a transient mode of communicability and affective passage, an openness dancing precariously during the transitional phase of absenting, the burning away of the body of the incense, paralleling the absenting of the medium's full conscious presence. An emptying of the medium's body to make room, so to speak, for the copresence of deities and other unseen personae.

Zheng Yulan closes her eyes and begins yawning. In Hexian, as in many other regions of China, yawning is a sign that the spirits had arrived and were entering the medium's body, given the airy, pneumatic quality often described of otherworldly presences. "What is the name?" she asks.

Cai Huiqing responds with Li Hanwei's name, on whose behalf she is consulting the deities. As is often the case, the main supplicant of a session is not assumed to be the person who arrived at the altar; consultations are often initiated for others in the family. The reading of one's own cosmic circumstances is not uncommonly left until last, after having inquired for others.

Zheng Yulan asks of Li Hanwei's whereabouts. In an era of rural outmigration, family members are not always assumed to reside locally. Cai Huiqing says that he is away, on the road, driving a large truck, delivering goods.

"Where does he drive?"

"From here to other counties, at times much farther, via the highway, to make deliveries." Zheng Yulan contemplates this; then her right hand begins shaking as she whispers rapidly under her breath, conversing with her tutelary spirit. Another yawn hits her, and her eyes snap open. "He hit someone while he was driving."

"An insider or outsider?" Cai Huiqing asks—someone within the community that the family knew as opposed to a stranger. It was neither: it was a xian. As noted, while xian often refers in Daoist texts to human immortals who have self-cultivated to the point of deathlessness and liberation from the body, in contexts like this in Hexian, *xian* often refers to an old ghost who has been deceased for more than thirty years and evokes themes of danger and malevolence. For those who "walk Mao's path," *xian* might indicate not only old, malevolent ghosts but also corrupted gods, touching on an evil tied to the greed, corruption, and imperialist invasion that Mao had once kept at bay. In sessions of incense seeing at altars, *xian* are less often described in terms of a generalized evil and greed infecting all spirits and more often in terms of particular desires tied to particular demands, with no lower stakes for those who encounter them.

After inquiring about Li Hanwei's local truck route, Zheng Yulan chuckles knowingly. "That corner—don't you know that's the ten-thousand-man pit, the *wanrenkeng?*" She is speaking of a major intersection, which for decades prior to the reform era was known locally as the site of a mass grave. During the famines of the 1940s and 1950s, it is said that those who simply collapsed of cold and hunger and died in the street or those whose families did not have the land to bury them in were simply tossed into the pit. Later, during the Cultural Revolution, it also served as resting place to those accused of political dissent—they were killed point-blank at the edge, I was told.

Now the ten-thousand-man pit lies beneath a Sinopec gas station. It is no longer so actively feared as it once was yet still houses countless hungry, wandering ghosts from decades past. Without proper burial and identity, these are abandoned ghosts, those not taken in by the heavens nor kept by the earth *(tian bu shou, di bu liu)*. They are stuck between realms, at times filled with vengeance, at times drifting aimlessly, colliding into unfortunate human bodies. As Heonik Kwon (2008) suggests in his work on postwar ghosts in Vietnam, following modern modes of mass death, abandoned ghosts must be taken more seriously in theorizations of social relation and reciprocity, and the Durkheimian neglect of ghosts who fall outside of the logic of genealogical kinship must be troubled. As Arthur Wolf (1974) puts it, one man's ghost is another man's ancestor.

The ten-thousand-man pit is but one among many sites for spectral collisions in Hexian. Ghosts are also said to be common at intersections where their souls had been released during mortuary ritual; their personal gravesites; homes of women who recently miscarried; sites of past wrongs, reminiscences, and ghostly sociality (in one village, a group of ghosts were said to enjoy spending their time chatting on a particular tree); and simply arbitrary places along their driftings. The history I address here—that of the 1940s—is just one among many histories that may return. There are also ghosts of the more recently deceased and ghosts stretching back from reform to imperial times. I heard the story of one female ghost, for instance, who returned to haunt a woman in her village. When the woman visited a local medium to decipher her affliction, the ghost revealed the names of neighboring villagers who allegedly sexually assaulted her in the Cultural Revolution era. While the assault incident, according to those I spoke to, was an open secret in the village, the haunting precipitated reinvestigation and redress of an event that had been neglected in the zone of half remembrance.

Here I turn to the site of the ten-thousand-man pit and the history of the 1940s, not as the sole geographic or temporal origin of ghosts in Hexian but as a singular encounter through which to consider how histories may be carried by ghosts, and how we might follow ghosts in an attempt to trace the histories for which they act as remainders and reminders.

NO MAN'S LAND

From his trip to Henan amid the Second Sino-Japanese War (1937–45), U.S. journalist Theodore White writes,

> My notes tell me that I am reporting only what I saw or verified; yet even to me it seems unreal: dogs eating human bodies by the roads, peasants seeking dead human flesh under the cover of darkness, endless deserted villages, beggars swarming at every city gate, babies abandoned to cry and die on every highway. Nothing can transmit the horror of the entire great famine in Honan [Henan] Province, or the irony of the green spring wheat with a promise of a bumper crop which is not ripe for harvesting for two more months. Most terrible of all is the knowledge that the famine might have been averted.[5] (1943, 21)

White's travels and eyewitness accounts, newly heroicized in the 2012 Chinese film *Back to 1942*, brought international attention, not to mention national embarrassment, to the then Nationalist government's neglect of Henan Province during the war: "Nobody knows or cares how many refugees die on this road. They say two million people have moved out along this route since fall; by now probably 10,000 a day are drifting along westward. Of [Henan's] 34 millions we estimated that there have been three million refugees. In addition, five million will have died by the time the new harvest is gathered" (1943, 21).

During the war Henan was treated as a no-man's-land, a buffer zone between Nationalist and Japanese fronts. On May 11, 1938, an order was sent for the Nationalist army to demolish the dikes of the grand Yellow River in eastern Henan to form a barrier against the rapidly encroaching Japanese forces. In what has been called the largest act of environmental warfare in history, the Yellow River rushed to overflow the Huai River. The resulting flood succeeded in momentarily delaying Japanese troops but took with it almost nine hundred thousand of those living in villages and towns of the region, who were not forewarned of the scheme, and left over four million seeking refuge (Dutch 2009; Wou 1994, 218–19). By the time White reported on Henan several years later, the combination of drought and the Japanese destruction of crops had brought on mass starvation, compounding the effects of one disaster after the next.

When we arrived in Chengchow [Zhengzhou,] the snow-covered, rubble-ruined streets seemed full of ghosts in fluttering grey-blue rags. They darted from every alley to screech at us with their hands tucked in their gowns to keep warm. When they die they just lie down in the slush or gutters and give up. We prodded one or two of them gently to see whether they were still alive. . . .

That afternoon we heard of a cannibalism trial. A Mrs. Ma was being tried for eating her little girl. Parts of the baby's flesh were brought in as evidence. The state charged she killed the child and ate it. Her plea was that the baby had died from hunger first and then was eaten. (White 1943, 22)

Despite such wrenching accounts, Liu Zhenyun, author of the book on which *Back to 1942* was based, tellingly notes in a reflection on his research process:

My grandmother lived through the famine. When I ask her about 1942 she responds: "1942? What about it?" I tell her it was the year many people died of starvation.
"People died of starvation all the time," she replies. "What's so special about that year?" (2012)

In the same vein the year 1942 did not seem to constitute a signifier of pain around which recollections gathered for those in Hexian who lived through it. When I asked about 1942, the response often came: "You mean the Old Society?" Used in parallel with "feudal society," the Old Society (Jiushehui) was the term employed for all that came before Mao's New China. And it was not uncommon to hear that one could not compare China with the United States, as China had been a country for "merely sixty years." Upon noting my surprise at the number, some would respond that, of course, there are the thousands of years of Chinese history *(lishi)* but only when Chairman Mao founded New China did China truly emerge as a nation *(guojia)*. Imaginaries of the nation in Hexian thus centered around the moment of Liberation, around Mao and the Chinese Communist Party. The Maoist state was not seen as one regime among others but as the very grounds for existence of China as a national entity.

In contrast to New China, Old Society was described, among those I met who still carried memories from that era, as a time when corpses scattered across village roads (depictions not unlike those of Theodore White's). The square at Fuxi Temple, I was told, was filled with those seeking refuge and salvation, and many died of cold and hunger while begging on the square. It was a time when young men hid from the Nationalist army in fear of being snatched for involuntary service, and young women covered their faces in ash to appear less enticing, in fear of "bad" soldiers, both Nationalist and Japanese. In contrast to Nationalist troops, who were said to demand entry into villagers' homes and dine on their scarce grain, the People's Liberation Army of the Chinese Communist Party was often recalled with fondness. Camping outside of villagers' homes rather than intruding, they said, the People's Liberation Army offered assistance and supplies rather than seizing them.

Such accounts of Old China and of Liberation, of course, must be considered alongside narratives formulated by the Maoist state in the act of state building and for the quelling of political opposition (M. Cohen 1993). Such periodizations have the capacity to powerfully transform the language of memory, augmenting the very experience of time. Yet it would be off the mark to consider the renderings of those I met in Hexian mere narrative reproductions of state ideology. Reflecting on an older debate surrounding "peasant nationalism," Odoric Wou (1994) writes that during the years of the Second Sino-Japanese War, the Chinese Communist Party mobilized the rural movement, building solidarity with peasants in face of flood, drought, famine, and warfare, as well as the "boisterous" behavior of Nationalist-commissioned bandits and warlords.[6] In Hexian recollections of the pre–Maoist Old Society, transmitted through oral accounts and corroborated in national media, together with the sense of precarity and moral collapse in the post-Mao present, heightened the sense of safety and exceptionality of Maoist times.

To raise the themes of history and the ghost also raises the question of the event. In anthropological writings two sets of contrasts have often been put forth, pointing to two dimensions of the event: that between the event and the everyday and that between event and structure. On the one side is an extraordinary quality, whether in terms of scale and universality, violence and traumatic effect, or the transcendental and otherworldly. On the other side is a simultaneously contingent and rupturing quality, in its disruption of existing systems (and what is nameable and legible within them), and the emergence of new forms, of new names. The event and everyday pairing carries a transmuted echo of the sociological distinction between the sacred and profane, in which the extraordinary is set apart or forbidden from mundane concerns. The event and system pairing extends the linguistic question of synchrony and diachrony, mapping onto the historian's perennial dilemma of continuity and change.

For those I met in Hexian, the rise of Mao with the founding of New China, articulated through its distinction from Old Society, seems indeed to constitute an event in both of these senses, in its extraordinary dimension and in its rupturing of a previous order; it is a recognizable event, a world-changing event. By contrast, what appeared to external observers as the extraordinary violence and event-like quality of the 1942 famine and the Cultural Revolution are often described in Hexian with a timbre of the ordinary, no different from other moments that surrounded them. Rather than 1942 or the Cultural Revolution, Maoist Liberation, the 1958 Great Leap famine (spoken of locally as "year '58"), and the death of Mao punctuate the local sense of historical time. To sustain inquiry toward events and their unmarked counterparts is thus to follow the movement of disjointed gazes. Moreover, it is to attend to the forward and backward motions of event making, the anticipatory and retroactive forces that invoke questions of deferred action. The event (and quasi event) unfolds through various moments of reactivation, which also complicates and puts into question the site and temporality of the event proper. What is it, for instance, to hit an old ghost, amid present concerns seemingly distant from this past?

DREAM OF A DYING HEN

The mood of the room grows tense as Zheng Yulan reveals the collision with the ghost. Cai Huiqing looks worried. "I/we/he hit the ghost? I/we/he can't see them on the road *[an kan bu jian]*." In contrast to the "I" in standard Mandarin *(wo)*, "I" in the Henanese dialect *(an)* doesn't distinguish between first-person singular, first-person plural, and third-person singular except through its contextual deictic usage—in this case, the "I" of Cai Huiqing herself, the "we" of the family, and the "he" of her husband, who was the only one in the truck at the time of the incident. She is thus apologizing as and for the whole family, her husband in particular. The ghost, says Zheng Yulan, was smashed to a pulp and is very angry. Cai Huiqing rushes to the kneeling mat south of the altar and begins to kowtow northward.

"Let me/us/him kowtow to you. I/we/he collided into you. I/we/he are sorry," she continues as her head begins hitting the floor. "I/we/he are sorry. I/we/he couldn't see you." The Henanese "you" *(nen)*, as counterpart to *an*, signifies a pluralized or pluralizable second person—the you of your relational being.

This gesture of kowtowing seems insufficient.

"He is furious," Zheng Yulan relays, squinting into the flame, referring to the ghost. "You see?" She points to a single blackened, scorched stick of incense, towering above the rest. "You see how angry he is! He wants your husband's life!"

Cai Huiqing begins tearing up. "That won't do! Tell him to leave! Whatever he wants, we'll give. If he wants money, we'll give him money. Keep talking to him!" She runs over to the mat and begins to kowtow again.

Here we're brought to the significance of burning incense—what might be considered a hermeneutics of incense. In many mediumship sessions I saw, when one or several sticks of incense stood darkened above the batch, each marked a sign of trouble to be deciphered. In this case the single blackened stick that stands above the rest was a manifestation of anger arising from a history of bad deaths paved over for a gas station, directed toward Cai Huiqing's family, through Li Hanwei as a truck driver in an era of rising product exportation and traffic accidents.

Zheng Yulan's exegesis is spoken amid the blazing transformation between the two states of incense: from solid, undifferentiated stems into the fine, almost liquid gray powder of ash. It is as if the singularity of the situation—the collision of life histories, human and ghost, carrying layers of collective history and geography—is together summoned to the present and made visible momentarily through the ephemeral dynamism of flames before crumbling into a pile of ash, atop the ashes left by previous negotiations and pleas. This ash, materializing the encounter, can then be taken up in certain cases for further ritual purposes, through ingestion or strategic placement. But, in this instance, another modality is invoked.

"Have you dreamed of this person?" Zheng Yulan asks. Cai Huiqing has not. "You will, then."

That night, after receiving instructions from Zheng Yulan for the desired offerings to spare her husband's life—six hundred ingots folded from gold spirit money to placate the ghost and ten reams of yellow spirit money to show gratitude to the deities—Cai Huiqing indeed has a dream.[7] In fact, she has several. The first involves her two mothers: her birth mother who had passed away some years prior, whom she called Ma (mother), and her adoptive mother, whom she called Niang (another term for mother and for the maternal natal home [niangjia]). The second dream is brief, of an old hen. Upon our next visit to Zheng Yulan several days later, accompanied this time by both myself and her mother-in-law, Cai Huiqing recounts her dreams:

On the road, I saw a man. A tall man, southward, with a face not quite square and not quite round. Then I saw our Ma. The two of them, our Ma is walking on the west side; he's walking on the east side. And I thought, yeee! How could I be seeing our mother?

They approached, right in front of me. I called out, "Ma!"

Our Ma said, "Yeee! I have been searching for you. I missed you so much." Our Ma cried and cried, and I cried too.

I said, "Why did you leave?"

She said, "I did not leave. I am here at home." Then someone came to pull her away, pulling her hand, it was our little sister, and they left.

This man, this man stiffly stood there. Our Ma . . . she is crying, crying, crying, toward the south, near the wall where there was a water pipe. Crying, crying, I hear our Ma cry. I run toward the pipe, to let the water out.

Our Niang said, "Where did you go? You have been gone for years and have not returned."

Our Ma said, "Mmnh! You are here?"

Our Niang said to my Ma, "Here is a hundred RMB. Here is a hundred RMB. You go buy yourself something to eat. We haven't seen each other for so long."

Yeee! I thought—our Niang has eased up [xiang kai le]. In the past she always harassed [nao] our Ma.

Our Ma said, "I don't want your money! You stay here and take care of our daughter." Our Niang kept insisting and nudging the money toward her. Our Ma said (yelling), "I do not want your money!"

Yeee, this dream was so clear.

Then . . . our Ma wanted to eat our Niang! Our Niang asked, "Why eat me?"

I yelled to my son, "Our Ma is going to eat our Niang! Hurry! You cannot eat that; you cannot eat a live person!"

She said, "I will drink her blood. I will drink her blood."

Our Ma blew a breath of air. With this breath, yeee! It blew our Niang into the distance. Our Niang's face turned sallow. Our Ma was on the north side, facing south, and began inhaling. Inhaling, inhaling, and our Niang began floating into the air. I faced south, with my back to our Ma, facing our Niang.

I said, "This is not acceptable. I have to stand in the middle. I have to keep both of these two mothers. It's not acceptable." Even now, my back is chilly. I can feel the whoooo of the chilly air. Then I suddenly awoke.

I said, "Yeee, the Old Mother [*laoniang*, referring to the medium's tutelary spirit] said [that I would] dream [*tuomeng*]. These dreams must be conveyed [*tuo*] by one's family, must '*tuo*' the family. This dream must have emerged through '*tuo*,' right?"

Tuomeng is a term common in Hexian, indicating what might be called a mediumistic dream—a dream used by deities, ancestors, and other spirits to convey a message or plea from the other world.[8] *Tuo* is to entrust, to hold in one's palm, to plead, to rely, or to serve as a foil to, and *meng* means a dream or to dream. Together they signify the conveying of a message from one persona to another, across visible and invisible realms. Across historical moments and textual and oral traditions in China, the dream has been a site of engagement between humans and spirits. As Carolyn Brown (1988) muses, the dream seems to take on inverted temporal significance across Western psychoanalytic approaches and pre-twentieth-century Chinese approaches to dream interpretation. Amid the centrality of future-facing visions of progress at the dawn of the twentieth century, she notes, Freudian approaches to the dream yielded attention to questions of the past. Amid a broader tendency to cite the foregone golden age of sage kings, various strands of Chinese dream interpretation strongly emphasized futurity and prognostication. In Cai Huiqing's case the dream brought together her own life history, caught between two maternal figures, and the desires of ghosts from times past, while also carrying the prognostic dimension of how to proceed.

In early Chinese texts such as *The Book of Songs (Shijing)*, *Spring and Autumn Annals (Chunqiu)*, and *The Commentary of Zuo (Zuozhuan)*, whose compiled contents date from twelfth century BCE through fifth century BCE, diviners were involved in the explication of dreams (Hegel 1988). Heavenly entities guided rulers through imperial dreams, portending auspicious and inauspicious political decisions and world events. Records of such dreams were detailed even if their immediate implications were unclear, as the significance of some may be realized only with the passage of time, when the relevant occasion eventually arises.

Yet the potential significance of dreams was treated with strong ambivalence, as their divine status was by no means guaranteed—"There are [also] *yemeng*, wild dreams, and *kuangmeng*, freak dreams, both caused by demons who seize the soul while one is asleep and lead it astray, or perhaps abscond with it altogether"; thus, "danger lies in only retaining those parts [of the dream] one can understand and interpret," given their true divine origin (Wagner 1988, 16, 19). With the general increase of written texts during the Warring States period (475 to 221 BCE), dream narratives were increasingly recorded at length, invoking documentation and interpretation by various advisors, military strategists, historian-astrologers, and spirit mediums (Strassberg 2008).

Demonic entities were also cited in medical treatises as a cause of nightmares, either through their physical lodging in the human body or encounters with humans in dreams, given the tendency for the human's *hun*-soul to wander during sleep. In Chen Shiyuan's 1562 *Lofty Principles of Dream Interpretation* (translated in Strassberg 2008)—a heterogeneous compendium drawing on Confucian, Daoist, and Buddhist texts; philosophical essays; dynastic histories; medical texts; anomaly accounts; poems; dramas; and popular dream manuals—an excerpt resonates with a common rendering of ghostly intrusion by mediums I met in Hexian: "What is meant by 'demonic presences'? Death-dealing demons attach themselves to people as disastrous influences. Ghosts of people with grievances will seek revenge against those responsible. They appear in dreams because the thoughts of the dreamer are filled with doubts and his spirit and qi-energy are in a state of confusion. Then, demons take advantage of these weaknesses to let loose their strange forms of retribution. Thus do calamities and disasters arise, and it becomes difficult to pray for blessings and well-being" (94). Combining themes of retribution and cosmological correlation with the state of human qi and emotional state, demonic entities both induce and exploit sites of vulnerability. Because of the uncertain and potentially multivalent status of the dream, a range of techniques were deployed to verify it, including imperial and popular forms of divination, as well as corroborations with waking occurrences (Wagner 1988).

Not unlike the cosmological accounts of postreform chaos and indiscernibility in Hexian, the sense of uncertainty and risk was at times attributed to changing times. Chen Shiyuan cautions in his sixteenth-century text, "Ever since the ancient methods disappeared, there has been no definite way to fully interpret dreams. . . . Alas, the ancient methods of interpretation have not been transmitted. Later generations of people have been unable to govern their emotions and natures. Their conduct during the day is muddled, deluded, ignorant, and confused. They are lacking in self-awareness. Thus, what appears in their dreams is chaotic, perverse, and evil—by no means that which flows in accordance with the qi energy of heaven and earth." Chen further describes a temporal shift from prognostication to corroboration in the interpretation of dreams resulting from this loss of hermeneutic capacity: "Even if there were omens that could be used for confirmation, they would be incongruent and barely intelligible, so that one must wait for the consequences to appear before realizing what the dream meant" (cited in Strassberg 2008, 85). Dreams thus opened up a portal between the living and the nonliving;

shifted the coordinates between past, present, and future; and raised concerns over the problems and techniques of interpretation.

. . .

After Cai Huiqing's recollection of her two dreams, Zheng Yulan proceeds to request some clarifications—that it was Cai Huiqing's birth mother in the dream who wished to extract blood from her adoptive mother, who wished to take her adoptive mother's life. The birth mother in the dream, Zheng Yulan says, was hateful, spiteful. Cai Huiqing gives her own interpretation—that her birth mother, in a gesture of acknowledgment and sympathy, must have meant that after all these years, her adoptive mother is still tormenting her (zhemo). Throughout Cai Huiqing's childhood her adoptive mother had been verbally and at times physically violent toward her and remains demanding and temperamental in her old age. Her birth mother, when she was still alive, had often conveyed remorse for giving Cai Huiqing away, for subjecting her to a deeply painful life under her adoptive mother's watch. Despite Cai Huiqing's own sorrow toward her separation from her birth mother, she tries to stay firm in her sense of filial duty, cooking three meals a day for her adoptive mother, a finicky eater who often pushes her bowl aside in staunch dissatisfaction.

Zheng Yulan asks about the tall man in the dream. The man stood to the side, Cai Huiqing says, and did not take action for the remainder of the dream. "He just stood there. Very tall. His face . . . to say it's round, it's not quite round; to say it's square, it's not quite square. His skin was quite white. Eyes not big, not small." Cai Huiqing then relays a second dream: "The next day in the morning, I began dreaming again. I felt muddled [mi], muddled and dreaming, muddled and dreaming, early in the morning. I dreamed of an old hen [laomuji]. It laid an egg. The egg comes out; the egg sits to the side of her. The old hen dies. The old hen dies, and her mouth even spat out liquids. Yeee! When I went to grab the egg, yeee! The egg was cracked and spoiled [tangle]."

Upon hearing the second dream, Zheng Yulan reveals the true identities of those in the first. The birth mother in the dream, Zheng Yulan says, is a female ghost disguised as Cai Huiqing's birth mother, here to trick Cai Huiqing and enact vengeance on Cai Huiqing's family to save her own son—the tall, pale man in the dream. It is left somewhat ambiguous whether this tall, pale man is the same ghost as the one hit by the truck. Regardless, this ghost has been hovering around Cai Huiqing's home for seventy-some years—that is, since the time of famine and warfare in the 1940s. The tall, pale ghost's mother has traveled a long way to find her son, who is now trapped and choked by a certain arc-shaped object, stuck beneath Cai Huiqing's home, in the southwest corner. Cai Huiqing will have to unearth and get rid of this object to free the ghost son and avert revenge from the ghost mother. This would be the rusted pipe clamp Cai Huiqing excavated, when she came pounding at my door several days after.

As for the old hen and the egg, this is a message from the ghost mother, an ominous threat to the future generations, to the *houdai*. The hen stands for Cai Huiqing's mother-in-law, Zheng Yulan explains; thus the egg at once gestures toward Cai Huiqing's husband and their children—a threat to the patriline and the conjugal family, through the figure of the paternal grandmother. The story of supplication and appeasement sits uneasy, as one ghost's woes linked to another's, and the family's fate remains uncertain. The catastrophes of one era threaten to become the catastrophes of another. Cai Huiqing later laments in tears that, indeed, her children are failing. Her son, who lives in Beijing, is in his thirties and divorced, and his ex-wife refuses to let him visit their child. The tales of two mothers and two sons, human and ghost, thus grow entangled. Moreover, her elder daughter, who lives and works in Shanghai, is reaching thirty and appears, Cai Huiqing says, to have no prospects for marriage despite her intelligence and beauty: a curse on future generations.

DISTANT INTIMACY

Between the ghost from the mass grave beneath the Sinopec station demanding her husband's life and the famine-era mother-son ghosts threatening her children and adoptive mother, histories of the twentieth century, of ghosts abandoned by heaven and earth, become copresent with the temporality of Cai Huiqing's life and that of her family, mediated through the work of Zheng Yulan, her tutelary spirits, and the flickers of flaming incense. As with other women I met in Hexian (women tend to be more involved in such matters than men, but by no means exclusively), Cai Huiqing visits mediums in times of trouble or at life junctures, even while Li Hanwei and at times her children disparage these visits as a superstitious squandering of time and money.

"He doesn't believe it," Cai Huiqing says of Li Hanwei, "but I already 'saw' on his behalf." The risks posed to and accumulated through Li Hanwei's life on the road by those who entered the yin realm decades ago, she is suggesting, are mitigated by her ritual engagements, whether or not he himself professed conviction in their efficacy. As Erik Mueggler (2017) writes, rather than a Western secular ontological divide between the living and the dead in which the former is taken as real and the latter is taken as imaginary, both the living and the dead can instead be thought to move between material and immaterial forms, particularly in certain ritual contexts. For Cai Huiqing, her ongoing negotiations with the spirits constitute an ethical labor for her family and for the next generation—neither of which are materially present in the here and now of the hometown—a distant intimacy of the "I" and the "we" heightened in an era of labor migration.

Here I use distant intimacy to ponder forms of life available to those residing in regions figured as left behind in an age of global capital and labor mobility. Given the dislocation of geographies and lifeworlds, spirit mediumship provides one mode through which closeness is engaged from afar. It opens up an intimate zone of effectivity, not by proximity but from a distance; Cai Huiqing stakes a claim on the "he" of her husband and "we" of her family through a parallel, invisible world, with the medium as proxy. In an era of deep uncertainty, Cai Huiqing works to ensure the safety of her husband, marriage prospects of her children, and continuity of future generations in part through her engagements with mediumship, work that may be dismissed and admonished by them in the wake of state antisuperstition campaigns. Her dealings with the ghosts—dreaming, digging, pleading, appeasing—keeps the present afloat, skirting catastrophe.

The "we" of her family is thus entangled with the "we" of specters to China's long twentieth century; tending to desires of the present involves tending to the desires of ghosts. To release the ghost mother's son is to save her own son; to ask forgiveness from the abandoned ghost is to reckon with violent histories paved over by the roads and gas stations so applauded as signs of rural development. It is to lend one's body to the passage of histories that have, like the ghost mother in search of her son, traveled a long way.

Distant intimacy also raises the question of mediation beyond the particularities of contemporary migration, even if newly instantiated. Rosalind Morris writes of the very institution of mediumship as marked by some degree of anxiety, of being positioned as the vessel and voice of magical efficacy while artfully staying out of the way: "Total mediation appears to be no mediation. . . . To speak and not be the subject of speech, to know and not be the subject of knowledge: this is the medium's predicament" (2000, 101–2). The ideal medium, in this sense, conveys the message of the spirits without intervention, passing on the other's desire without contamination. Through the movement of amnesic forgetting during possession—in Hexian, as in many other places, many mediums spoke of not knowing what was said during a session—mediumship effaces its own traces, in a transmission of knowledge and action that marks a deferral of origin.

Mediumship might then be considered a technique of indirection, of access through detour. It is to act on the present via passage through other persons, places, and times—humans, deities, ghosts, and the temporalities and geographies they each bring to the table. As François Jullien (2004) writes, drawing on various strands of Chinese aesthetics and political strategy, detour needs not represent constraint but can be deployed for heightened effect. The act of lending and borrowing, of citational distance and speaking by proxy, can open up a space for maneuver and allow for a mobilization of energies through its partial anonymity.

In contrast to the tendency to fully name spirits in Morris's (2000) work in northern Thailand or the generic spirits of unknown biographies she cites of James Siegel's (1978) work in Sumatra, there is often an intermediate degree of identification of the ghosts conjured in Hexian. Certain elements and attributes are named without others, as the medium and supplicant together move toward a partially spoken specification of a localized death. A ghost might be said to be from inside or outside one's village, along with the manner of death—drowning, hanging, starvation, cancer, car accident. A surname, as in the case of the ghost named Liu, might be posited, but rarely the full name. Facial and bodily features might be described, but the full personage is often left to the searchful corroboration on the supplicant's part. The mediumship session, then, can open up inquiries into semi-occluded histories of the dead that have been partly but not entirely forgotten. The medium acts by and as proxy, offering a pathway of historical return through which the bad deaths of bygone times stake their claims after years of invisible, purgatorial cohabitation with the human realm.

While it is not explicitly discussed during incense-seeing sessions, within the contemporary cosmology at large, in which dangerous, corrupt spirits are said to have returned after Mao's death, distant intimacy also finds its counterpart in imaginations of a former mode of relation, one between the sovereign and the self. In the time of Chairman Mao's reign, it is said, spirit mediums were not needed, as gods and ghosts momentarily vanished—there were no spirits to mediate. In their place stood the Chairman—as a virtuous figure of cosmic sovereignty who kept the ghosts at bay.

In her work in North Korea, Sonia Ryang (2012) writes of a sense of self formed through a direct sense of closeness with and dedication to the sovereign. It was a sense of individuation cultivated in face of the virtuous Great Leader, through the humbled cultivation of one's own virtue. Similarly, for many in Hexian, Chairman Mao not only holds a position of political authority but stands as exemplar for virtuous emulation. The loss of the Chairman, many felt, was accompanied by the loss of virtue in the People. Moreover, with the dawn of economic reform, the revolutionary, future-facing peasantry so central in Maoist formulations are now refigured in postreform discourse as the rural "left behind." The ghosts that reappeared in the postreform era, in this sense, reconfigure contemporary time and space, creating a differently mediated mode of distant intimacy with the passage of history.

As discussed earlier, whereas the Maoist era is recalled as an interval of alignment between heaven and earth, cosmic order is said to be disjointed in the historical present. With the return of ghosts amid moral doldrums, spirit mediums work through a series of detours, traversing with their tutelary spirits to the hells and back, through geographies near and far. They work to conjure a new sense of cosmic potentiality, amid anxieties that safety and virtue no longer emerge from a sovereign assurance imagined of the past but require reckoning with the thousands upon thousands of ghosts that now swarm the landscape, from years, decades, and centuries past. It is as if the distance between heaven and earth was narrowed for a moment through their alignment, then split once again after Mao's death, severing the realms and reopening a vast space in which ghosts and other entities swarm.

Mediumship, then, might be said to occasion distant intimacy amid several simultaneous dimensions of the present: dispersed kinship and community conditioned by postreform rural outmigration, the problem of otherworldly mediation at once old and new, and the implicit loss of a virtuously sovereign self once mirrored and secured by the earthly presence of the Chairman, now disrupted and dispersed in a post-Mao proliferation of ghosts.

SPECTRAL COLLISION

What is it, then, to collide into such a ghost? In Hexian ghosts and potentially demonic entities tend to be euphemized into a most generic noun when one is potentially implicated: *thing*. In times of suspicion that an illness or situation may be linked to an otherworldly entity, the hushed phrase arises: "there is a thing/to have a thing" *(you dongxi)*. In the case of direct contact with a ghost, the most common phrase is "colliding into (some)thing" *(zhuangdao dongxi)*. Such collisions are not always felt at the moment of contact; only those sensitive to the movements of the yin world might take notice. To be a medium, then, is to be capable of perceiving and rendering perceptible the unspeakable thing spectrally driving a given situation.

Ghost encounters are often known by unsuspecting humans only through the signs and symptoms they produce—illness, mishaps, interrupted life paths—but not their cause. When they cross the threshold of perception, spectral collisions pry open the meaning of the present, propelling a search for new strands of mutual implication between occurrences past and present. The ghost, as Avery Gordon puts it, not only gives notice to itself but provides a symptom of what is missing— a loss, a life, a path not taken (1997, 64). The collision sets off signals, announcing the invisible presence of the specter while hinting at absences beyond itself.

Spectral collisions thus speak to recent articulations in anthropology and in affect theory of occurrences that do not quite reach the threshold of an event in a classic sense yet may force one to take notice and affect how one goes on to make adjustments or care for one another (Berlant 2011; Das 2015).[9] Alongside the folding of the violent and evental into the ordinary (Das 2006), spectral collisions also have the capacity to redraw threads and momentarily intensify ties between various scales of time and space, human and nonhuman. The inquiries, excavations, and procedures put into motion by mediumship produce links across events recognizable to official history—the start and end of the Maoist era, times of known famine and warfare—and occurrences that might be deemed more ordinary but no less significant: a suicide, the particularities of a truck route or walking path, the moseying and nudging of half-forgotten ghosts.

In the language of mediumship in Hexian, spectral collisions are considered one among several forms of calamity *(zai)*, distinguished from another form: natal calamity *(benming zai)*, even if the two could at times coincide. Natal calamity is linked to the cosmic-numeric conditions of one's birth, according to one's eight-character birth date and time in the lunar calendar. It is a meeting point between calculable forces—yin and yang, cardinal directions, and such elemental forces as fire, water, and earth—and potential relations with deities prior to being born on earth.

Spectral collision, by contrast, touches on themes of contingency and intentionality not determined at one's birth, involving spatialized coincidence and historical returns in encounters with unseen others. On the one hand, ghosts are often driven by desire and spite—longing for the humans they have departed, hurt and anger for their neglect, wishes for goods and riches in the afterlife, indignation and vengefulness for the wrongs from their former life yet to be set right. On the other hand, ghosts also evoke the motif of accident. Tending to travel in straight lines, ghosts are said to inadvertently collide into humans who happen upon the same place at the same time on a shared landscape hosting both yin and yang realms.

Thus, even when not pursuing justice or revenge, the very aimless drifting of ghosts poses a potential risk to those who unwittingly cross their paths. Their era, their time, their pain, and their yearning are carried in their ethereal existence, invisible amid a shared landscape. Stretching across human lifespans, their spectral presence brings multiple histories into a shared "now," making the past an effective force in the present. A spectral collision, in this sense, has the capacity to reactivate events past, even if in a subthreshold manner. Cai Huiqing's family is put at risk on account of a bad death from another era, reactivating the force of a prior moment by putting the present at stake. Such an encounter might be thought not only as a present reference to the past but as the reanimation of desires and pains coming from another time, with its own set of horizons, transported into a given present. To think through ghosts, then, is also to revisit the temporal status of the human persons living among them.

In Jean Laplanche's (1999) elaboration of "afterwardsness," he describes three usages of *nachträglichkeit*, which has also been translated in the past as "deferred action," across Freud's texts: the notion of the further or secondary, the sense of movement from the past into the future, and the movement from the future to the past. The second usage points to the progressive or deterministic—a time bomb from earlier in one's life history waiting to be set off by an external element—while the third suggests the retrospective or hermeneutic. These usages coexist without being reconciled in Freud, maintaining a degree of ambiguity. To these Laplanche adds his own: of the desire and message of the other—of afterwardsness as something *deposited* from the past by a third, which demands to be deciphered. Rather than choosing between one or another, Laplanche holds on to these aspects of afterwardsness as the back-and-forth movements of translation.

Likewise, dealings with spectral collision in mediumship maintain a translational tension between forward and backward movements of personal and historical time, attending to repetitions, deferrals, and desires of the other, human and nonhuman. The wishes and woes of ghosts from eras past, the pains of Cai Huiqing's childhood with her adoptive mother, and the precarity of the postreform present are mutually set off by the run-in between the living and the ghost, set to the contemporary motif of the car accident. Negotiations with the ghost, such as that staged at Zheng Yulan's altar, constitute a second or third or fourth encounter, as the ghost would have already encountered the supplicant, with or without the latter's knowing. From the initial collision with the truck to the mediumship session, a hermeneutic process begins, a search for the ghost's desire. The translational movements between human and nonhuman realms reach toward the enigma of the message, drawing together disparate moments in time to reconfigure the present.

Questions of spectral passage through human bodies and psyches also evoke themes of intergenerationality. In their work on mourning and melancholia, Nicolas Abraham and Maria Torok (1994) articulate a concept of the phantom as a mode of intergenerational transmission, in which secrets and losses of the dead leave a gap in representation, moving across generations in ghostly form. Unlike losses within an individual lifespan, which may or may not be available to one's own conscious knowing, the person haunted by the phantom is afflicted by the unfinished business of others, without access to what is transmitted. Pains from the ghost's life, sealed and encrypted, are lodged in the living.

In Hexian, spectral collisions distribute the ticking time bomb of afterwardsness and intergenerational passage across a spatial plane through the unseen movement of ghosts. Personal and collective histories drift latently across landscapes of potential encounter. To turn the corner and bump into a ghost could be to have their woes seep into your life. The abandoned ghosts hovering about the ten-thousand-man pit could intensify their anger and demands when hit by a truck. Famine ghosts from the 1940s, trapped under Cai Huiqing's home, could resurface through Cai Huiqing's dreams, setting histories of loss back into motion.

While the clinical task of psychoanalysis, for Abraham and Torok (1994), is to eventually discover and release the message encrypted in the phantom, the wishes and woes of ghosts are not always fully deciphered during a mediumship session. Losses and longings are partially unraveled, with efforts aimed at bargaining with the ghost—at a good-enough offer that would bring a momentary truce. When a series of engagements comes to a close, then, the specter and its secrets may not be fully decrypted, and the ghost might not be annihilated. Instead, knotted entanglements between human and ghost are loosened after a partial recognition of the desires of those involved, making some room for each to move along on their way.

THE I, THE WE, THE GHOST

A while after our visits to Zheng Yulan, Cai Huiqing's childhood friend, who grew up in Hexian but spent much of her adult life in the urban South of Guangzhou and Shenzhen, comes to visit. Upon hearing about Cai Huiqing's worries over her husband and children and about her visits to the medium, the friend tries to convince Cai Huiqing that she must learn to be "independent," to stop uselessly troubling herself with her family's business, to tend to her own desires: "Make yourself happy; find your own hobbies," she says, using the singular "you" of standard Mandarin. Cai Huiqing retorts, "What would *I* want?" switching to the register of the singular standard Mandarin "I" of *wo* rather than the "I/we" of the Henanese *an*.

The question of the "I" conjures classic anthropological discussions of personhood. In his 1938 lecture on the notion of the person, Marcel Mauss points to the historical contingency of the rational, reflective, self-contained notion of the self, across a genealogy of Roman law, Christianity, and modern psychology, in contradistinction with, yet linked to, notions of the *personage*, the latter of which gestures toward the significance of the role, the mask, and the name as relational determinants. In the case of China, Mauss calls the name a "collective noun," in its elaborations of birth order, rank, and social class, and the individual as a composite of and correspondence to ancestral transmissions, of "something springing from elsewhere" (1985, 13).

The work of missionary Maurice Leenhardt in New Caledonia, among those whom the French colonists glossed as Kanaks or Canaques, registers the ambivalence that accompanies the shift from the relational person to the "I," at once freeing and devastating. Leenhardt writes of the Kanak notion of the personage, which knows the self through relationships. It is not a self that affirms itself through the "I am" but a body that is a vessel and support for a set of relationalities collected throughout a life. Yet, upon colonial encounter and Christian conversion, this very structure of the person begins to fatally disintegrate. Leenhardt gives several examples of this, but of particular interest here, he writes, "The Canaque ceases to mix first and third persons when he speaks. He says 'I' and he recognizes 'one'" (1979, 169). Such subtle yet fundamental avenues of linguistic conversion, in conjunction with forms of military and political violence, tears the Kanak notion of personage apart with the newly individuated self, resulting in a sense of arbitrariness, loss, and anomie.

In China the question of the "I" was also central to an earlier moment of encounter, a moment when mediumship and other forms of healing were in the midst of being variously demarcated into zones of medicine and superstition, of legitimacy and illegality. Part of the broader search for modernity and national self-determination in the early twentieth century following military invasion and occupation, the "I" of *wo* constituted both a contentious site in the struggle for a newly imagined body politic and a linguistic sign capacitating rising modes of mass communication.[10] Movements to vernacularize and nationalize language struggled to move away from both classical Chinese and the multiplicity of regional dialects in the service of communicability. In these vernacularization movements, first-person pronouns such as the Henanese "I/we" were considered overly localized, thus to be subsumed by the standard national "I" that was to rearticulate the citizen self vis-à-vis the nation state (Kaske 2008).

Yet in spite of such efforts in official and pedagogical domains, dialects still reign in many regions, in coexistence and mutual influence with standard Mandarin. In Hexian the general usage of standard Mandarin in daily life immediately marks one as an outsider, while its selective usage creates a sense of an uncanny deliberateness—an emphatic seriousness in gratitude or in apology, a wink to the strictures of officialdom or simply an ironic pointedness.

"*I* don't want anything," Cai Huiqing continues. "What is there to want?"

Her friend retorts, "So then, you have to learn how to want for yourself."

As Cai Huiqing later reflects to me, with a sigh and a laugh, "*I* just want to complete my duties, *renwu!* When your elder brother and your sisters all have their own families, have their own children, then I can be finished. But until then my duties are not yet complete!" She was speaking of her children—my brother and sisters in our fictive kinship during my stay.

Rather than a mere question of unwanted obligation as it may connote in translation, Cai Huiqing's evocation of "duty," at once playful and serious, points toward a sense that her own life would not reach completion without what she saw as the makings of a full life for her three children. Beyond a sense of relational obligation that assumes an autonomy of the "I" from the "they," taking the atomized individual as its primary unit, Cai Huiqing's sense of personhood, articulated through the Henanese *an*, gestures toward a fundamental distribution of the person, in which the familial other is deeply infused with the self, and an incompletion of the other simultaneously marks an incompletion of the self.

Between the "I" and the *an*, between the demands of the ghosts, the work of mediumship, and accusations of superstitious squandering, sits Cai Huiqing's dilemma of how to imagine a life, a life in which the "I" once again contends with the first-person plural of the "I/we," this time mapped onto an uneven postreform landscape, in which places like Hexian, dialect and all, are drained of symbolic and economic value, ripe for departure. And it is in this scene, between the gas stations, trucks, and abandoned ghosts, that those like Cai Huiqing navigate a splintered world, between yin and yang realms, in hopes that someday in the distant future, her grandchildren and great-grandchildren continue burning batches of incense after she becomes an ancestor, not forgetting the desires of another ghost.

4

A Soul Adrift

Tan Suzhen's daughters do not know just how their mother lost her soul. But ever since the four sisters moved off to the city a decade ago—first to the southern factories of Dongguan, then to those of Beijing—she seems to have been looking for it. A former brigade leader during Maoist years, Tan Suzhen now wanders the dirt paths of their home village, at times for short jaunts, at times for hours on end. Her daughters bring her to the psychiatric ward, hoping the doctors can help bring her back, in one sense or another.

In the southern city of Guangzhou, Liang Ming sees a ghost on the stairway of his factory dorm. Overcome with fright, he returns home to Hexian, no longer able to carry on with his night shifts. His mother and father bring him to several village elders to call back his soul, to no avail. They go to the psychiatric ward seeking his recovery but soon begin planning for his discharge. Schizophrenia, they sense, is not the true problem. They would find another path to save their son, outside the hospital.

Down the hall Guo Hongjun cannot sleep, mired in anxiety. He built a two-story house for his eldest son, but something went wrong with the design. The stairs were built on the outside, with no correlate on the inside. Bearable in the summer, perhaps, but laughable in the winter. A retired local official, he had the funds to build the house, but it seems a waste to rebuild. His wife tries to reassure him, saying that the house is fine, that he needs not be gripped by minor imperfections. He shakes his head, bitter that no one—himself included—caught the mistake on the blueprint. All the while, his wife whispers to me, their son lives in the city and has shown little interest in moving back to the hometown, back to the village.

Xia Peizhi sulks in bed in the open ward, exhausted in the wake of her near collapse. Her test scores had been dropping. She withdrew from high school. Family finances are teetering. Her father is a migrant laborer, a construction worker in Shanghai. He returns home just once a year. He does not know how to speak to her, how to comfort her, how to convey his affection as she wants him to. He does not know how to sustain a sense of safety in her. He cannot not grasp what it means to have an ideal, to have a dream. When he talks, all he talks about is money, she says.

In the locked ward Wang Weihong shivers in his bed, body stiff, facing the ceiling, eyes wide with terror, darting side to side. He has been seeing ghosts. He is a man of few words, never one to complain, his wife explains. In his quietude he has been filling with anger and fear. He injured his back working in the coal mine. His father taunts him for failing to earn a decent living. He feels the whole village looks down on him. He does not know how he will support his family. He does not know how he will build a house for his eldest son; a young man without a house is not a marriageable man. Acute psychosis, his wife, Liu Shuhua, repeats after the psychiatrist. She urges Wang to let go of his "New Countryside dream" *(xin nongcun mengxiang)* and to be content with what they have. When he talks, he talks about money.

THE PEOPLE'S PSYCHIATRIC UNIT

During the fifth plenary session of the Sixteenth Central Committee of the Chinese Communist Party in 2005, the policy framework of "building a New Socialist Countryside" was announced by the administration of Hu Jintao and Wen Jiabao. A broad-reaching proposition, the New Socialist Countryside renewed existing calls for combating the so-called Three Rural Problems: agriculture, the countryside, and the peasant. Undergirded by visions of impoverished villages slowly receding and rural surplus labor gradually absorbed into urban industrial and service sectors, the New Socialist Countryside conjured once again the spectral dimension of the rural, in which the problem of rurality could be resolved, in the call to modernization, only by its imagined vanishing (Day 2013).[1]

Whereas the return to family farming after decollectivization through the household responsibility system was first lauded in the 1980s, a sense of failing development and rising rural dissatisfaction took hold across the 1990s and the first decade of the 2000s, despite apparent progress by economic measures. It was a moment in which wealth accumulation led to new concerns over rent seeking and bureaucratic corruption rather than celebrations of peasant entrepreneurship as was first imagined in the early reform era. After a loosening of media censorship in 1992, alongside announcements of staggering Gini coefficient growths, a wave of publications and public debates arose on themes of social stratification and inequality. From the Marxist analysis of class *(jieji)* to the language of social strata *(shehui jieceng)*, the problem of inequality shifted from the notion of antagonism and revolution in the Maoist era to one of developmental time in the reform era: "Those who prosper before others must not become the targets of class resentment but models for others to emulate; they are the avant garde of a more generalised prosperity to come" (Anagnost 2008, 502). New social-engineering projects arose, aimed at expanding the middle class through consumption practices and a sense of middle-class identity.[2]

Amid these debates Li Changping, a rural cadre from Hubei Province, sparked further discussion in 2000 with his open letter to Premier Zhu Rongji: "The peasants' lot is really bitter, the countryside is really poor, and agriculture is in crisis" (cited in Day 2013, 119). By 2003 and 2004 the rural "problem" came to be framed as the greatest obstacle to China's continued development, and discourse around the peasant shifted from the early reform language of success to one of crisis. A thread of unresolved tension underlying disparate conceptual and policy accounts thus remained: "How do we understand history, Chinese intellectuals asked, if the peasant is not viewed as on the path to disappearance?" (6). And, as W. E. B. Du Bois puts it, "How does it feel to be a problem?" (1996, 7).

This chapter traces a constellation of stories drawn from conversations I had with patients and their attendant family members at the psychiatric unit of the county People's Hospital. It dwells on the hesitations and ordeals facing what Liu Shuhua called the New Countryside dream, between the grand China Dream—which implicitly distances itself from rurality—and strained visions of a modernized countryside. As mentioned in the introduction, the urban population in China came to surpass the rural for the first time the year I arrived in Hexian, amid what has been termed the largest migration in human history—the post-Mao movement from villages to cities by the "floating population." While residents of Hexian were categorized largely as agricultural, most families had at least one member away, "floating" in the city. The stories here pivot in one way or another around the paradoxes posed amid these movements of dispersal and return.

Through these accounts I consider the larger forces meeting at the site of a life and how these reverberations, at once singular and collective, might help us think otherwise about grand projects of global health (Das 2015; Stevenson 2014). In spite of the sense that Western institutions, economies, and languages of mental health have insinuated themselves across the globe (Watters 2010), terms of therapeutic articulation, patient and family engagement, and legislative debate continue to involve entanglements of translation, experimentation, and subversion in the so-called West and beyond (D'Arcy 2019; Giordano 2014; H. Huang 2018; Z. Ma 2012; Zhang 2014). The hegemonic potential of the psy-disciplines is to be contended with but not to be presumed, even within the clinic. I approach psychiatric symptoms as the edges of experience, not external to questions of time and place

(Jenkins and Barrett 2004), while also gesturing beyond them (Corin 2007; Pandolfo 2018).

The logics and practices of the hospital system, psychiatric diagnoses, and pharmaceutical cures necessarily inherit, to some extent, the disciplinary dimensions of modern reason (Foucault 2006). And some patients, as in the case of Xu Liying, discussed in the next chapter, more explicitly describe the hospital as an institution of unwanted medicalization and detention. At the same time, for other patients, the hospital offers a tentative site of retreat from the entanglements of economy and kinship, experienced as an unbearably tense present. Rather than exhibiting a hegemonic reign, psychiatric terms are copresent with vocabularies drawn from various nonpsychiatric worlds, including spirit mediumship, among patients and their families, even if the latter is often evoked in hushed tones in the ward. As in the case of apparently secular Communist slogans, writings, and images in the chapters before, psychiatric symptoms potentiate a spectral doubling, acting as cosmic operators pivoting between yin and yang realms.

· · ·

Established just a few years prior to my visit there, the psychiatric unit of the People's Hospital is operated by three psychiatrists and a staff of nurses. Before the unit's founding as an independent department, psychiatric cases were treated in the department of neurology, whose doctors had received some training in psychiatry, or, in more severe or difficult cases, through transfers to larger city- or provincial-level hospitals. Even after the establishment of the psychiatric unit, many patients continue to be transferred to the psychiatric unit from the departments of neurology and internal medicine. The search for care through other departments is due more, according to the unit director, to the sense of uncertainty surrounding the nature of illness and a lack of awareness of psychiatry as a field than to a fear of stigma, although this is not to say that a sense of stigma was absent. Several linguistic slippages shape these circulations. The colloquial term used for madness *(shenjing)* maps onto the term for neurology *(shenjingke)* more than the formal term for psychiatry *(jingshenke)* does. Then there is the sense that madness seems more of an "inner" *(nei)* ailment than an "outer" *(wai)* one, mapping onto the term for internal medicine *(neike)*. The very encounter with psychiatry, even when patients wind up at the hospital, often begins with a minor detour.

Near the entryway of the ward sits the psychiatrists' office, where outpatient services are provided. Unlike the urban psychiatric wards I have visited in the past, where psychiatrists each worked in individual offices—doors closed—with individual patients (who were also often accompanied by family members), the psychiatrists on staff on any given day share the office, and patients and families crowd into the room, at times listening to one another's accounts to the psychiatrists, at times chatting among themselves or simply waiting with an air of urgency. The inpatient ward consists of twenty-some rooms down a long narrow hallway, turning at a heavy opaque metal door separating the open and locked wards. The psychiatrists make two rounds a day, once in the morning and once in the afternoon. Across the day the ward fluctuates between the murmur of conversation, the quiet of afternoon naps, and occasional outbursts of argument.

Dr. Yuan, the psychiatrist who helps introduce me to patients during my time at the hospital, often speaks of the ward as a space of repose for the patients. "Come take a rest here" (ge zhe'r xiexie), he would say, to those with eyes glazed as if in another world, to those glaring in fury, to those trembling in fear. A common euphemism for a hospital stay, the notion of rest hints at one dimension of the significance of the ward amid tensions of life outside. While contemporary global mental health relies much on the neuroscientific as the site of conceptualization and intervention (Kirmayer and Pedersen 2014) and while psychopharmaceutical prescription constitutes the primary mode of treatment at the ward, Dr. Yuan rarely emphasizes biological causation—neuroscientific or otherwise—in our discussions or in his conversations with patients and families.

Unlike the tendency toward biological reductionism Zhiying Ma (2012) finds among psychiatrists in urban Guangzhou, when I ask Dr. Yuan for his thoughts on causes of illness, he says that he does not consider biology to be the main issue in most cases. Rather, he reflects on the difficulties facing many patients who arrive at the ward. He speaks of the young people who leave for the cities for work, fall ill, and return to the hometown after confronting the trials and tribulations of the labor market. He speaks of those who wind up at the ward because of anger, which he considers the most common lead-up to illness. In the myriad complexities of family matters (jiawushi), it's often those sparsest in words, he says, those who do not usually argue or complain, who at last collapse into illness. In such cases in particular, he considers hospitalization itself a form of healing, beyond pharmaceutical specificities—a temporary retreat from the world facing the patient outside, a moment of quiet and clarity, an extrication from the unbearable entanglements of shifting familial tensions and obligations, amid the decline of agricultural life and precarity of wage labor.

Like Cai Huiqing in the previous chapter, the families of most patients I meet are scattered between Hexian and elsewhere for much of the year. If consulting the spirit medium from afar on her family's behalf in Cai Huiqing's case offers a form of distant intimacy, hospitalization often brings family members together momentarily, a gesture of care through transient proximity. In both sections of the inpatient ward, patients are often accompanied by family members, as there is a sense that patients need to be attended to beyond the basic care provided by the staff—to communicate with doctors and arrange for payments, to bring fresh clothing and desired food, to keep them company and tend to their requests.

Save weddings, birth celebrations, and funerals, hospitalization—psychiatric or otherwise—seems to be one of the few occasions in Hexian that draws local extended family and immediate family near and far, along with select friends and neighbors, into a circuit of visitations. In this sense hospital visits also take on ritual shape, one punctuation among others in the broader rhythms of life. Visitors bring gifts of food and drink, and at times money, sitting with the patient and their accompanying family members for an hour or two or three. For the patients, their visitors, and even the psychiatrists, illness engages a sociosomatics, in which the "exhausted, painful, vertiginous body" often speaks to questions of moral and political appeal (Kleinman and Kleinman 1994, 716), at once encountering and moving askew from biomedicalization and pharmaceutical reason (Clarke et al. 2010; Lakoff 2006).

Despite the expectation and uptake of psychopharmaceutical treatments, patients, families, and psychiatrists convey skepticism toward the exclusive or primary status of neurobiological causation and rarely speak of symptoms in terms of an individual affair of a psychologized, pharmaceutical, or secular self. The spatial and symbolic reach of the clinic is thus not simply what meets the eye. As the yin realm of spirited forces can invisibly infuse any phenomenon given to perception, the agency of effects cannot be presumed on the grounds of physical place or material substance. The symptom maintains a polysemic density not exhausted by a single clinical hermeneutic (Good and Good 1981). Even within the ward transformations in symptom presentation can constitute evidence of otherworldly interventions from afar, and pharmaceutical efficacy may hinge on conditions of divine benevolence or demonic expulsion enacted in another locality. Women of the family often visit spirit mediums and other healers on behalf of the afflicted before, during, and after hospitalization, with or without the presence of the patient. When faced with the potential otherworldly status of psychiatric symptoms, those I meet at the hospital often maintain a stance of the *perhaps or perhaps not*; uncertainty, as Lisa Stevenson (2014) writes, can offer an ethnographic mode that attends to the hesitations of one's interlocutors, as well as one that allows itself to be thrown into a shared existential frame.

Many patients and families speak of the illness for which they come to seek treatment in terms of possession, soul loss, and ghost encounters or as the blurred boundary between madness and otherworldly happenings. As a young woman diagnosed with schizophrenia poses to me, how is one to "know"—how is one to apprehend the nature of any given affliction—if demonic spirits are tricksters that aim to confuse and bring illness, and psychiatric disorders can conjure hallucinatory percepts of intangible beings? Caught between two agents of duplicity, it is impossible to be sure.

Beyond particular symptoms, in the contemporary cosmology in Hexian, the broader sense of social disintegration and crisis in filial relations—what would otherwise be understood through accounts of sociohistorical causation—constitute not only worldly changes but manifestations of cosmic chaos. The death of Mao, as noted, is said to inaugurate a return of corrupt gods and ghosts, mirroring and propelling humans in madness and greed, including the greed of sons and daughters that leads to the collapse of filial piety. The potential doubling of signification and efficacy across yin and yang realms must thus be kept in mind when considering the psychiatric, social, and historical dimensions of these stories.

A SOUL ADRIFT

Tan Suzhen has been searching for her soul ever since her four daughters migrated to distant cities for work a decade ago. She traverses the village in search of it, murmuring to herself. Other villagers, while not hostile, have stopped speaking to her. For the most part Tan Suzhen doesn't stray far from the perimeter of the village, less than a mile crosswise. Although troubled at first, her daughters say they no longer worry too much about her journeys. She doesn't wander into neighbors' houses and thus far has returned home unharmed. The strolls vary, and the sisters do not see a pattern or logic to her destinations. Yet each time, they say, she moves with conviction, knowing precisely where she needs to go—not to local temples or spirit mediums' altars where others might seek healing but to this patch of shrubbery today, that turn of the road tomorrow.

In spite of her arduous hunt, the task appears ceaseless, and her soul seems to succeed in escaping again and again. Inside her house, where she now lives alone after her husband left years ago, she places objects here and there, a lump of soil, a chunk of bark, or, more recently, a handful of feces, in an effort to *ya hun'r*, to "press" her soul beneath the objects to keep it from floating away. Soul loss (*shihun*) is an old term, found in texts dating back at least to the first century BCE, in medical and ethical, as well as political, contexts. In Hexian soul loss is often described as the exiting of one's soul upon the fright of seeing a ghost, and most villages have several of those who know the technique for soul calling.

While her daughters do not agree with Tan Suzhen's own account of soul loss and consider her idiosyncratic rituals part of her diagnosis of schizophrenia, they did not seek hospitalization for their mother until their recent concerns over hygiene. After more than a decade of affliction ebbing and flowing in severity, it is only in the past five or six years that the four sisters had begun taking turns, stepping away from their work, husbands, and children in Beijing to return to Hexian and tend to their mother.

But Tan Suzhen no longer wishes to be bothered. She does not allow her daughters to live in her house during their visits and strikes in anger if they move any of her meticulously placed objects. So when the sisters come to Hexian, they stay in a house across the road, bringing her three meals a day and surreptitiously attempt to clean the house bit by bit, when she is not looking. As An Mei, Tan Suzhen's third daughter, says with a tinge of regret, "Maybe if we had been around, to respond to her words, to chitchat with her, she would've been better. But now she can't even respond when you say something. . . . She no longer communicates with the external world and speaks only to matters in her own thoughts."

The humdrum practice of everyday chitchat (shuoshuohua), literally "speak-speak-words," is considered fundamental to well-being, thus fundamental to care—a staple of existence alongside that of a shared meal. Speech and food, words and grain, both are sustenance for maintaining a life, a life necessarily mutual. And in an era of labor migration and increasing individualization, they are at once the most simple and most difficult of gestures for sons and daughters, many of whom have left the village to seek work in the city. While some parents join their adult children in the city, it is not always seen as a desirable option, since for many, such as Tan Suzhen, home is deeply tied to place, while the city is often associated with boredom and a lack of social life.

While public health concerns over the "left behind" often focus on access to health services in rural regions, Tan Suzhen's daughters offer another way of contemplating a life well lived among those who remained, and what's at stake in the disintegration and reconfiguration of local moral worlds under broader conditions of lopsided economies. As Arthur and Joan Kleinman (1997) write, local moral worlds mediate between large-scale shifts and sociosomatic processes through everyday rhythms and rituals. In Chinese contexts, they note, moral-relational concepts as reciprocation (bao) speak to such flows of social experience.

Commonly used to describe the return of care from adult children to aging parents, bao speaks to the daughters' efforts to keep Tan Suzhen company at the hospital. The sisters remain in the inpatient ward with their mother from morning to night, bringing food and chitchat, even if unsolicited—gestures of attempted reciprocation are not always acknowledged or experienced as such. Not entirely uncommunicative, and by no means quiet, Tan Suzhen engages at times with the conversation in the room, but more often with another world, a world of characters past.

An Mei sits with me on the hospital bed, as we watch her mother pace back and forth in the room.

"Bring this mo to your elder aunt!" Tan Suzhen walks toward us with a bag of steamed buns, nodding toward the ward hall. Their aunt—Tan Suzhen's older sister—has long passed. Aside from her husband and children, Tan Suzhen has no immediate living kin.

"Our aunt? Where's our aunt?" An Mei retorts. Tan Suzhen stares at her without response, then continues pacing.

I try numerous times to speak with Tan Suzhen, but, for the most part, my mode of questioning is disregarded. The subject of psychosis, as those who have worked in such settings know, does not always engage with the other's questioning or desire for knowing. At times Tan Suzhen approaches me, asking of my age, my hometown, my family. Then she wanders off once again, back to her own conversation.

"Why did you come to the hospital?" I try asking at one point.

"Old representative, 'struggle the landlords,' did you participate?" Tan Suzhen asks in return. I shake my head. She is referring to struggle sessions of the Maoist era, when those suspected of bad class politics were publicly examined, humiliated, and at times violently tortured to the point of death.

"Ma! *Why* did you *come* to the hospital?" An Mei tries to assist with my banal line of questioning.

"Manage the trains. Manage the cars. Traffic policy. Draw the lines where? How many people are there now? How many?"

"Ma!" An Mei scolds. "She's speaking of fixing the public roads now. She's always going off on tangents. She thinks she's still a leader," An Mei shakes her head.

Prior to marriage, during the Maoist era, Tan Suzhen headed a local brigade and organized youth in their daily work. Although she seems to speak often of these times as she paces back and forth, her daughters are uncertain which elements are drawn from her actual past and which are drawn, as they call it, from her imagination. "We've never experienced that kind of society, so we've only heard her speak like that, that she's the head of the brigade and so on. We don't really understand either," An Ling, the youngest of the four sisters pitches in.

A gap between the generations presents itself, signaling the disintegration of a prior kind of world and a prior kind of promise—in this case a Maoist promise of political significance, where the village constituted the future of New China, and women held up half the sky. Yet the two worlds are also copresent in the contemporary. As Tan Suzhen dialogues with kin and cadres past, old dreams of a socialist utopia waft into the room, joining our conversation.

The Maoist world, lived as the present in the case of Tan Suzhen, is reminiscent of the temporal disturbance common in phenomenological descriptions of schizophrenia, both clinical and autobiographical, in which a socially shared sense of time begins to disintegrate. As Anne Lovell puts it, it is—akin to Fredric Jameson's (1991, 16) description of late capitalism—to experientially "inhabit the synchronic" (1997, 362). The past, present, and future are compressed into a "now, now, now" (Fuchs 2013, 84). Here, rather than an exclusion of historicity complicit with the cultural logic of late capitalism, as in Jameson's account, I consider the compression of time in Tan Suzhen's case as an uncanny presencing of the past—a symptomatic reminder that creates a disturbance in the smooth fading of socialist dreamworlds. But, unlike reformulations of Maoist and post-Mao times in spirit mediumship, Tan Suzhen's voicings of the Maoist era remain somewhat outside of more shared accounts.

While the vocabularies and rituals of spirit possession and mediumship—or soul loss as a form of spirit dispossession—can offer a manner of reconfiguring a world, through the realienation and reinstantiation of the position of the person (Corin 1998), in psychosis, "the *koinós kósmos,* the common world," also "gives way to the *ídios kósmos,* the ego-centristic and self-referential world" (Fuchs 2005a, 139). But here, rather than containing the *ídios* within the egocentric as such, I think with Jacques Lacan (2007) on the fundamentally collective and often unconscious dimension of the symbolic out of and against which the subject emerges. Thus, even seemingly idiosyncratic manifestations of delusion speak to a collective dimension, both in the repertoires they draw on and the histories they register—including histories of disruption or transformation of those very repertoires.

In Tan Suzhen's pressing of her soul beneath collected objects and her strolls tracing the perimeters of her village, ritual resonates idiosyncratically with Chinese cosmological renderings of soul loss, but without effective healing from soul callers or spirit mediums when other relatives brought her. Instead, a parallel world has been carved out in search of the soul struck out of her by unnamed forces, a world no longer fully available to those around her. Yet in its own fragmented way, this other world insistently insinuates unresolved dilemmas of time into the conventionally shared world, without a full narration of loss or what was to be made of such worlds out of joint.

The second of three sisters, Tan Suzhen grew up in a farming family, one considered "middle peasantry" *(zhongnong).* Under Maoist-era categorization, middle peasants were those with more land than the poor and landless peasants. But unlike the rich peasants and landlords targeted by numerous punitive campaigns, middle peasants tilled their own land without employing labor and were not considered of a "bad" class background. Yet Tan Suzhen married into a landlord family. Tan Suzhen's daughters say they do not know much about the circumstances of the marriage, but do know that it was not a peaceable one.

After marriage Tan Suzhen never returned to her position as brigade leader and focused on raising her children. The family situation worsened after she gave birth to four daughters and no son. Society those days, the sisters quip, valued men more than women. Those who gave birth to no sons were not well regarded by the husband's family. Moreover, their father did not bother taking their mother's side; thus, she was bullied by her in-laws (*shouqi,* literally the receiving or bearing of anger). Paralleling theories of affective escalation in mediumship and Chinese medicine, the daughters relay that anger begets anger, and Tan Suzhen's own fury at the situation gradually led to her illness.

But lest this begins simply resembling a cliché of Chinese patriarchal traditionalism, there was another dimension marked by historically shifting strategies of marriage arrangement. During the Maoist era families from "bad" class backgrounds (such as Tan Suzhen's landlord in-laws) at times strategically arranged marriages with those from "good" class backgrounds (such as Tan Suzhen's middle peasant natal family) to minimize potential political punishment (see Croll 1984). These political marriages often led to complications and disruptions in kin relations, whose impacts were also received by the next generation—those like An Mei and An Ling.

Between a bad-class marriage, the scorn of in-laws, the short-lived promise of socialist leadership, and the departure of her four daughters in an era of factory work, it is as if Tan Suzhen's soul was dislodged at the collision between multiple symbolic and economic worlds—a cosmohistorical collision. She often says that her soul was "struck" out of her, though she does not say by what or by whom. "Look, look, look . . . can't find it. . . . My next generation . . . I . . . I lost my soul. . . . Four mouths . . . Four mouths," Tan Suzhen mumbles what her daughter takes as an accusation.

"Ma! But aren't we good to you? Aren't we good to you?" An Mei's eyes moisten, though she laughs it off and continues. "She's always saying that she had four mouths to feed, but that 'one person can raise ten, yet ten people cannot raise one'"—an allegation of failure in filial duty, a failure in reciprocation.

Although the four sisters maintain a constant rotation between Beijing and Hexian, their mother does not appear satisfied. It was a dilemma shared by many of Tan Suzhen's generation, one that viewed itself as given short shrift by the transformations of the times. Bounded by respect for filial piety to the elderly above them, yet becoming elders in a generation that they feel lacks such regard, aging parents in Hexian often lament their position as one of unreciprocated care, as a generation that tended to both the young and the old yet will receive nothing in return. Meanwhile, for their children, who learned that their economic future—and with it the future of China—is located outside of the village, there remains no easy resolve.

LOVE AND LACK

Xia Peizhi was diagnosed with depression after her mother brought her to the hospital. A third-year high school student, she was slated to prepare for the national college-entry examination but withdrew from school amid preparations several months before her hospitalization. For most secondary school students in China, the three-day exam marks the culmination of their educational endeavors, a pivotal moment considered determinative of their very horizons of possibility. For those in rural regions and small towns, it is seen as the path up and out, toward an economically, not to mention symbolically, more viable life. Xia Peizhi says that her mood grew low (xinqing diluo) after she switched to a more advanced-level course at school and her test scores began dropping. She felt a mounting pressure, given the cost of education and her family's difficult economic circumstances.

"I felt I could not bear it anymore. The pressure was high; I was about to collapse." Her voice is soft, tired, worn-out. Her sense of collapse is accompanied by a sense of fear, which from time to time deepens into dread and panic *(kongju)*. She links this dread and panic to her father's physical and affective absence. What makes her ill, she says, is the escalating pressure from school alongside her lack of paternal love *(quefa fu'ai)*. Her father is a construction worker in Shanghai and returns home only once a year, often during the agricultural busy season *(nong-mang)* to tend to the family plot. She feels that he has been away from home ever since she was young and that every reunion is fleeting. She can't seem to find a sense of safety *(anquangan)* and is always steeped in fear.

"My father is the 'honest' type. He doesn't know how to express his love, so I feel I have no support." The term "honest" *(laoshi)* marks an emblematic shift of the postreform era. Until the early 1980s honesty connoted a good person, hardworking and trustworthy, the ideal marriage partner, particularly when describing men. With the turn toward market competition and growing disparity in the reform era, the same term began morphing in connotation, pointing to a naïveté vulnerable to exploitation and duping, which would not fare well in the new moment and risks falling short of supporting a family amid the social games of the privatized world. Honesty also came to mark a caricature of the rural, of peasants too simpleminded for complicated times. As Yunxiang Yan writes of young women he encountered in rural Heilongjiang in the 1990s, "A number of them maintained that [honest] young men had difficulty expressing themselves emotionally *(buhui shuohua)* and lacked attractive manners *(meiyou fengdu)*" (2003, 78). By contrast, articulate speech, emotional expression, ambition, and a capacity for advancing one's social and economic position had come to be valued, reversing the previous connotations of similar traits as unsavory signs of empty words, lasciviousness, and aggression.

Xia Peizhi says that her father does not know how to console and coax her *(hong)*. She describes him as an "old peasant type," one who has never had "cultural quality" *(wenhua suzhi)*. Entering state discourse on population quality in the 1980s, in the same moment that the honest man grew undesirable for marriage, the language of *suzhi* came to account for China's failure to modernize, particularly vis-à-vis the theme of rural poverty. Accusations of a lack of "quality" pointed to a corporeal politics of bodies deprived of value from which surplus value was extracted, particularly in the denigration of rural migrant bodies in contrast to images of the urban, educated, middle-class only child (Anagnost 2004).

I ask Xia Peizhi what it would mean to express one's love. She says that it would mean to buy a few little gifts for your child, to ask how things were going, to call and ask how your grades were, to encourage you, to speak to you often, to comfort you. Instead, when her father does speak, all he speaks of is money.

"When he calls, he talks only about money. 'I earned this or that much money for you. I will send this or that much money home.' Nonstop: money, money. Earning money to the point that he forgot about his family! All you have is money, no familial intimacy—'Money cannot buy familial affection' *[jinqian maibudao qinqing].*" Xia Peizhi's phrase echoes an elementary school essay of the same title, circulated online around that time, written by and about those "left behind" by migrant parents: "In our class there are so many people waiting. . . . In this world there are yet how many people waiting. . . . Please don't let them endure the waiting; your love is the best nourishment. So-called money, your children do not even heed. They only heed your love" (Rongyao Mengping 2013). The essay's and Xia Peizhi's condemnation of parents in this era marks a painful split between a generation of labor migrants who departed from their hometown in the hope of a more economically sustainable future for their family—not to mention a symbolically viable place within their local worlds, as we will see later in the case of Wang Weihong—and a generation of children and youth coming of age through the language of psychology and emotional expression.

Although the postreform ubiquity of money is commonly linked to themes of envy, insecurity, corruption, and greed for many I met in Hexian, money also constitutes a language of care and social relation in the marketized world, particularly among those born in or before the 1970s and 1980s. Advice on well-priced goods and news of price fluctuations saturate daily conversations as a way of attuning one another to minor shifts in the economic landscape. Inquiries on the prices of purchases made—"how much money" *(duoshaoqian)*—followed by admonition or praise hinging on whether one spent wisely are nearly as common as the more classic greeting, "Have you eaten?" Given the regional history of famine and relative impoverishment, such materialist articulations and their attendant gestures—not external, of course, to their ideological dimensions—offer grounds for sociality and navigation, strategic and intimate.

By contrast, the younger residents I met in Hexian seem more repulsed by talk of money and pragmatics. Like Xia Peizhi, they articulate relationality through the language of dreams and ideals, tender love, and affective communication indicative of a modern, urban, middle-class quality, even as their families may embody the position of the peasant or the rural migrant, the very image of low quality from which they have learned to distance themselves.[3] In fear that their family may not survive in the new era if they failed to be among those who "got rich first," the parents of those like Xia Peizhi are caught between their own visions of what it would take to gift their children with an adequate life and their children's laments and resentment at their incapacity for modes of care other than that of cash remittances.

Xia Peizhi says that she no longer speaks on the phone with her father much, as there seems to be nothing to say between them. Speaking only provokes both of their tempers. Even when he returns home on those rare occasions, they don't talk much. "I feel he does not like what I say," she notes with some bitterness. "For instance, I tell him what I've done, what I think, what my ideals are. He says, 'Don't think about some *ideal*. Reality is reality. Ideals are too unreachably perfect.' He says, 'Don't dream and fantasize all day.'"

Xia Peizhi's father's words are reminiscent of the reform-era language of returning from heaven to earth, of trading the ethereal futuristic distance of the Maoist gaze for the immediacy of reality, economy, and pragmatics (Croll 1994). Yet this initial emphasis on reality had yet again been displaced by a new language of dreams, in both popular consumer and state discourse. Other school students I met in Hexian, like Xia Peizhi, also speak in the language of pursuing ideals *(zhuiqiu lixiang)* and likewise accuse their parents of not comprehending what it is to live for one's ideals. As one junior high student explains to me, she wants to pursue her goals and live a life with "waves" *(bolang)*, not the cautious, conservative life her parents live (an irony given the tumult of the decades her parents have lived through).

Across Tan Suzhen, Xia Peizhi's father, Wang Weihong, and younger residents like Xia Peizhi, there emerge disjunctures between multiple historical horizons of feeling, one articulated with or against the other across different moments—the Maoist promise of socialist modernity, the early reform promise of pragmatism and wealth, and the postreform promise of individual ideals and bourgeois affectivity. Yet each of these promises threatens to remain out of reach, both in the broader scene of ongoing disparity and in the fragmentations of kinship their very difference produces. Confrontations between these visions of the future emerge in the clinic, as both those who remained and those aspiring to depart are haunted by obverse sides of these fractures.

Xia Peizhi speaks about her mother differently than she does about her father. She feels that her mother cares for her, knows how to speak to her, knows what questions to ask. Her mother, she says, does not feel like a peasant woman. Her father, on the other hand, feels to her like the very prototype of peasantry—"just like those described in books." Despite the fact that her mother did not receive much more schooling than her father—neither completed elementary school—her parents were of divergent class categories in the past. In the Maoist era her mother's maternal family was considered at different moments a rich peasant or landlord family, while her father's parents were considered poor peasants. Her maternal grandmother's family faced campaigns of class struggle frequently and, in a reversal of Tan Suzhen's marriage, decided to betroth her mother to the son of a poor peasant family in hopes that it would improve their political lot.

Her paternal and maternal grandparents, Xia Peizhi observes, differ in their thinking. Whereas her paternal grandparents—those once labeled as poor peasants—are more "feudal" and "superstitious," her maternal grandparents are more "modern." And whereas her father does not hold the completion of her education in high regard and hopes that she will eventually be able to earn money and put food on the table, her mother and maternal grandparents have always been supportive of her pursuit of learning. Despite the disruption of prior class and educational divergence during the Maoist era, there remained an intergenerational transmission of educational attainment, due in part to a transmitted family orientation, regardless of the parent's own level of received education. In the postreform era the children of previous landlord and rich peasant families are thus more likely to move further along their educational paths than those of previous poor peasant families, despite the temporary equalization of parental education and wealth across class backgrounds (Deng and Treiman 1997; Sato and Shi 2007).

Inheriting these disjunctures of geography, class, and history, Xia Peizhi, whose desire for a departure from the scene of rurality is experienced as hindered by her "old peasant" father—a figure not unlike Wang Weihong—whose incapacity for an urban middle-class mode of affective communication hollows her of a sense of safety and competence. Like Tan Suzhen, Xia Peizhi lives at the crossroads of Maoist designations of peasant and landlord, but through subjective contours of the subsequent generation. Through tactics of cross-class marriage for evading political persecution, the failure of class struggle to truly erase the etchings of difference from prerevolutionary times is inherited by the children of such marriages, in whom this history of difference is reinscribed at the heart of a divided, collapsing self.

Despite the bifurcation of the modern and the superstitious in Xia Peizhi's perception of the matriline and patriline, she mentions that her mother has visited various "superstitious" guides since her illness, "those who ask for directions for you" (gei ni wenwenlu nazhong), who offer other modes of navigation. Her mother has visited spirit mediums and fortune-tellers—"those who see incense" and "those who calculate hexagrams," as Xia Peizhi put it—multiple times already. She is uncertain just how often or just where her mother goes for these consultations and has never accompanied her mother on a visit. All she knows is that a spirit medium has informed her mother that Xia Peizhi is a tongzi, a divine "child" sent to earth by a deity, who is wont to illness. Like Cai Huiqing, Xia Peizhi's mother engages with the spirit world on her daughter's behalf, in search of otherworldly forces shaping the predicaments of the present.

Xia Peizhi appears indifferent, for the most part, toward her mother's engagements and consultations. But she also feels that medication would not be sufficient for resolving her long, moody days; it would require some "psychological adjustment" (xinli tiaojie) on her own part or, better yet, some psychological counseling (xinli fudao), which she does not know where to seek. She does not feel such psychological forms of care would be available either in the ward or in Hexian, but rather in major cities like Shanghai and Beijing. In the previous month, she says, she had been prescribed olanzapine (an atypical antipsychotic usually prescribed for schizophrenia and bipolar disorder), which she felt to be ineffective. After requesting a change of medication, she was prescribed alprazolam (a benzodi-azepine used for anxiety and panic disorders, as well as depression-induced anxi-ety), followed by paroxetine (a serotonin-reuptake inhibitor used to treat depres-sion and a range of other disorders). There seems to be some degree of effect, she notes, but appears unimpressed, as indifferent as she is in tone toward her mother's visits to the spirit medium and fortune-teller.

Instead, within the purview of hospitalization, what she finds most comforting is the presence of the IV—"there wasn't much of a reaction (to the medication), but I felt that once the needle was hung, my heart was no longer panicked." As with many other patients I met, young and old, the materiality of "hanging the needle" (*guazhen*), referring to an IV injection and the hanging of the IV bag at the bed-side, often seemed to be accompanied by a sense of healing, a sense of being cared for, regardless of the precise substance injected, which the patients often do not inquire about.

With plans to return to school in the following school year, Xia Peizhi says that she hopes to move to Shenzhen one day, where she can live her own life, chasing after her own dreams. Yet it is not an easy image to hold; she feels like she is weak, that others look down on her, that she is incapable. She yearns to attend college, for what she imagines to be a "new situation," to be surrounded by those with "life experi-ence" and education, with whom she would be able to communicate. She wishes that she could do better at school, at examinations, so that she could gain a sense of safety—the sense of safety she feels she cannot receive from her father, the migrant worker who cannot but appear to her in the image of a textbook peasant.

HOUSE OF DREAMS

"Acute psychosis," Dr. Yuan notes as he left the room, leaving me with Wang Wei-hong and his wife, Liu Shuhua, sitting at his bedside.

"Since the start [of the illness], he has been sweating. His hands, his neck, his shoulders. He doesn't like to speak. He has never liked to speak." Liu Shuhua looks worried, dabbing her husband's forehead and neck with a small towel. He is forty-six and she is forty-two, but in his fragile condition he appears far more aged. Thin, shaking, with the blanket pulled up to his chest, Wang Weihong looks around with eyes filled with terror. He stares at the ceiling, his gaze snapping left and right.

"His illness came at night. In the middle of the night, I woke up and heard him crying. He kept saying, 'stop hitting me; stop hitting me,' and would not stop cry-ing. . . . He said he saw ghosts. I asked him where. He just kept saying he saw ghosts." The bout of sleeplessness and tears came a week prior, and since then he has continued in his insanity (*fafeng*) day and night, Liu Shuhua explains. She herself, she says, does not believe in ghosts and by extension had not consulted any spirit mediums. In her natal village most residents have converted to Christianity, including herself, which requires disengagement from such matters. But a female relative on Wang Weihong's side of the family did consult a medium on his behalf and relayed the message to Liu Shuhua. According to the medium, Wang Weihong had collided into a ghost, a woman from outside his village who had committed suicide, either by hanging or drowning. Suggesting that perhaps his soul was frightened away by the ghost, the medium came to their house and attempted to call back his soul, but his condition did not seem to improve. His eldest son then suggested hospitalization.

Wang Weihong has worked as a coal miner for more than a decade, spending most of the year away from the village and returning for a stretch of time only during the New Year holiday. Throughout the year it was just Liu Shuhua and her aging father-in-law living under the same roof, for whom she cooked and looked after. Having had eye problems since she was young, Liu Shuhua does not participate in formal employment or intensive farm labor, so the family relies for the most part on Wang Weihong's earnings. His salary was quite high, she says with an air of pride, rising from RMB 30 per day in the past to up to RMB 100 per day in recent years (approximately USD 16 at the time). But two years ago he injured his back in the mine. After undergoing spinal surgery, he recuperated at home for half a year and attempted to return to the work. But the pain in his back grew unbearable, and he could not continue.

The couple now lives in Wang Weihong's home village with his father—known for his bad temper—who reprimands him for failing to earn a decent living. Although his father's family was of poor peasant background during the Maoist era, upon reform his father assisted with various construction projects locally, helping build roads and other people's houses, managing to save RMB 10,000 over the span of a decade, to use in support of his children. Yet he feels Wang Weihong has failed in reciprocating, now that he has grown older.

"His father scoffs at him for not making money, for laboring all day for other people and not making any money. He says he is incompetent [bunenggan]," Liu Shuhua says in a hushed voice, to avoid provoking Wang Weihong. He does not attempt to dispute his father's verbal denigrations, she continues, and holds it all in. "He does not say a word. Whether you say he is good or he is bad, he does not make a sound, but he listens and deposits it in his heart [gezai xinli]." This gradual depositing and accumulation of anger, according to Liu Shuhua—in parallel with Dr. Yuan's description of patients who are sparse in speech but filled with anger—led to his illness today.

Throughout our conversation Wang Weihong pitches in: "No money, no money" (Meiqian, meiqian). Not only are Wang Weihong's earnings needed for supporting himself, his wife, and his father, but they must also sustain the cost of education and living for their two sons. Their younger son is in his second year of high school (boarding at a nearby school, a common practice in Hexian), and their elder son did well in the national college examination and has been accepted to a high-ranking university in Beijing. More than the pressure of tuition and living expenses, though, Wang Weihong is most tormented by the problem of building a house for his eldest son.

In Hexian the notion of house building is central to visions of patrilineal masculinity. To maintain the respect of both fellow villagers and of one's sons, the family—and the father in particular—is expected to build a new house for his son(s) as a central portion of his bride-price. During conversations with matchmakers, the question inevitably arises, "Is there a house [youfangma]?" Writing of rural Henan Province, sociologist Cao Jinqing notes, "Almost all the surplus product of the villagers, even that which they anticipate earning, went into housebuilding" (2005, 59). Cao reasons that the centrality of house building arises from both the relative lack of other avenues of investment in rural regions and the intense competitiveness of village social life, in which the house constitutes a symbol of wealth and status of the family.

Rachel Murphy similarly observes of rural Jiangxi, "The front of the house corresponds with the face of the family" and, amid labor migration, creates visible evidence in the home village of earnings gained from work in the city. Some migrant sons remit more of their earnings than migrant daughters to contribute to the parents' building of their own future house, to "improve their own eligibility in the marriage market" (2002, 103). The house thus creates a link between the urban and rural faces of life and constitutes an intergenerational thread between father and son.

In Hexian quarrels over house-related tensions are commonplace, between brothers and between fathers and sons, often also with the involvement of wives and daughters-in-law. Stories circulated of houses being built by or for one member of the family and demanded or occupied by another upon completion. And as Yunxiang Yan (2003) describes, adult children in rural regions carry an increasing sense of entitlement to family property, along with conjugal privacy. Thus, while the betrothal house becomes a sign of family dignity for the parents, it also becomes a material sign of the son and daughter-in-law's sense of right to property and privacy, no longer accompanied by an older style of filial obligation to care for their parents within a shared house.

Her husband, Liu Shuhua says, feels that everyone in the village looks down on him for being poor. Every other household is buttressed by an entire family of laborers, he often complains, while he is the sole laborer in their family. The neighbors have larger, multistoried houses (loufang). They wear better clothes, eat better food. The house the Wangs now live in was built more than thirty years ago. It is made largely of bricks, but Liu Shuhua calls it a straw house (caofangzi), out of her perception of its outmodedness, indicating an older and smaller style of architecture now deemed outdated. Most of their fellow villagers have built newer houses since, more in line with the ever-changing styles favored as symbols of status, unlike their old "straw" house, with cracking roof tiles.

During the sleepless nights of his illness, Liu Shuhua found her husband out in the yard in the middle of the night, standing, squatting, pacing, hands outstretched, then in a lifting motion. He was building an invisible house. Overhearing our conversation, Wang Weihong pitches in, voice trembling, halting, cracking: "Make money. . . . The children . . . need to build a house, take in a daughter-in-law." His son tells him not to worry about the house, to focus on getting well. But it is too late. "No money. . . . No money to build the house. . . . What to do if it can't be built? . . . No money," he continues, no longer in sync with our conversation, drifting into a staccato loop of his panic.

Wang Weihong's terrified utterances amplify the predicaments of rural dwellers after the reform era. Once part of the politically lauded poor peasant class of the Maoist revolution, those like Wang Weihong are hailed by new demands of being a good father and filial son, as the decline of peasantry and devaluation of agricultural labor renders tenuous the status of the honest peasant-turned–migrant laborer. His pained, repetitive enunciations and terrifying encounters with ghosts disfigure and render uncanny linear imaginations of continual progress in the New Countryside dream, making perceptible their haunting quality for those abandoned by its promises.

Liu Shuhua tries to reassure him—that their children will soon be able to work, to earn their own money. Since their elder son was admitted to the university, things will turn out fine; everything is fine now. Everything is fine. The brothers will eventually find work and finance their own houses, even buying a house for their father in the future, she says buoyantly. Her mustered optimism drops into a quiet grumble when I ask if the two of them ever disagree on things. She says that a while back, Wang Weihong came up with the idea that he wanted to get new blankets made—nice, wide blankets for their sons, rather than the old, small, narrow blankets they had been using since their childhood. The large, wide comforter and duvet sets she speaks of, customized by local shop owners according to fabric and filling, cost approximately RMB 200. Two blankets would cost around RMB 400, which, while not an unthinkable expense, is still seen as an investment, particularly for those like Wang Weihong, for whom it would amount to at least four days' worth of earnings.

"I said, why? Why have this New Countryside dream? We all have blankets to cover ourselves with right now. The two kids are still young; they can be covered for now with the blankets we have. There is no need to make new blankets. The kids are still in school. We have no money. Stop thinking about making blankets." Aside from Wang Weihong's wages from the coal mine, their other source of income is the wheat and corn grown on their family plot, approximately five *mu,* slightly less than one acre. In the case of a good harvest, the crops can be sold for upward of RMB 7,000 to 8,000 in a given year, according to Liu Shuhua. Her husband's hospitalization costs for the month, which they paid in advance, is RMB 7,000.

Fortunately, the New Cooperative Medical Scheme, referred to in Chinese by its abbreviation, Xinnonghe (New Rural Cooperative), has just been fully implemented in Hexian, promising to cover around 80 percent of qualified rural medical costs. The system operates by reimbursement; thus the finances needed to be fronted by the patient and family to receive treatment.[4] Liu Shuhua says that she does not understand the details of insurance coverage and awaits her son's visit to manage the paperwork. Like many other family members I met at the hospital, Liu Shuhua speaks of the new policy in the tone of rumor—she heard in the halls that 70 to 80 percent of costs was indeed being reimbursed, despite many hospital goers' initial skepticism. Amid our conversation her younger son arrives. I ask him if he feels that the hospital stay would be affordable for the family. He says that there is some difficulty and that they will have to borrow money from kin. Then there was tuition—his own is RMB 1,750 per semester, and his older brother's would be over RMB 6,000 per year. I ask him what they will do to in face of these costs. He shakes his head and simply says he does not know. Between the blankets, tuition, houses, and hospitalization, talk of money sounds out the desires and impossibilities of care amid the New Countryside dream.

A CRISIS OF FILIAL PIETY

In the literature on postreform transformations in intergenerational relations, the effects of decollectivization on the family often pivots around the continuity, change, and reformulations of filial piety (xiao). A contemporary iteration of an "anthropocosmic" vision of Confucian moral education (Tu 1998, 122), filial piety points to one among ten modes of relation within the five sets of cardinal relations (wulun): ruler and subject, father and son, husband and wife, elder and younger brother, and that between friends. It marks the proper stance of the child toward the parent, particularly the son toward the father—the written character places the graph of the elder above the graph of the son.

Shaken by pained iconoclastic intellectual confrontations of the early twentieth century, the question of filial piety, along with that of Chinese tradition as such, came to occupy a space of ambivalence, of petrified origin. Against classical formulations of the filial relation as one's earliest encounter with moral understanding and thus the source of all cultivation of virtue, amid New Culture and May Fourth Movements of the 1910s and 1920s duty and reverence toward the parent came to be condemned instead as the origin of all evil, as that which promises to leave China's new generations in exile from the modern world (Schwarcz 1986).

Yet renewals of filial piety, in the name of traditionalism and modern national consciousness, abound (Chan and Tan 2004; Hsu 1971a).

In her review of ethnographic and survey studies across East, Southeast, and South Asia, Elisabeth Croll finds that in contrast to modernization theories of gerontology (e.g., Caldwell 1976), which predicted unidirectional paths toward an increase of nuclear families and a flow of resources away from the older generation, "the intergenerational contract, albeit renegotiated and reinterpreted, is no inherited relic but remains resilient" (Croll 2006, 484). High rates of intergenerational coresidence remain in both urban and rural regions across Asia, despite the rise of nuclear households. Even among generationally split living situations, elderly parents are often incorporated into the households of adult children once widowed or incapable of self-care. Against models that rely on the household as an economic unit, a high resource flow between generations residing in separate households has been found across numerous studies.

Extended families often live in proximity within the same city or village, providing mutual support despite split residence, creating what has been called "embedded" nuclear families (Croll 2006, 484), "networked" urban families (Whyte 2003; Unger 1993), and "aggregate" families (Croll 1994). In terms of explicit stance toward filial relations, Martin Whyte found in his survey studies in a medium-sized city in the northern province of Hebei that parents and children generally shared a sense of support for notions of family obligation. In some cases the younger generation was significantly more likely to disagree with the notion of prioritizing their own children or careers over their own parents. While some minor differences exist, Whyte concludes that within his study there is "little sign that parents and children are separated by a 'generation gap' when it comes to these attitudes" (2003, 89).

A stark contrast is found in Yunxiang Yan's reading of rural China. Tracing transformations of private life from the Communist Revolution in 1949 through the late 1990s in a village in the northeast province of Heilongjiang, Yan writes of a "crisis of filial piety" accompanying a rise of the individual and of conjugality (2003, 162). An increasing sense of entitlement and individual rights with relation to family property along with a desire for privacy of the conjugal family is marked by earlier family division and the shortening or abolishment of patrilocal residence. Whereas parental coresidence with an adult married son was an expected manifestation of family cohesion and reciprocity in old age both before and since 1949, Yan finds increasing rates of what he calls "empty-nest families" among elderly parents across the late 1980s and 1990s (145).[5]

While early family division would have previously been considered a sign of failure to raise filial sons, alongside other sweeping changes of the reform era, prolonged coresidence came to be regarded as evidence of the incapacity of parents to assist married sons in establishing independent households. Building a new house for one's son soon after marriage, or even prior to marriage, became an increasingly significant expectation. And while an empty nest was once considered a form of misfortune in old age, it had become a new norm by the late 1990s. Nonetheless, the new norm is not without a sense of mourning. One of Yan's interlocutors, a father of four married sons, worked with his wife to finance the marriages of each son, before every couple moved out into the newly built houses, leaving the parents alone to their old, small, original house, without rights to enjoy the new homes they built: "All the gold and silver have been taken away by my sons. What is left is only a shaky, empty storehouse, guarded by an old man and an old woman. It has been like a dream, a bad dream" (2003, 144–45).

Lone living among elderly parents tends to change only when they grow very old, when they might then move in with one of their married sons. Beyond changes in coresidence, more than 80 percent of parents Yan (2003) surveyed considered their married sons and daughters-in-law "unfilial." Across materialistic and non-materialistic gestures—from petty cash, food, clothing, and shelter to other gestures of respect and care, like conversation and cooking—many found their situations to be unsatisfactory, even if they did not yet constitute more severe cases of parent abuse. When not residing with their children, parents often found that they are visited only when there appeared a concrete need, for instance, for the child care of grandchildren.

Rather than Whyte's (2003) sense of continuity in the endorsement of filial obligation across parents and children, Yan (1996) finds a deep shift in notions of intergenerational reciprocity. The parental generation (considered those generally above age forty-five) spoke of filial piety and elderly support as a manifestation of *enqing,* the most heightened manifestation of *renqing* ethics (see also M. Yang 1994). *Renqing,* which might be glossed as human feeling or affection, is considered the moral dimension that distinguishes humans from animals for the parental generation. It is a moral obligation as well as an affective bond, one that conveys a sense of limitless indebtedness, in which full repayment is indeed impossible. In contrast to the ordinary exchange of favors, the child is indebted to the parent for a lifetime, for the gift of life and the effort of raising the child to adulthood. Filial piety and *enqing* are thus immersed in a sense of vastness, an inexhaustible gratitude based on which respect and obedience toward the parental generation is expected. The deferential sense of infinite asymmetrical return is marked by a cyclicality that repeats the pact of limitless giving on the part of the parent and the impossible gesture of return by the child in the next generation. Filial piety is "unconditional and consistent" and "can never be fully repaid in money or material goods" (Y. Yan 1996, 174).

Among the younger generation (married adult children), Yan finds that a different vision of care and reciprocity emerges. While no one denied the moral legitimacy of elderly support, the notion of infinite indebtedness was rejected. Rather than a gift of life that propelled a uniquely human form of moral-affective relation, the younger generation saw human birth and child rearing as no different than animal reproduction and reasoned that the child has no choice but to be born. The fact of giving life, according to this new logic, does not constitute a gift, and care of the child is merely an expectable parental duty. Intergenerational reciprocity was equated with other forms of interchange, "to be balanced and maintained through consistent exchange" (1996, 178).

Whereas the child was, ideally, to demonstrate unconditional giving and deference regardless of the particularities of their parental relation in the formulation of filial piety, the sense of unsatisfactory parental care or relation on the part of the child now justifies the subsequent match of inadequate care. In anthropological terms it is a shift, as Yan (1996) puts it, from a generalized reciprocity of the gift that expects no immediate or equal return to a ruthlessly rational and self-interested notion of conditional exchange amid the shift to a market economy. In a more optimistic tenor, Croll terms this a shift from filial piety to filial care, in which the latter consists of "more practical expressions of mutual need, mutual gratitude and mutual support for two-way exchanges of support and care" (2006, 483).[6] For Yan, though, the crisis of filial piety not merely is the turn to a new form of care but also signals the very collapse of the former symbolic world.

WORLDS APART

This sense of failed reciprocation, from both parents toward their children and from children toward their parents, infuses accounts of affliction and collapse at the hospital in Hexian. While any structure of reciprocation is undergirded by its potential failure, the sense of fracture I encountered also rendered the grammars of reciprocation discordant and at times illegible across generations. Between Maoist and post-Mao eras, between earlier categories of good and bad classes and contemporary discourses of high and low quality, horizons past and present etched their incongruences into the troubled intimacy of kinship. As is at times quipped, the qin is no longer qin, which might be glossed as "the familial is no longer familiar or intimate," marking a sense of both disappointment and distrust in kin relations as foundational grounds.

As Nicholas Bartlett (forthcoming) writes in his work on addiction and recovery in Yunnan Province, the lack of transmission of the Maoist way of life can be seen in distinct generational modes of inhabiting China today. Drawing on the work of Karl Mannheim (1952), Bartlett describes two of his interlocutors—a father and his adult son—as cotemporal but not contemporaneous, living in the same moment with different understandings of the past and future. Similarly, intergenerational fissures appear here in imaginations of mutuality, amid a non-contemporaneous sense of familial and national time.

The expectation and desire for residential proximity of one's grown children, from prior to the post-Mao surge of outmigration, can be seen in Tan Suzhen's utterance of the four mouths she fed that cannot feed her back, despite her daughters' efforts in visitation and cooking, at least during periods of illness. The valorization of house building as a fulfillment of parental duty can be seen in Wang Weihong's and Guo Hongjun's panic, yet in the latter's case it is unclear whether his son wished to return to the hometown, house or no house, given visions of futurity increasingly appended to the city. Attention to cash remittances so central to migrant workers' sense of sustaining the family, in Xia Peizhi's case, is seen as her father's failure of paternal support, in lieu of psychological languages she and others of her generation have come to perceive as care.

The sense of fractured generations—and with it the sense of a fractured self—come to the fore as a symptom of what it means to live out the "problem" of rural China today, between a collapsing symbolic world encapsulated in the crisis of filial piety, an uneven geography of value awaiting the disappearance of the peasantry, and bifurcated provisions of state welfare rendering precarious those who remain. Alongside literary and political figurings of the peasant, cosmological formulations of post-Mao spirits, and returns of history through the ghost and the medium, the cases here offer another way of considering registers of experience amid disjunctures of time. As in the case of Cai Huiqing, the "I/we" of kinship raises questions not only of the self in relation to others but of one's sense of personhood as such, where the fullness of the familial other is constitutive of the fullness of the self.

Intergenerational gestures, whether through house building or through cash remittances, would in this sense not simply be acts on behalf of the other but another form of address to the question Cai Huiqing had found so uncanny in the individuated standard Mandarin "I": "What would *I* want?" Instead, the Henanese form "I/we" that Cai Huiqing and others deploy hints at a plurality constituting the subject of desire. Rather than any simple sense of self-abnegation that the question might seem to suggest, it helps to recall that classical Chinese conceptions of the person begin with not the egocentric self but a force field of multiple centers, dynamically shifting into positions of relation with one another (Hall and Ames 1995). The unit of the person *(ren)* simultaneously entails intimate selves and others, straddling what would be articulated in modern vocabularies separately as the individual and the family (Hsu 1971b; see also Markus and Kitayama 1991). In spite of modern campaigns against classical conceptions of kinship and piety, the sense of personhood beyond the boundaries of the atomized individual remains central to many I met in Hexian, even if articulated differently across generations.

When gestures of reciprocity grow stilted, the status of one's own personhood also comes under question. On the one side, parents and grandparents who experience themselves as sacrificial and their children as unfilial thus experience themselves as incomplete in their life phase. On the other side, children who experience themselves as effortful and their parents as incapable of registering their own wants and needs are thus unable to reach either the status of filial son or daughter or their own imaginations of personhood in accordance with shifting notions of the self. While failures of filial reciprocation are by no means new, they take particular forms in the contemporary. Filial piety comes to be caught between notions of inexhaustible gratitude and conditional exchange, manifested in part through tensions surrounding coresidence, across house divisions and labor outmigration. Grammars of care lose their mutual legibility, between the status of money as gift, particularly among those shortest of it, and denouncements of money as a form of care that buttresses rising psychological genres of affectivity.

Across my conversations with patients and families, the language of psychiatry is present but, to some extent, sidelined. For most the psychiatric ward is one stop in a broader search for healing, and psychopharmaceutical cures are one hope among many. In the case of Xia Peizhi, a transient sense of comfort and protection is secured from the IV bag hanging by her hospital bed, while she imagines healing in the faraway form of urban psychological counseling. Her mother, meanwhile, consults spirit mediums and fortune-tellers on her behalf, to her relative indifference. For Liang Ming's mother and father, the lack of their son's response to medication and the nature of his affliction seem more properly addressed by appeals to otherworldly means than what the hospital can offer. The hospital stands as but one site of transient respite for patients and family members exhausted by the times, collapsed in fury. Madness spins out from the fissures of kinship and economy, from troubled forms of life and care, burdened by disappointments and debts toward pasts and futures—rifts that eject one from the sense of a livable present. It is with this sense of fractured temporalities and generations in mind that I turn now to the cosmological rendering of madness in the present, signaling a cosmic time out of joint.

Vertiginous Abbreviation

It has been eighteen years since Xu Liying was called to the divine task of revolution, which marked the beginning of what she calls her illness—an otherworldly affliction beyond the psychiatric diagnosis offered at the Hexian People's Hospital. She was strolling down the street one morning, between her home and the small noodle shop she ran with her husband, when she felt a gust of wind sweep toward her. She lifted her gaze toward the sky to see the Ten Great Marshals descend from the heavens, along with Old Mao himself.[1] They had come a long way, from the Jinggang Mountains—birthplace of the Chinese Communist movement—to summon her for the revolution. Knowing it would be immensely difficult work, she stood reluctant. Yet she could not refuse, she says, as it constituted no less than a divine command *(lìng)* issued from the heavens.[2]

Now, eighteen years later, she continues to carry out her allotted work. Her task is an urgent one, one that torments her as she opens herself to the copresence of malevolent spirits, embodying them to destroy them, preventing them from causing further harm in the human realm. Such tortured struggles with evil were not always necessary. Back when Chairman Mao reigned, she says, ghosts and other demonic spirits were absent. For Xu Liying, as with others in Hexian who engage in spirit mediumship, "the time when Chairman Mao reigned" marked a hiatus for spectral stirrings, and the Chairman's death made way for the return of dangerous, corrupt spirits. The return of spirits after his death, according to the mediums, is accompanied by a sense of mutual delusion, in which deception and decadence are mirrored between earthly and heavenly realms. While possession by spirits is diagnosed through rubrics of psychiatric disorder in the clinic, the language of mediumship provides an inverted diagnosis: it is through today's precarious cosmos that psychiatric symptoms can be understood.

This chapter considers the contemporary cosmological significance of the psychiatric and the psychiatric rendering of the cosmological in Hexian. It reflects on the time I spent with Xu Liying in the locked ward, her fraught position as spirit medium and psychiatric patient, and the temporal horizons that come to meet in the space of the clinic by way of her hospitalization—a diagnostic modernity and messianic anticipation amid spectral returns. The figure of the *medium* and the figure of the *patient* thus allow for several passages of thought here. They allow us to pass through the anachronization of culture in the modern diagnostic gaze, as well as the rendering of psychiatry by mediumship as a symptom of the times.

To be sure, psychiatry and mediumship do not always overlap in Hexian. Plenty of those in Hexian who have experienced possession by deities or ghosts do not wind up at the psychiatric ward, and many at the ward do not describe their ailment in terms of the invisible yin world. At the same time languages of madness pervade contemporary mediumship, and talk of possession is very much familiar to psychiatrists and patients at the ward. Amid the epistemic murk (Taussig 1987) posed in the ward and beyond, symptoms act as a pivot between earthly and cosmic registers. As Xu Liying describes, psychiatric symptoms gesture toward the horizon of a revolution incomplete, in which the present is to be understood in terms of the coming end of the world.

THE HOSPITAL AND THE TEMPLE

The hospital and the temple sit across the road from each other. Both face south, an auspicious architectural orientation, as emperors faced south toward their subjects. On the temple square a large television screen stands tall, facing the front of the temple. It blares a loop of advertisements from dawn to dusk. They are mainly for real estate developments in the making, but one stands out: an advertisement for the psychiatric unit across the street. An arrow points in the direction of the ward—"500 meters," it reads, so that the proximity cannot be missed.

The advertisement draws on a well-known sentiment in Hexian toward the expansive square outside of Fuxi Temple. While the square is known as a central, legitimate space for ritual engagements, it is also reputed to be a space of strangeness and chaos, one where questionable characters and those beyond the bounds of sanity gather. Exemplary of such mad figures are the spirit mediums—those spending their days on the square, murmuring, singing, reciting, or performing rituals beyond more common forms and rhythms. In the language of mediumship, they are performing the work of walking, running, and guarding *(zougong, paogong, shougong)*—of pilgrimage and tending to the deities.

The spatial face-off of the temple and the hospital follows a series of encounters between health and religiosity throughout the twentieth century. Across China the hospital as a modern medical institution was introduced by Christian, particularly North American Protestant, medical missions. The first Western-style clinic in Hexian was established in the first decade of the twentieth century by a Chinese Christian physician from a nearby city. In the 1920s the Nationalist Party established the first public hospital in Hexian, the Civilian Hospital, with fewer than ten staff members. On the eve of Japanese occupation in 1938, amid the Second Sino-Japanese War, staff evacuated the Nationalist-run hospital, and the Japanese puppet government set up the Prefectural Hospital at a new location across from the Fire Deity Temple, later to be moved into the Fire Deity Temple itself. With the end of the war in 1945, the puppet government–run hospital switched hands to the Nationalist Party and relocated several more times. After the founding of the People's Republic in 1949, several clinics were combined into the Division Public Hospital, forerunner to the People's Hospital, with a staff of approximately thirty. Historically, then, the hospital as an institution arrived and moved with the ebbs and flows of religious and political encounter.

In 1952 the Hexian Division People's Hospital was built across from Fuxi Temple, where it remained until my time in Hexian. Its renaming as the People's Hospital came as part of the Chinese Communist Party's mass Patriotic Hygiene Campaign in the 1950s. Such public health mobilizations across the country were infused with medical metaphors of a national body infected with superstition, transposed to the medicalization of individual Chinese bodies (Nedostup 2010). The link between hygiene and patriotism was not new to the Communist era. Soon after the arrival of armed imperialism in the nineteenth century, health and hygiene sat at the center of debates on the possibility of China's modern existence, bringing questions of bodily cleanliness and racial fitness together with those of scientific progress and state power, away from those of Chinese cosmology (Rogaski 2004). In the late imperial period, prior to the widespread establishment of modern hospitals, spirit mediums and ritualistic healing were commonly sought for various forms of illness, madness, and spirit possession in urban and rural China. With the expansion of missionary access, opened in part by the continual threat of foreign military invasion, such practices as mediumship and possession were widely denounced as idolatry and superstition. Medical missionaries drew a link between madness and possession, equating the two on the one hand and attempting to distinguish between instances of mental illness and superstition on the other (Baum 2018). These tensions and ambiguities between health and religiosity, articulated in part through the language of superstition, would find their echoes in the psychiatric unit in Hexian.

A LUCID MADNESS

At the time of our meeting, Xu Liying is sixty-five years old. She is diagnosed, notably, with what's known in the psychiatric literature as "culture-bound syndrome" in English—more telling in its back-translation from the Chinese psychiatric textbook used at the hospital: "psychiatric disorder intimately related to culture."[3] Of the fifty-some patients staying in the inpatient ward at the time, Xu Liying is the only one granted this diagnosis. While possession is far from uncommon as a dimension of other patients' experiences of illness, they more commonly receive diagnoses of schizophrenia, bipolar disorder, or acute psychosis. Xu Liying is exceptional, in some sense, on account of her lucidity.

Xu Liying's husband and son brought her to the hospital after she began performing rituals in the middle of a major street intersection, for fear that she would be injured by passing vehicles. It is not the first time they brought her to a psychiatric hospital, but it has been many years since their last effort to seek a psychiatric solution to what they see as her excessive engagement with ritual. She was often out day and night, at times coming home for a meal, at times skipping meals altogether. Xu Liying knows of her family's concerns and voices her own regrets for not being home, for not assisting in the care of her grandchildren. But she doesn't sway. She remains dedicated to her divine task, even from within the walls of the ward. For Xu Liying psychiatric disorders are demonological symptoms, symptoms of the times that point precisely to the urgency of her task. During her hospitalization several fellow mediums come to visit, urging her to return to the temple square to continue carrying out her work. To them the doctors are mistaken in their diagnosis, as she is simply undertaking the spiritual work they all share, day after day. They try to convince the doctors to release her, to no avail.

The psychiatrists themselves are caught in an obverse conundrum. Like many others in Hexian, they at times joke that all those who frequent the temple are, in some sense, mentally ill. But when I ask about the precise boundary between what they would consider mental illness and what they would call culture or tradition—whether all engagements with temple ritual would, for instance, be seen as psychiatrically tinged according to that logic, or whether normative and mad engagements could be distinguished—they concede that it is a riddle without a clear answer. Their laughter stages an unease, of discerning the fraught boundary between "tradition" and "psychopathology" after a century of antisuperstition campaigns. Moreover, these conversations at times lead to stories of one of the psychiatrist's own visits to a select fortune-teller—one more knowledgeable and reliable, they would say, unlike those who lingered at the temple square.

Dr. Yuan, one of the psychiatrists, introduced me to Xu Liying in part due to her limit position, a liminal figure in the blurred zone between categories. She was, as he put it, an interesting case. Beyond what the psychiatrists and her family saw as Xu Liying's excessive engagement with the spirit world, she shows few other signs warranting diagnostic attention. The ambivalence emerges throughout her intake form:

> *Occupation:* Peasant.
>
> *History of Present Illness:* Patient felt pressure in life eighteen years ago, felt society was unjust, gradually lost mental normalcy.... Three days ago illness severity increased, main presentation of chaotic language, speech does not follow path, does not sleep well at night, feels society is unjust, society needs reform, the world is going to end etc., often kowtows and pleas for protection at front gate of temple. Recently kowtowed on major street intersection considering it efficacious, hard to manage....
>
> *Cognition:* No sensory disability, no delusions, no hallucinations, thought process and association normal, logic normal, language and thought activity normal, content of thought damaged . . . attention normal . . . insight lacking.
>
> *Severity:* Personal and family life affected, social functioning damaged.
>
> *Diagnosis:* Psychiatric disorder related to culture.
>
> *Differential Diagnosis:* Although hallucinatory delusional thoughts are present, content adheres closely to real life, not systematic, not absurd, carries superstitious coloring, thus can be distinguished from schizophrenia.

At once delusional and logical, at once damaged and realistic in thought, the status of Xu Liying's engagement with spirits—and with it the status of the contemporary cosmology—stands at an impasse, between superstition and schizophrenia, coded in the third term of cultural psychiatry.

HAVOC IN THE UNDERWORLD

Thinking back, I am uncertain why Xu Liying accepted my presence in her hospital room. In Hexian one is never entirely sure what a spirit medium sees in a human that approaches, which entities might be guiding the human's desires, speaking in the human's name. Sitting cross-legged on her hospital bed, Xu Liying assigns punishments rhythmically under her breath, as she flicks sunflower seeds one by one, a technique for accounting: "Hack the hands off, hack the feet off, down the eighteen strata of hell." She is enacting *dianming,* the naming and annihilation of ghosts and other harmful spirits that inflict madness, illness, and death, ghosts the doctors can't see. One by one, she culls them away—this is both the source of her affliction and her divine task.

"Others don't understand what I'm doing, mired in this all day, this underworld [*yincao difu*]." Although Xu Liying does not agree with the doctors' approach to her illness, she does consider the question of madness intimately linked to her otherworldly task. "These psychiatric disorders, how does one wind up with them? When humans die, they have a breath of air, and this breath of air can reincarnate; at times it does not reincarnate into a person and remains in the underworld. Now, through this breath, they become demons *[xian]*. They stick and attach themselves to human bodies, to quarrel and fight. . . . And it's not just one or two. If there are only a few, the person won't make much of a ruckus. If there are many, they wreak havoc; they force you to do things. They control you, as if they were a deity."[4]

For Xu Liying and other mediums in Hexian, as well as many others who engage in the ritual economy of propitiations, the actions of human beings are not fully—if at all—within the jurisdiction of a self-conscious, self-transparent human subject. While humans are born with the breath of their soul—*hun* or *língqì* (lit. "spirit-breath/air")—the body is a vessel that may be inhabited by multiple spirit entities and thus is driven to speak, think, and act by voices and desires beyond the boundary of the skin. As noted, the mediums often say that deities "borrow your body" *(jie ni shenti)* to carry out deeds and "borrow your mouth to speak" *(jie ni zui shuohua)*. Whether a deity makes its presence and desire known to the human whose body it occupies is under its own discretion, and even when such knowledge is provided, it is often through forms of unwanted mental and corporeal torment, ranging from pain and loss of appetite to madness. Thus, in the cosmological thinking of mediumship, a fundamental precarity and divisibility undergirds the very constitution of the person (see Corin 1998; Crapanzano and Garrison 1977; Strange 2016). Possessed persons are not in command of themselves.

Xu Liying explains, "Heaven's will *[tianyi]* arranges for you, tells you to go somewhere, at which temple to cultivate. They need you to go to this or that place to do this or that work. . . . The heavens above and the earth below, they arrange for you; you're no longer in command *[bu dangjia]*. And if you are going to heal others, you'd better go where they want you to. We do not know in our world; we only walk here and there, passing like a film. The path in this world, full of curves, a harsh road, high as a tall mountain, sunken like the sea, but we must pass through."

Yet the loss of command over one's actions and desires grows hazardous with the presence of ghosts and other malevolent spirits. According to Xu Liying, such demonic entities commit murder and arson, cause traffic accidents, dupe and steal, and bring a wide array of illnesses—psychiatric disorders; cancers; arm, leg, back, ankle, muscle, and bone pain; shoulder infections; eye and nose problems; and bleeding of the ears. I ask her why the ghosts made her ill in particular.

"You think these people all around us [at the psychiatric ward] are not the same? They are! To be frank, if they weren't, who would come here?" For Xu Liying other patients in the ward are similarly afflicted but simply remain unaware of their true condition because of the invisibility of spectral presence—demonic entities become perceptible to human beings at their own discretion, unless they have been "processed" *(chuli)*. Those who have not yet been processed nestle in one's body, impervious to perception. Suffering at the hands of such entities, one must avoid responding in anger—the escalation of anger only begets the escalation of demonic invasion. Among many mediums I met in Hexian, anger is considered a major risk and portal for both the intrusion of spirits and madness. The afflicted can only attempt to rid of demonic spirits gradually, Xu Liying said; there is no simple way.

"I name them, and the moment one is named, one is slain *[kandiao]*. For instance, some guy named 'Mr. Li' committed murder, and the sun orders for him to be decapitated, to be thrown into prison, to be melted by fire, to never reincarnate again. This is how they are gotten rid of. . . . If you don't name them, you cannot rid of them." Thus, to complete her own task and to rid herself of her own illness, she must remain patient—"day by day, little by little," naming ghosts and corrupt spirits one by one, from account books *(zhangben)* kept by the sun deity, documenting the crimes each has committed. Through the ledgers as well as the assistance of the very few deities she trusts, particularly the sun, the moon, and the Eternal Mother, she names the demonic spirits one after another, expelling them by naming them. At times, she says, she is sending them into the next round of reincarnation; at times they are prevented altogether from future reincarnation, never to affect the human realm or even the underworld again.

Xu Liying's account of the underworld resonates with visions of hell in China depicted particularly since the ninth or tenth century. Often enumerated at eight, ten, eighteen (as in Xu Liying's description), thirty, or sixty-four, Chinese Buddhist hells combine Indian concepts of karma and Chinese principles of bureaucracy. Humans receive retribution for their deeds, and bureaucrats of the underworld collaborate with earthly and heavenly offices, keeping records of the deeds and "forwarding the log-books at death to the appropriate court of hell, where the results were tabulated and a just reward meted out" (Teiser 1988, 460).

For Xu Liying, as for other mediums I met, the abundance of demonic entities today and the madness they induce are symptomatic of a particular conjunction of history, politics, and the cosmos. Usurping human bodies, demonic spirits attempt to seize power and take reign. "Why psychiatric disorders?" Xu Liying poses. "For instance, you or I become mentally ill; we all become mentally ill. What's the aim? Before Old Mao died, he said, 'In the future a million madmen will storm the palace—sweep out all cow ghosts and idiotic gods!'"

Returning throughout our conversations, this line brings together two Maoist sayings. The first comes from Mao's 1949 poem "The People's Liberation Army Captures Nanjing," a triumphant account of the occupation of the then Nationalist-ruled Presidential Palace, signaling the Communist Party victory in China (Mao 2019). The second is the title of an official editorial in *Renmin Ribao* (*People's Daily*), published on June 1, 1966, which publicly inaugurated the Cultural Revolution and became a slogan for denouncing the Four Olds—old ideas, old culture, old customs, and old habits.

Yet the phrasings each took a new turn in Xu Liying's account. Whereas the original line from the poem reads, a "million-strong mighty army crosses the great stream,"

Xu Liying offers a symmetrical, nearly rhyming, iteration, "a million madmen storm the palace." And whereas the original slogan reads, "sweep out all cow ghosts and snake gods," Xu Liying displaces *she* with *sha*—"snake" with "idiotic."[5] Moreover, while the original 1949 poem refers to the then-recent military victory and thus is at times translated in the past tense in English, the grammatical flexibility of tense in the Chinese version allows for its poetic transformation from history into prophecy.

The "million madmen" that will "storm the palace," for Xu Liying, refers to the contemporary moment, in which deluded and sinister spirits—including corrupted gods—have come swirling back after Mao's death. This precarious cosmos is the origin of madness today: "When Mao died, once Deng Xiaoping took office, how did he put it? Regardless of whether it's a black cat, whether it's a green cat, as long as it catches mice, it counts as a good cat. Once this phrase was uttered— whoosh!—the monstrous *[guai]* appeared in the world." Giving a slight twist to the reform-era maxim on black and white cats—oft-cited in everyday laments in Hexian directed at the postreform era, as noted—Xu Liying paints a scene of chaos, in which humans are possessed by duplicitous spirits masquerading as deities.[6] "This god, that goddess, all from a fake family . . . swindling people, extorting people, duping people, deluding people. And there are those clever ones, making you hazy and confused." Fraud, delusion, and madness intertwine with the motif of corruption: "The Southern Heavens, the Northern Heavens, the Middle Heavens, they have all been corrupted! All idiotic gods, not one upright righteous god. If they are righteous gods *[zhengshen]*, they would not ask for money from people, would not ask for pigs, sheep, mule, horses, would not ask for gold, ingots, and buns *[mo]*."

Speaking from within Henan, which faces the characterological indictment of charlatanism, Xu Liying gestures outward instead toward a cosmic geography saturated with greed. Her rendering points to two themes that fill postreform imaginaries of China at large: fakery and corruption. In Yu Hua's (2012) *China in Ten Words*, Copycat and Bamboozle stand alongside the Revolution and the People, sketching tragicomic scenes of the people swindling the state, the state swindling the people, and imitative proliferations between the market and the state. In national discourses, paralleling Xu Liying's cosmological account of the death of Mao and the rise of Deng, concerns with corruption heightened with the dawn of the reform era, intensifying across the 1980s and 1990s (He 2000), and remained central to official anticorruption languages of Xi Jinping's administration during my time in Hexian.

In both Xu Liying and other mediums' accounts, the opposite of the fake deity is not only the "true/real" *(zhen)*—the usual linguistic counterpart to the "fake" *(jia)*—or the "original" *(yuan)*. It is most often the "upright" *(zheng)*, as in the distinction discussed between *zheng* (the righteousness of moral emperorship or orthodoxy) and *xie* (cosmic evil or heterodoxy). Xu Liying and others thus offer a pairing of the fake and the upright—opposing modern and late capitalist notions of the fake not simply with reality but with moral rule. The fake deity refers not only to spirits who disguise themselves as deities, thus a question of false identity, but also deities who have lost their moral standing. Fake deities are characterized by greed, exploitation, and the desire for harm—in other words, the fake brings us back to the theme of corruption—of not only those who falsify but those who abuse their identities in the struggle for gain and power.

MUTUAL DIAGNOSIS

The language of fakery and the links drawn between madness and spirit possession find their counterpart in psychiatric and antisuperstition literatures. The former points more to the epistemological error of outmoded beliefs than to explicit questions of morality, while the latter mixes questions of error with those of falsification for gain. I return now to the diagnosis given to Xu Liying by Dr. Yuan, the full name of which is found in the psychiatric textbook used for reference at the ward (Shen 1982): "psychiatric disorder intimately related to culture," with an elaboration of subtypes. Whereas Xu Liying's mediumistic accounts diagnose the presence of psychiatric disorders through the status of the cosmos after Mao's death, cultural psychiatry diagnoses the spirit world through a series of modern temporal displacements from the primitive to the scientific, pointing to the other life of socialist time making more familiar to academic accounts. Following a section on the "Asiatic psychosis" (English in the original text) of koro and qigong deviation psychosis, the final section is dedicated to the "Subcultural Hysterical Possession State."[7] "Superstition and religion are common among the world's nations and ethnicities," the section begins. "As Marx indicated, religion is a type of social concept . . . yet is a type of illusory reflection, originating from the narrow and ignorant concepts of the age of barbarism" (Shen 1982).

Faith in deities, it went on to explain, constitutes "folk belief" (minjian xinyang; in both English and Chinese in the original). Pithy descriptions of Yin Yang, the Five Elements, Confucianism, Buddhism, Daoism, and "ancient" witchcraft and spirit worship in China across millennia are told in one breath midparagraph, bookended by two explanations for the tendency toward superstition: first, the lack of scientific thinking among the ignorant, uneducated "lower strata" of the population and, second, China's high rural population and rates of rural illiteracy. Then comes an anthropological justification: "According to the famous anthropologist Malinowski . . . the function of [witchcraft and witchdoctors] is to 'increase belief that overcomes fear and, more valuably, to provide people with self-confidence, [and] conquer pessimism with optimism. If it were not for witchcraft, primitive people would not overcome practical difficulties and would not progress to a more advanced culture.' Thus, witchcraft was very common in primitive society; witchcraft held common authority" (Shen 1982).

The section continues, describing a Jungian view of therapeutic potential in witchcraft, but quickly warns that possession is often exploited for social harm. It closes with a reminder of the distinction between illegal superstition and legal religion before moving on to case examples. Condensed in Xu Liying's diagnosis is an extended history of ambivalent translation: Marxian and social evolutionary analyses of religion and world history; functionalist anthropological accounts of witchcraft; Jungian considerations of psychological efficacy; modern Chinese renderings of a backward, rural national body; and legal-political distinctions between religion and superstition inherited from missionary movements.

The notion of culture-bound and culture-related psychiatric disorders arose alongside colonial efforts at the turn of the twentieth century, when missionaries and physicians came to document "peculiar" illnesses among their non-European counterparts: *amok, latah, koro, pibloktoq* ("Arctic hysteria"), and *witiko*, among others (Tseng 2006).[8] Coined by Hong Kong psychiatrist Pow-Ming Yap first as "mental diseases peculiar to certain cultures" (1951) and eventually as "culture-bound syndrome" (1967), this uncanny categorical remainder continues to linger at the edges of mainstream psychiatry.[9]

Paralleling other faces of colonial encounter, the awkward concept of the culture-bound syndrome resembles at once the remnants of colonial curios and the implicit threat posed to the very core of modern Western epistemology and ontology, now sought, now contained. Work continues to improve the formulation of culture in the fifth edition of the *Diagnostic and Statistical Manual of Mental Disorders* (American Psychiatric Association 2013; see also Lewis-Fernández et al. 2014), though some have also suggested that—given the growing international hegemony of *DSM* discourse, the transnational pharmaceutical industry, and the rise of Global Burden of Disease approaches—the very meaning and relevance of debates over cultural classification must be rethought, and efforts should turn instead to practicable strategies of care provision, advocacy, and stigma reduction (S. Lee 2002). Between calls for a new cross-cultural psychiatry (Kleinman 1977) and the rise of global mental health (Kirmayer and Pedersen 2014), old questions continue to haunt new approaches (Hopper 1991), and practices of cultural and ethnopsychiatry may engage in both the reification and critical rethinking of difference (Giordano 2014).

The links drawn between madness and mediumship were by no means produced by the institutions of psychiatry alone. Notions of psychiatric illness were central to debates on religion and campaigns against superstition throughout the twentieth century. Following late Qing writings on the reform of Chinese customs and the replacement of temples by modern schools, a series of essays and pamphlets in the name of "eradicating superstition" *(pochu mixin)* were produced from the 1920s onward by the Nationalist government, Christian evangelists, and some reform Buddhists.

The original 1924 text, *Pochu Mixin Quanshu* (lit. "eradicating superstition compendium"), with the English title of *Superstitions: Their Origins and Fallacy*, was drafted by Chinese Methodists Li Ganchen and Luo Yuanyen and designed as a tool for evangelism, with categorizations drawn from church members' observations of non-Christian engagements. The text and the iterations that follow draw often on social evolutionary and functionalist theories of religion, including theological views that begin with "primitive" religions and end in Christianity (Nedostup 2010). Such antisuperstition texts continued to be published in the Maoist era, and new versions have been published well into the reform era. Ideas and practices to be debunked and combated range from the existence of gods and ghosts and the efficacy of feng shui masters and spirit mediums to reincarnation after death. A 1964 edition of *Pochu Mixin Wenda* (Questions and answers about eradicating superstition), for instance, dedicates a chapter to the question of possession and mediumship, titled "What Is the Situation with 'Possession by Ghosts and Gods'?"[10]

"So-called 'possession by ghosts and gods,'" the chapter begins, "is the attachment of ghosts and gods to the body of a living person." It then immediately moves to the link between the lack of empirical reality of spirits and the theme of falsity: "As discussed previously, there are no ghosts and gods in the world; thus, it is clear at first sight that so-called possession by ghosts and spirits are nonsensical words [*guihua*, lit. 'ghostly words'] for duping people" (*Pochu Mixin Wenda* 1964, 60; my translation). In this the medium becomes the charlatan par excellence: "Some witches [*wupo*] in fact play the trick of 'possession by ghosts and gods' to swindle for money and belongings . . . pretending that they themselves are possessed by 'so-and-so god' . . . yawning continuously, stretching, rolling their eyes back, squeezing their fists tight, uttering phrases" (61).

In these renderings mediumship and possession are cast as a self-conscious strategy of deception for gain, displaying the outward signs of possession without a corresponding experience of possession. Yet the chapter goes on to describe another form of apparent possession: "There are those very few people [whose] mind/consciousness [*shenzhi*] is originally clear and abruptly lose mental normalcy [*jingshen shiqu changtai*]; their voice while speaking and their movements almost seem like they are those of relatives who died; upon awakening, they themselves do not know what has just occurred. What is the reason for this?" Here the language of psychiatry enters. "We know that the brain [*danao*] can also get ill; the severe version is psychiatric disorder, [when one is] mad [*fengfengdiandian*] all day; the mild version is the condition of losing one's consciousness in the short term" (*Pochu Mixin Wenda* 1964, 62–63).

While these forms of madness and loss of consciousness are described as common, the chapter describes a final, more rare circumstance: "There is a type of patient who regularly yearns for relatives who have passed away and cannot seem to forget their tone of voice and their demeanor. Once their brain function becomes disordered, and they recall these impressions particularly vividly, that person might display the relative's comportment." The chapter is resolute regarding the status of these instances: "This is a particular expression of a nervous disorder, absolutely not some 'possession by ghosts and gods'" (*Pochu Mixin Wenda* 1964, 64).

Lacking a home in the post-Enlightenment ontology of the modern sciences, the perception of spirits and other unseen forces came to be relegated to the domain of psychopathology and claims of possession to equal charlatanism. While caution and suspicion toward the efficacy of any given spirit medium and fortune-teller predated antisuperstition articulations, the very effort to define and elimi-nate superstition in the postdynastic era newly placed notions of fakery, swindling, and trickery within a Protestant-inflected symbolic universe.

Entering the Chinese lexicon as neologisms at the turn of the century, the mod-ern Chinese bifurcation of "religion" (*zongjiao*) and "superstition" (*mixin*) shifted the terms of the prior debate. Nation-building efforts following the collapse of the dynastic system involved the imitation of Japanese and Western constitutions, founded on Christian conceptualizations of religion—and superstition as reli-gion's other. Officials and scholars worked to impose new distinctions between "genuine" Daoism from "superstition" (including mediumship and possession), the results of which would determine, for instance, whether a temple was pre-served or destroyed (Goossaert 2005).

In imperial times the distinction at stake centered on the righteous (*zheng*) and the improper (*xie*) rather than religion and superstition. *Zheng* rested on a sense of Confucian righteousness and moral emperorship, whereas *xie* marked that which strayed into the realm of improper cults or improper sacrifices. These mapped onto notions that might be translated as orthodoxy (*zhengjiao*) and heterodoxy (*xiejiao*), respectively. While strands of Buddhism and Daoism were at times accused of het-erodoxy by the imperial state, the terms *zheng* and *xie* were by no means limited to the official realm. They were employed in parallel as spiritual-religious concepts by the very groups condemned as heterodoxy by the imperial state (Nedostup 2010). Buddhist messianic traditions, for instance, used *zheng* in reference to the True Doctrine practiced in accordance with the principles of the Buddha and *xie* to describe the evil that would ravage the world in cosmic crisis (Zürcher 1982). Between the vocabulary of psychiatry and antisuperstition campaigns on the one side, and those of Buddhism and mediumship on the other, there has thus been a history of mutual diagnosis. Here I turn to Xu Liying for her account.

CORRUPTION, CULTIVATION

After Xu Liying's initial encounter with the call to revolution and as she continued in her illness, she began to grasp the complications of a cosmos in chaos, a chaos too complicated for full explication, she says. "Except for Old Mao, who did indeed cultivate to fruition toward goodness [shanshishanguo], cultivate to achieve the fruits of righteousness [xiucheng zhengguo], the rest of the Ten Great Marshals did not cultivate and have all become corrupt. Premier Zhou, Zhu De, Jia Long, none of them cultivated to the point of fruition, and all grew corrupt."

Beyond the recent return of demonic spirits after the death of Mao and the rise of Deng, the cosmic temporality of corruption is layered, rolling across multiple dynasties. Xu Liying continues, "Tang, Song, Yuan, Ming, Qing—five dynasties; [yet] they are seven. Ordinary people know only five dynasties. Five periods of chaos [hundun], seven dynasties. The old white turtle took hold of the five dynasties. The son of the white turtle family is Zhou Guoshi, Zhou Enlai; he took reign for two dynasties, with the girl. The sixth is the ancient who split heaven and earth, is sister and brother. The old white turtle is their mother. . . . The imperial palace is not the imperial palace; it's a chaotic dynasty."

The old white turtle Xu Liying speaks of is the mythological origin of the eight trigram divinatory system employed in the Book of Changes, the shapes of which were revealed by the heavens to Fuxi on the back of the white turtle around the time of the rebirth of humankind. Locally, the turtle is at times said to still dwell in a lake adjacent to Fuxi Temple. Xu Liying's lament thus brings together the Maoist time of Zhou Enlai, the primordial time of the white turtle, and the rolling chaos of one dynasty after the other, propelled by power struggles in the underworld. Weaving modern historical and mythological times, Xu Liying conveys a tangled tale of power and betrayal, of coups amid swarms of demons. "Old Mao should not have died. In the underworld they found someone to infect him with illness. [Zhou Enlai] had many connections in the underworld. He wanted to kill everyone else, kill Old Mao, leaving only himself. Can this be? To tell others to stray toward corruption, toward murder and arson, can the Communist Party allow for this?"

Her task, then, is to continue Mao's revolution, to clear the current moment of cosmic decay by returning to an ethics of which he was exemplary. "What I do is not domination! What I do is not Chiang Kai-Shek's work. I do Old Mao's work! I follow Old Mao. Old Mao doesn't swindle, doesn't cheat! Not greedy or corrupt, not rotten! He eats based on conscience and labor, eating and living collectively, right? I have been meditating in this direction for eighteen years now, and I never scrounge off of other people's food. I eat what I carry with me."

Not eating others' food (buchi renjia fan) is a common phrase in Hexian, at times explained as a carryover from a moral economy of scarcity (see E. Thompson 1971). Given the local history and memories of mass starvation, both pre-Liberation (before 1949) and during the Great Leap famine of 1958–59, to consume one's rightful share constitutes the foundation of everyday morality. In contrast, the wealthy and powerful today are perceived as those who consume the fruits of others' labor, the grain they did not sow. For mediums such as Xu Liying, to "walk Mao's path" signals a striving toward an ethics now out of reach, given the state of contemporary greed and corruption, in a crisis of morality and sovereignty of cosmic proportions.

"Whatever task he [Mao] gives me, I will finish it for him. Gloriously complete my duty, do good for the People my whole life. Those who do evil will forever be evil. Those who do good, let us show them. . . . Old Mao acts and speaks honestly, for the sake of the People in all regards. Who are the officials today acting for the sake of? All for themselves. Eat, drink, get the money into their own hands, sitting there enjoying themselves. You as a commoner, you don't have a path of wealth; he has a path of wealth, then what? Let me say this, I am not philosophizing. I've been mad for eighteen years. I say this all day—we the People must maintain conscience; we cannot scam people and dupe people."

Echoing accounts from the temple square, Xu Liying speaks of Maoist antisuperstition campaigns as an act of divine intervention. "When Mao was to be sent down to the earth from the heavens *[xiafan]*, he did not want to. But they insisted, saying he must descend. Once Mao took office, he banned religious faith *[xinnian]*. After he reincarnated as a human *[zhuanren]*, he smashed all the temples, no? Heavenly command was given from above, telling him to smash them all, keep none of them. They were filled with demonic spirits *[xian]!*" The undiscernible identity and moral status of the spirits, in temples and beyond, both before and after Mao's reign, explains the presence of psychiatric afflictions. "Yeee! You don't know who is in there, is that the Goddess of Mercy or not the Goddess of Mercy? You cannot see them, you cannot touch them, and you wind up in the hospital."

I ask Xu Liying about the other mediums at the temple square, thinking that perhaps she considers them to share in her task of transforming the present. Yet she remains dubious of the others. With the Chairman gone, the very act of mediumship cannot be trusted. "They sit there—even on a cold snowy day, they cannot help but sit there. They are not in control . . . the humans, running north and south with their satchels, crossing every which way. [But] it's all demons *[jing xian]!* Not one is an upright god. . . . No one can say for certain when it comes to these matters. . . . If they're real, they don't swindle others, don't take things from others, don't eat from others, don't drink from others, and can even help when one is suffering. This is called accumulating morality and enacting good deeds. Other [spirits] pressure you, lead you to death; that's different. . . . Who is in command? No one's in command! Heaven guides you; earth guides you. This time around, it's demons. No one is in command!"

A WORLD AFLAME

Xu Liying tells me what must be done under such circumstances of moral and divine corruption. The task at hand, she says, is to assist in the "dynastic revolution" *(chaoge)*, combining the imperial language of dynasties with the modern use of revolution. In line with imperial Chinese political thought, each dynasty is seen as likely to be efficacious and virtuous at its initiation but gradually disintegrates. And the "dynasty" of which the contemporary moment is a part of has reached an unbearable point of decadence, in the mirroring of earthly and heavenly corruption. According to Xu Liying, given the degree of corruption and chaos today—from politicians to temple goers to spirits—the human race is headed toward the apocalypse of a world aflame *(huoshao shijie)*. Throughout our conversations one of the few figures Xu Liying considers uncorrupted, aside from the sun, the moon, and Mao, is the Eternal Mother. And while Xu Liying does not elaborate on their link, eschatological anticipation is central to the spiritual texts dedicated to the Eternal Mother.

Historically, the Eternal Mother, also translated as Unborn Mother (lit. "without birth or beyond birth") has been the central figure in what's known in the literature as the White Lotus Society in northern Chinese regions (including Henan). More a state-imposed appellation than a term of self-reference, it points to small, scattered groups across time and space, whose resemblance centers more on their cosmology than their name or systematic organization. First used in the fourth century, then borrowed as a term in the eleventh century, "White Lotus" came to be seen as a more distinct tradition from the sixteenth century onward, partly due to imperial efforts in the Ming and Qing dynasties to brand and purge such "heretical" doctrines (Naquin 1976; Overmyer 1972; Haar 1992). The Eternal Mother has thus historically occupied the space of rift and heterodoxy with relation to the state, and her mythologies have been seen to speak dangerously to this rift.

In various collections of scripture, as Susan Naquin (1976) describes, the Eternal Mother is described as giving birth to a son and daughter who married and became ancestors to all humankind. (In some versions her son and daughter were none other than Fuxi and Nüwa.) But after she sent her children—the humans—to the Eastern World, she grew anguished as she observed their growing decadence and confusion *(mi)*. She watched her children lose their original nature and grow more indulgent in vanity. She sent them messages and letters to ask them to return home, where their mother was, to no avail. For a human to return home was not only to return to the mother's side but also to "confirm that he is unborn and will not again turn in the wheel of transmigration" (9). To return her children to her side, the Eternal Mother would send a series of gods and Buddhas to "teach a new system of values" and "come home" (10). She first sent the Lamp-Lighting Buddha, followed by the Sakyamuni Buddha. Each were only able to save a few of her children. The Eternal Mother would thus have to send one more Buddha to save the remaining humans—the Maitreya Buddha.

In the accounts of spirit mediums in Hexian, the historical arrival of Mao is at times linked with the arrival of the Maitreya Buddha, in a moment when China had reached the brink of ruin and calamity. Among those at the temple square,

Mao is often said to belong to the Western Heavenly Gate (Xitianmen), referring to Buddhism, as Buddhism arrived from the west, from India—"Mao and the Buddha, the Buddha and Mao: they're all one family," as I heard several mediums at the temple square put it.

As described earlier, the Chairman is said to be sent down from the heavens in human form to spark the Communist Revolution, armed with the divine task of destroying temples and icons, clearing existing decay, and preventing China from full foreign domination. He was sent, some whispered, by none other than Maitreya. Indeed, some said he was the very manifestation of Maitreya. As Wang, the disseminator of the Chairman's biographic booklet, puts it, "Mao is Maitreya; Maitreya is Mao. They are the same person. The Eternal Mother is their mother; they are the same."

But, according to some mediums, saviors like Mao are sent only in moments of crisis, of absolute threat to China's sovereign existence. It is as if, to borrow from Walter Benjamin (2007), the messiah arrives just when tradition is on the verge of being overwhelmed. In a flash of danger, a vision of the ruinous past crystallizes in the here and now, shattering illusions of a homogenous, progressive time, and opens up attempts to deliver tradition anew. The miraculous arrival of the Chairman and the proliferation of corrupt humans and spirits in his wake gesture toward an eschatological horizon, paralleling the calamitous end of the world following human decline in the scriptures of the Eternal Mother.

For Xu Liying, like other mediums at the temple square, the coming end must be understood in light of foreign imperialism and Communist Revolution. As I describe in the opening of the book, Xu Liying speaks of the coming end in terms of a moral-spiritual periphery—of foreign nations that participate in domination, the United States and Japan in particular. These outer edges of the world will burn, while those in China—the center of the world—will be the last to be affected. Hexian—the center of Henan, which is in turn the center of the Central Plain region, which is in turn the center of China—will be the last place to remain, she says, from which the virtuous few will be chosen to inaugurate the new world to come.

Through this apocalyptic geography, Henan Province, which in the national discourse is considered peripheral and left behind precisely because of its landlocked position, is reinstated as a powerful center around which all else will collapse and burn, and figures of political and military domination are rendered as the ultimate spiritual, moral, political periphery. Only after this burning and culling of the world, she explains, will the revolution reach its aim—that of true socialism (zhenzheng de shehuizhuyi). As Xu Liying describes it, true socialism is a world of equality, in which there will be no corruption, no cheating, and no stealing. "If today I have a hundred mo, a hundred buns, and there are a hundred people, each of us gets one bun. Even if there's only one piece each, it still must be distributed.

What's equality? That's equality. This bowl of water, wherever you go, you can prop it up for [the other person] to drink. Isn't that a good thing?"

Yet, for all the simplicity and clarity conveyed by this utopian image of the next world, the path is long, arduous, and without a clear end. Xu Liying has been toiling in her revolutionary task for eighteen years, and there is no knowing how much longer. There is a radical gulf between the daily *work* of revolution and the eventual arrival of its apocalyptic achievement, and Xu Liying carries on her rituals daily, knowing she might not be around to see the end.

VERTIGINOUS ABBREVIATION

Perhaps this is also what Jacques Derrida (1994) means by the radical heterogeneity of the future, in his proposal of the "messianic without messianism," in which ethics, after the sense of disappointment and horror toward socialist states, especially among those who had been previous proponents of Marxism, may reside precisely in a nonexpectant, nonpresumptuous, future-facing mode of anticipation. It would be an anticipation open to a profound alterity, to a sense of the ever-arriving marking the impossibility of ever arriving. Yet if Derrida's work is in part an effort to augment Benjamin's (2007) "weak messianism," in which the angel of history turns its back to the future, with a gaze toward the *demands* of the catastrophic, ruinous *past*, the spectral force of history, of foreclosed and deferred promises, also cannot be sidestepped in Hexian.

As David Ownby (1999) writes, millenarian imaginations across Chinese history constitute responses from within, often to times of war, famine, invasion, and calamity. Following stretches of regional strife and famine, and amid the sense of corruption and loss of moral-political guarantee since market reforms, those who walk Mao's path like Xu Liying transmit the spectral returns of catastrophic histories while facing a future unknown. In their accounts waves of chaos across heaven and earth reach back toward the very (re)birth of humankind and up to the historical present, washing over the borrowed bodies of humans. Plays of expectation and nonexpectation are articulated through languages and rituals of esoteric knowing and open-ended waiting, committed duty and reluctant deployment through the loss of self-mastery.

Without trying to collapse the heterogeneous span of Chinese millenarianism with the Jewish mystical traditions inherited and renewed by Benjamin (2007) and others, I want to consider how ethical imaginations of the end of time—from both spirit mediums in Hexian and critical philosophers in Europe—are inflected by struggles with the dilemmas posed by the gradual shattering of twentieth-century dreamworlds. In these cases the lingering hope and trepidation toward the ever-deferred promises of Communism after the so-called end of history interlace with anticipatory genres of spiritual-religious traditions, together raising questions about the possibility of rethinking culture, politics, and ethics today. Now, a century after the initial throes of what early twentieth-century Chinese intellectuals called semicolonialism, decades after many French and other European Maoists dropped this self-reference following the tremors of the Cultural Revolution, specters of Mao return to Xu Liying and others, awaiting the apocalyptic return of a revolution incomplete.

Here I'm taken to Giorgio Agamben's (2002) indirect response to Derrida's (1994) formulation of the messianic as a forward-looking embrace of infinite deferral, which Agamben sees precisely as a source of the danger and catastrophic failures of historical revolutions. Agamben suggests, in contrast, that messianic time doesn't lie fully exterior to chronological time. Rather, it constitutes a peculiar *portion* of chronological time, the time it takes to register the always-already here, yet ever-still not-yet temporality of the apocalyptic, *the time it takes for time to come to an end,* for time to accomplish itself. "Or, more exactly," he writes, "the time *we need* in order to accomplish, to bring to an end *our representation* of time"—a "contraction" of chronological time that "transforms it entirely," a "vertiginous abbreviation" imploding the now into the eternal. But it is also a time in which prophecy must remain silent: "there is no one to ask: 'how long'" (5, 2; emphasis added).

While those like Xu Liying would veer away from the transformation of human-represented time as the chief aim of their task, the unfolding of messianic time in and through chronological time—which produces a vertiginous abbreviation of the "now" in face of the eternal—resonates with my encounters in Hexian. Between the missing sovereign and the sovereign-to-come sits a dizzying era saturated with specters, while spans of cosmohistorical time condense and congeal into various forms in the present. To be a medium to the present is to carry out one's allotment, *ming*—a *portion* of time marked simultaneously by lifespan and duty (Lupke 2005).

In a reflection on violence and social life, Barend ter Haar describes a thread of what he calls a demonological messianism in certain Chinese religious traditions, which he traces historically up through its influence on Maoist times. Such traditions often center on the demonic nature of apocalyptic disasters, which await a savior backed by divine armies, often located in a mythical West or Western Heaven—although the earthly locales onto which these mythical sites mapped varied. Unlike what he terms "ordinary demonological thinking," demonic messianism points to a grand scale of immanent attacks that span the "entire cultured world," while also tying events to "a specific chronological and administrative context of dates and locations," in which a new divine ruler and the ruler's divine generals are "identified as actual people" (1992, 66).

While Haar distinguishes this strand of messianism from those surrounding Maitreya and the Eternal Mother, those in Hexian seem to merge these elements. For Xu Liying and others in Hexian, the demon-infused chaos of the world-historical present points toward chronologies of foreign imperialism, Communist

Liberation, and market reform, while anticipating the (re)appearance of Mao or a Mao-like figure, associated with a Maitreyan-inflected Western Heavenly Gate. As noted earlier, the merging of Maoist and cosmological themes is not surprising in what some have called atheist secular worlds (Ngo and Quijada 2015). Indeed, the Chinese Communist Party drew explicit inspiration from such messianic movements as the Taiping Rebellion, centered on notions of egalitarian moral obligation and pitted against those with wealth (Thaxton 1983).

In Hexian, what stays with me is the reworking of time by those like Xu Liying, in the encounter with other temporal renderings—psychiatric, developmentalist, or otherwise. I think about those at the temple square waiting for an enigmatic *someone,* with no final word on the "how long." I think about Xu Liying, who toils at her task, without knowing when the revolution will truly arrive. Yet does not the very time it takes to "process" the ghosts "one by one," as Xu Liying puts it, and the time it takes for lost gods to travel from one body to another before they reunite, constitute a certain portion of messianic time? Does not the very language and ritual of mediumship regarding the time it takes for time to come to an end hint precisely at this mode of transformation, in which assumptions accompanying homogenous progressive time might be quietly or dramatically refigured, through the daily work of walking, running, guarding, and seeing in Hexian?

Perhaps in their very insistence on cosmic toiling—now deemed superstitious or psychopathological in the aftermath of modern encounter—Xu Liying and others in Hexian register the deferred Maoist promises of peasant political subjectivity after semicolonialism, of postreform economic and symbolic dispossession in an era of uneven capitalist investment and labor outmigration, and of much more than any ethnographic retrospective can reconstruct. The progressive time of the socialist promise merges with horizons of eschatological anticipation, together carried in a spectral temporality of returns. The vertigo of history, including the encounter of thought across times and spaces, is abbreviated and transfigured through the borrowed bodies of the mediums. Anticipations of end time and cosmological realignment reach forward and backward, resounding the very disjunctures of time collected across China's long twentieth century and beyond, carving out a portion of intensified time that attempts to register the very meaning of the "now," between catastrophe and eternity.

Coda

Those Who Remain

Back at the temple square that night, Wang has just finished reciting Mao's poem "Snow" and is now reading from Mao's unofficial biography. Twenty or so people have gathered around him. The younger businessman who felt bewildered *(mi)* by the scene has wandered away. The group of elderly women are still there, listening. A man with thinning gray hair walks up to the growing crowd, shaking his head, mouth curled in disdain—a theatrics of skepticism. He looks to be of a similar age as Wang, in his sixties or so.

"Prattling on about these things? These are all matters of the past," he mumbles. Wang glances toward the interruption but continues without pause. The skeptic lingers at the edge of the crowd, half listening. Now and again he repeats his interjection: "These are all matters of the past." Wang's eyes grow defensive, his voice louder, fighting to keep the attention and confidence of the crowd. After several more muffled interjections from the periphery, the skeptic at last steps forward, center stage in the small crowd, and blurts out, "These are all matters of the past! Why don't you speak of some matters of the present?"

"The present?" Reluctant to engage the detractor yet clearly agitated, Wang snaps, "The present is chaos! The present is you give me ten thousand; I give you twenty thousand! The present is selling political seats and buying political seats, without any decent politicians to go around!"

"Ay! That's right!" The skeptic retreats, nodding in satisfaction.

"But"—now Wang is roused—"they are one and the same! The past is the present, the present is the past, and history cannot be neglected!"

"History is history," scoffs the skeptic. "The present is the present."

Wang seems to have exhausted his supply of ripostes. "But . . . you cannot forget history," he manages and turns back to the booklet: "1921 . . . "

After some moments of peaceful recitation, the skeptic returns to the scene. Moving intensely close to Wang for a final face-off, the skeptic spits, "Then tell me, in the end, is it the living that reigns or the dead?"

Wang fumbles for words. A spectator pitches in laughingly, "Does such a thing even need to be discussed? Of course it's the living!" The skeptic shushes him and turns back to Wang: "This is the last question I'll pose to you. There's no need to discuss anything else!"

Cornered into the choice between two, Wang musters up his conviction and hollers, "The dead!"

"Then there's nothing left to say!" And with that the skeptic smugly steps back once again.

"And you?" I ask the skeptic. "Who do you think reigns, the living or the dead?"

"The living and the dead both reign!" It's an evasive response—or is it?

"We Chinese have this tradition, always looking toward the dead," he continues. "Even in reading we have to read texts by the dead. And the living? Isn't it still the living who are reading the books?"

One of the spectators begins to snicker at Wang, "Are you ill?"

"Indeed I am! I'm a madman, a *shenjingbing!*" The crowd bursts out in laughter, including Wang himself, breaking the tension for a moment.

"Elder Uncle, how is it that you believe in gods? Invisible and intangible, where do you find them?"[1] Addressing the orator, a woman, perhaps in her late twenties, dances into the crowd, miming sweepingly with her hands as if blind. The crowd begins to chuckle.

Wang again fumbles for words: "Well, gods are people, and people are gods!"

"Why do you not believe in gods?" I ask the woman.

"Of course I believe in them! I merely wish to seek counsel from Elder Uncle as to how to find them! How do you find them if you cannot see them and cannot touch them?"

I realize I had misunderstood her query. At first, I thought her question to be a challenge in the spirit of skepticism. But I would come to learn that such debates edge on what those at the temple square call *duigong,* the "facing off" of spiritual powers, not merely a restaging of the modern rift between the religious and nonreligious. It is a mode of searching, a genre for discovering spiritual affinity and kinship, identifying guides and disciples, and discerning between friend and foe—between those carrying with them virtuous spirits and those housing demonic entities.

Recalling this scene at the temple square brings me back to some of the conundrums facing the contemporary cosmology and among those who remained. As mentioned earlier, if we turn to an older translation of the so-called left behind (*liushou*), we come to a double meaning of those who stay and keep guard while the emperor is away. The problem of the relevance of the past and of the dead, as raised by the skeptic, calls to mind efforts of Chinese reformers and revolutionaries from the twentieth century onward of the pained desire and fraught attempt to "shake off the ancient ghosts" carried on one's back, to quote Lu Xun, in the movement toward a "progressive, ever ascending" future (J. Lovell 2009, xxx).

Yet the skeptic's satisfaction at the orator's indictment of the present also suggests that to leave the past behind by no means secures a splendid future. Rather, a present has been reached that leaves its observers *mi*—lost, confused, bewildered—like the young man returning to a place he once knew. Under such conditions what is to be sought and how is one to seek it? As the dancing disciple asks, how might one encounter the invisible and intangible forces infusing yet eluding the world? And are such questions, as the crowd's laughter raises in both unease and relief, simply mad? Then, at the center of all such questions and doubts, there is the orator's voicing of Mao, which signaled to many who gathered around that his speech is an address emanating from above, from beyond the human realm.

A veiled emperor at once timely and untimely, for spirit mediums in Hexian, Mao seems to have arrived and departed in a flash of eternity, a glimpse of earthly divinity stretching toward visions of a revolutionary end time, leaving the present in the afterglow of the absented sovereign. This might seem counterintuitive considering the wealth of writings on the harsh realities of so-called actually existing socialism. But, as I hope to have shown, the figures of the rural and of the peasant have been at the heart of literary and political reconstitutions of the "actually existing" again and again.

Against the grain of outside accounts—or, rather, absorbing and transforming such accounts from within through their cosmic doubling—spirit mediums who "walk Mao's path" offer a different vision of the contemporary real. The post-Mao world, in their rendering, is a postscript to an interval of divine sovereignty, marked by a sense of loss left by an unfinished revolution. In lieu of sovereign guarantee, the hollowed present has been filling up with ghosts and false deities. The sense of rising material abundance is accompanied by a growing sense of material desire, a desire that constitutes both vehicle and evidence of demonic corruption that returned with the Chairman's departure. Among such dangerous entities drift true, virtuous gods—lost gods who seek one another through the human bodies they occupy.

Through their ventriloquized laments, the mediums who walk Mao's path speak not only to a sense of loss but also to the nested temporalities constituting the "now." By placing statist politics and market reforms within grander movements across yin and yang realms, across the earthly and heavenly, the contemporary cosmology inverts the space-time of the very terms of history. To shift our gaze—seeing, for a moment, like a medium rather than seeing like a state—is to imagine differently the nature of the world being inhabited, in which an earthly state, for instance, is but one force among many in a series of reversals and might itself be subject to deployments beyond its own knowing. In this rendering the purported periphery of such "small places" *(xiaodifang)* as Hexian marks a new, virtuous center, home to the end and the beginning of the world. This address implicates not only those in Hexian but those in its peripheries—figures of invasion and domination, including foreign researchers like myself that the medium Zheng Yulan from the introduction would call "propagandists." To see like a medium is thus also to surrender one's own sense of self-knowing and to be rewritten by the other.

Thinking back also brings me to the world of academic psychiatry, where I encountered the ambivalence of culture in the contemporary. Back to the conference hall in Shanghai, where psychiatrists and psychologists pondered the incorporation of culture into the field of mental health in a time of social change. Formally linked through national-level policy decisions to the network of state-run psychiatric hospitals across provincial, city, and county levels, the patients and families I encountered at the psychiatric ward in Hexian felt at once near and far with relation to the concerns of academic mental health.

The nearness is marked by the distance: the train ride separating the two scenes is a reminder of the rural-urban difference produced under conditions of market reform, by the geographic splitting produced by diverging imaginaries of Maoist and reform eras. It is partly this symbolic history, in which the rural was first valorized as a force of revolutionary futurism, then diminished to a space of land-locked backwardness, that forms the landscape for the contemporary "social change" the academics and clinicians spoke of. At the same time distance is evident in the differential forms through which the cultural question manifests. Among the urban clinicians and scholars, efforts at reincorporating culture into psychological theory often pass through schematized renderings of such concepts as Confucian moderation. In the rural clinic ghosts and deities—the other side of "tradition"—seem to enter without a proper place to go, hovering between modern vocabularies of psychosis and superstition. Yet they also find simultaneous or overlapping spaces of enunciation, at times from within the ward.

In the clinic "moderation" arises through the "maybe" and the "both" on the part of patients and families, challenging the possibility of analytic finality in the epistemological and ontological status of madness. To return to the musing of one patient, how is one to know the origin of one's own affliction, if both spirits and psychiatric disorders act similarly to delude? Somewhat like the "epistemological double register" of those who are religious in a secular world described by T. M. Luhrmann (2012, 372), though diverging from the centrality of sincere faith in the Christian context there, many I met at the hospital and elsewhere approached the otherworldly through a zone between belief and doubt, marked by the phrase "[one] can't *not* believe but also can't *fully* believe" *(buneng buxin ye buneng quanxin)*. It is a sensibility more resonant with an "ontological pluralism" (Aulino forthcoming) that does not prioritize the production of mutual exclusions or a singular reality that can be known and mapped.

Moreover, for many in Hexian, psychiatric and spiritual afflictions often operate in tandem. Vulnerability in the body and psyche invites the entry of demonic entities, which in turn gradually drive one mad through their duplicity and duplication and, with time, chronically wear away at neural capacities. If psychiatric discourse was meant to displace the world of so-called superstition by proclaiming the ontological illegitimacy of ghosts and deities, ghosts and deities in turn take up psychiatric discourse for their own purposes, hiding behind the language of psychiatry while continually afflicting those who may eventually wind up in the ward.

Meanwhile, conditions of the yin realm are described as inextricable from the times—the impossibilities and fractures facing intergenerational ties, the sense of dissolving filial piety, the strains of labor outmigration. For the mediums a resurgence of psychiatric afflictions comes in the wake of the Chairman's departure. With the collapse of sovereign guarantee, demonic entities once kept at bay return to induce madness among a sea of humans who have lost moral ground.

Amid the entanglements of contemporary paradox, of a world at once too much and not enough, the ward at times becomes a space of fleeting respite. This is not to claim the psychiatric unit as a desirable destination, but, not unlike other inpatient hospital spaces, there is an evocation of needed rest and care—kin and neighbors arrive with gifts of food, and sons and daughters return home from offices and factories to sit by the bedside, watching the IV, drip by drip, ensuring the liquid rotation doesn't cease. And it is here, fleetingly, that the patients, families, and psychiatrists live out the conundrums of the times together, knowing full well there is no quick fix to what faces everyone outside the walls of the ward.

I cannot say whether these scenes, at the hospital, the temple square, or beyond, have the capacity to make way for a hearing of the sort that Michel Foucault announced to be foregone. But it does seem that madness as a question of truth beyond psychiatry is not lost on the mediums or the psychiatrists in Hexian. The psychiatrists in the county clinic share the world of their patients as well as the world of global mental health. They speak skeptically of fully biological or individual accounts even as they prescribe daily doses, describing instead those who carry the burdens of their families, falling ill from accumulations of anger circulating through troubled relations. The symptom in this sense does not speak merely in the service of reason but also to the pain of fractured collectivities facing an impasse of the times.

The mediums, having been written out of modern religious and medical legitimacy, continue to address madness in their consultations and ritual repertoires. Symptoms, for the mediums, are not merely indications of biological truth or psychiatric reason but signs of cosmopolitical disarray. Possessed bodies and disturbed dreams link the present with its hauntings, reinvesting the most local of geographies with significance across national, world-historical, and cosmic scales.

Recalling Wu Dongliang, the foreign-educated artist-entrepreneur in Shenzhen who informed me that nothing would come of my journey to Henan—that such remnants of the past as mediumship are not to be found in China today—I think about what he would say of those such as Xu Liying, Zheng Yulan, and Wang from the temple square. They are surely not quite the figures he imagined, not quite the subjects of traditional religion I should be looking for, not quite shamans (see Pedersen 2011). As discussed at the beginning of this book, rather than a space of possibility or tradition, Henan Province in postreform years evokes a sense of rural abjection and cultural evacuation in the national imaginary—once the ancient center of the Chinese cultural-cosmological universe, now a petrified and petrifying core to be purged from new formulations of a cultural China. Lips tightened at its mention before my departure—"It is not really a good place." Eyebrows raised once I returned—"Quite the feat." What, then, is the possibility of writing such a place, without its reincorporation into more of the same? And, between the risk of betrayal and what Zheng Yulan called my duty as a propagandist, how is one to proceed? I cannot pretend to answer. It seems that I can, as she put it, only walk forward; there is no retreat.

Given the reverberations of twentieth-century dreamworlds and catastrophes, the mediums in Hexian are among the inheritors of its many specters. Alongside the possibility of radical openness afforded by spectrality, the spectral here is also tethered to a collapse of the cosmocratic mythologic and the demands of its ghosts. Despite Chinese and Western intellectual tendencies to focus on the excesses of the Cultural Revolution as emblematic of the Maoist years, most of those I met in Hexian spoke with reverence for the Chairman and spoke of the Maoist era as a time of dignity and virtue despite material scarcity.

To the mediums, it is precisely the sidelining by a world of market advance that leaves those within Hexian the rare and the righteous. If "the China of China" is a place of symbolic self-negation for those trapped between the impossibilities of a barred tradition and full foreign assimilation, mediumship in Hexian transforms this negation between Maoist languages and marginalized repertoires of practices deemed "superstitious," carrying within it this history of abjection. The figure of the poor peasant holds on to its older ethicopolitical status according to Maoist class ranking, registering its devaluation in the post-Mao world as a site of struggle against the corruption of the times. Together activating messianic elements of a socialist teleology and a Maitreyan Buddhist eschatology, they invert the symbolic geography of a spectralized rural, placing Hexian at the center of a cosmopolitical future.

It is a practice of remaking time, of shifting the mark for the end of history, thereby also inverting the geography of value claimed by current national and global discourses and economies. In this sense, I might respond to Wu Dongliang, that there are mediums in China today, but indeed not mediums of the imagined past. Those like Zheng Yulan, Xu Liying, and Wang are mediums of the historical present—of multiple temporalities that collide in the present—recrafting ever-shifting terms, remaining on guard. They engage the world of lost gods, vengeful ghosts, and duplicitous humans, receiving the divine and demonic with an eye toward revolutionary horizons.

. . .

A few days before I leave Hexian, I catch sight of Xu Liying, sitting by herself at the edge of the temple square, with a small bag of foodstuffs and a pile of sunflower seeds. It has been months since her discharge from the hospital. We chat for a bit, then bid each other farewell. As I walk away, she goes back to work, chanting under her breath, killing ghosts, continuing to struggle for the revolution. But when the revolution will reach completion, no one knows, not even she. It is not for us to know.

FIGURE 2. Cartography of loss. Stitching with neon yellow thread on red fabric, from the temple square in Hexian. In the center is the character *zhong* (middle), shared by Zhongguo (Middle Kingdom) and Zhongyuan (Central Plain). Photo by the author.

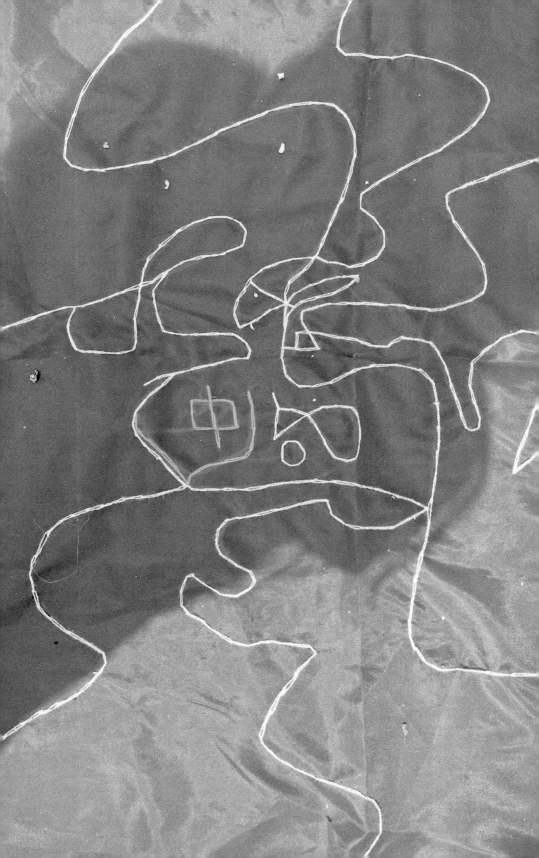

ACKNOWLEDGMENTS

I thank first and foremost those in Hexian. I cannot do justice to what they have gifted me in time, thought, and unspoken lessons. Deepest thanks go to Cai Huiqing, Li Hanwei, and their family, who generously hosted me, sharing company, conversation, and meals with me, engaging me in spite of my differences. Zheng Yulan helped me understand the stakes of this work through her initial invitation and warning, for which I am grateful. Xu Liying brought me into an entire world through the space of the ward, patiently bearing my questions. Wang and many others at the temple square shared not only words and lived concepts with me but an existential space of dwelling day after day, facing the abyss of life and sociality with eyes toward the horizon. Dr. Yuan and the other psychiatrists at the hospital were incredibly kind in supporting my work. Tan Suzhen, An Mei, An Ling, Xia Peizhi, Wang Weihong, Liu Shuhua, Guo Hongjun, Liang Ming, and others I met in the ward shared with me their hopes and concerns, at a moment when things were, to say the least, not so easy. To all those in Hexian, I can only hope that in my rendering, a shattered mirror, they might find a fragment faithful to their visions and struggles.

My gratitude also goes to all those in Shenzhen, Shanghai, and Beijing—friends, scholars, clinicians, interlocutors—who, each in their own way, inspired the questions that have given shape to this work. I have kept them and their words in mind, returning to them across different moments for illumination. For the sake of anonymity, I am not naming those throughout China who have helped me along the way. I can only say that my gratitude is not scalable by the length of words here and, in its brevity, is immense.

This book grew out of my doctoral dissertation in the joint program in medical anthropology at the University of California, Berkeley, and the University of California, San Francisco. Stefania Pandolfo, so much more than an advisor, saw the contours and drives of this project before I could. To her I owe an entire way of tending toward a work, a life, a world, along with a political-poetic insistence to never forget why it is that we do what we do, even if we cannot fully understand. Liu Xin manages to turn the world upside down with his wry wit, all the while carrying the weight of history and thinking on his shoulders. He taught me how to read, and although I will never meet the task he set forth for himself and for his students, in him, I now understand what it is to be a scholar. Mark Csikszentmihalyi generously took me on, with openness to the peculiarities of my efforts. He has shown a warmth, kindness, and depth so rare, which in and of itself is a lesson in living. In that kindness resides a broad mind, which helped better my work. Finally, I would have lost my way at many crossroads without Vincanne Adams. She has been an exemplary guide—structuring, buoying, scaffolding. Her cogent counsel and precious encouragement gave shape and momentum to this project when they were most needed.

There are many others whom I have learned from in Berkeley and San Francisco, in particular, Nancy Scheper-Hughes, Aihwa Ong, Alexei Yurchak, Cori Hayden, Mariane Ferme, Lawrence Cohen, Pheng Cheah, Robert Ashmore, and Ian Whitmarsh, who always demanded that we be true to our curiosity. Among the staff, my thanks go to Kathleen Van Sickle, Tom Bottomley, Carolyn Frazier, Frances Bright, and, in particular, Ned Garrett, hoaxing students into tranquility with his curative nonchalance.

Samuele Collu has been there for it all. His friendship lit up these years and brought an oceanic dimension to the work at hand. Peter Skafish has been an astute companion in thinking through many worlds. Michael D'Arcy, Jason Price, and Jerry Zee offered forms of siblinghood and support for which I am grateful. Thanks go to my lovely cohort: Himali Dixit, Andrew Halley, Callie Maidhof, Rachel Niehuus, Carolyn Sufrin, Marlee Tichenor, Rosalynn Vega, and especially Jeremy Soh, for solidarity and for his depth of thought across registers. All those in the dissertation seminars led by the keen and tireless Nancy Scheper-Hughes gave generous readings of the initial drafts of what would eventually become the chapters of this book. They include, aside from those mentioned elsewhere, Alissa Bernstein, Rachel Ceasar, Sam Dubal, Ugo Edu, Ruth Goldstein, Noémie Merleau-Ponty, and Martha Stroud. Those in the Haas Junior Scholars Program in East Asian Studies helped me see important resonances across time and space. They are, aside from those mentioned elsewhere, Matthew Berry, Jesse Chapman, Paulina Hartono, James Lin, William Ma, Jeannette Ng, Sharon Sanderovitch, Jonathan Tang, Yunling Wang, Jesse Watson, Trenton Wilson, Linh Vu, and Yueni Zhong.

I would not have had the privilege of this journey without the initial encouragement and mentorship of Robert Lemelson and Douglas Hollan at the University of

California, Los Angeles, who introduced me to psychological anthropology and convinced me it was possible to pursue my own questions through it. They guided me through my research in Shenzhen with patient support and wisdom, which gave rise to the encounters that would later inspire this project.

Between my doctoral work and this book, it was a gift to have participated in the Mind and Spirit Project at Stanford University, which gave me room to engage a set of different but related questions. Thanks go to Tanya Luhrmann for insisting that I be more unapologetic in conveying my thoughts and for showing me what it is to tenaciously pursue a question. Cristine Legare offered new ways to approach problems with systematicity and openness toward the unexpected. The vivacious crew was like family: Felicity Aulino, Josh Brahinsky, John Dulin, Rachel Smith, plus Vivian Dzokoto, Nikki Ross, and Kara Weisman. Double thanks go to Felicity, who has been a crucial source of sustenance and laughter, and a sharp eye when needed. At the University of Amsterdam, where the last phase of rewriting was completed, I am tremendously grateful to Esther Peeren and Hanneke Stuit for their insightful comments and critical support. Lélia Tavakoli Farsooni, Tjalling Valdés Olmos, and Anke Bosma have animated my work with their companionship.

Hoon Song saw the spirit of this work and offered suggestions so crystalline that they bordered on the visionary. Stuart Strange gave a thorough and incisive reading of this text for which I am deeply grateful. Jason Price offered pivotal interventions in the final stages. Angelantonio Grossi was crucial in helping me round up the work. Nick Bartlett extended generous encouragement and feedback. Michael Puett has been a vitalizing source of inspiration. Many thanks go to others who have commented on or otherwise supported parts of this work in various forms and stages, helping me improve along the way: Elizabeth Bromley, Robert Desjarlais, Stephan Feuchtwang, Vanessa Fong, Byron Good, Mary-Jo DelVecchio Good, Janis Jenkins, Andrew Jones, Emily Xi Lin, Bessie Liu, Lisa Stevenson, Deborah Thomas, Jason Throop, and Dag Yngvesson. Much appreciation goes to Reed Malcolm at the University of California Press, who saw something in this project early on and has made this as smooth of a process as can be. Thanks also go to Susan Silver for her meticulous copyediting, Victoria Baker for her rigorous and collaborative indexing, Janine Baer for her careful proofreading, Archna Patel for her timely support, and Tom Sullivan, Emilia Thiuri, Aimée Goggins, and many others at UC Press for ushering this book into being.

This undertaking relied in different phases on the generous support of the Berkeley Fellowship, the Power Award, the National Science Foundation Graduate Research Fellowships Program, the Mellon/ACLS Dissertation Completion Fellowship, the Haas Junior Scholars Program in East Asian Studies, the UC Berkeley Dean's Normative Time Fellowship, and the George A. DeVos Memorial Award for Outstanding Graduate Student Research. Thanks go to all the staff and reviewers whose time this depended on.

Immeasurable thanks go to the kindred spirits without whom the world would feel less habitable: to Yuliya, who has been with me through it all, for decades now, and never stops questioning; to Carrie, for her inspiration across our many manifestations across that same stretch; to Ziska, who brought radiance to the joys and pains we shared these years; to Mike, who anchors me from a distance; and to those in the Great White North, whose shared leaning toward life at the edges of the world give me a sense of home. I send infinite gratitude to those who have patiently, profoundly sustained me, across parallel universes. Finally, there is Drew, whose grounding presence made this all possible and who has shown me what it is to care.

Everything goes to my family—my mother, my father, and my grandmother. To them I add my aunts, uncle, great-aunt, and great-uncle, who have offered me harbor across the years. It is for them I do, for them I try, even if not quite in the ways they had imagined.

NOTES

PROLOGUE

1. Here I am thinking with Laplanche (1999) on psychoanalytic notions of deferred action and his reformulation of Freud's "afterwardsness" in terms of the desires and demands of the third, reencountered across lapses of time. When thought alongside mediumship, afterwardsness offers a translational bridge for pondering nonhuman desires and temporalities beyond human knowing, which carry a prophetic quality of what is yet to come. What mediumship makes differently available conceptually is the crossing of beings beyond a single earthly lifespan, such that reencounters might draw a link across lives and realms. Across these articulations a zone opens up between retroaction and prognostication, contingency and destiny.

2. As Simpson puts it, to contend with such incidents is to consider how ethnography might take up refusal generatively, as the revealing of "a stance, a principle, a historical narrative," while keeping in mind who benefits from this anthropological need (2014, 107). See also the collection of papers in *Cultural Anthropology* on "Theorizing Refusal," addressing what one is *not willing to give up* to remain on good terms with particular forms of recognition and twisted reciprocation (McGranahan 2016).

3. Some from both within and outside of China raised this possibility when I relayed this incident: that minimizing engagement with a foreign researcher was a case of self-protection vis-à-vis the illegitimacy of popular religion under a secular autocratic state. While this could certainly be part of the picture, to take repressive state power as the only irreducible element in such multidimensional scenes flattens out the cosmology as mere representations of and responses to human politics. This would enact a severing of human production from cosmic unfoldings that, in my reading, misrecognizes the mediums' engagements with the political.

INTRODUCTION

1. Hexian is a pseudonym for a largely agricultural county in Henan Province. *He* here means river (shared by Henan, lit. "south of the river"). *Xian* is the term for county (a different Chinese character than the spirit entity *xian* discussed later, with the same transliteration).

2. An ethnography that engages the multiple realms of those in Hexian requires the imagination of the reader, in which those on both sides of the text are understood to live in worlds of doubt, including at times a mutual doubt targeted at the other. The peasant, as Favret-Saada (1980) puts it, is neither credulous nor backward, as the self-comforting myths of the scholar have often implied. See Desjarlais on the "phantasmography" as an anthropology attuned to the imaginary (2018, viii). See Price (2016) on the potential of prefiguration and engagements with texts that move beyond presumed legibility.

3. Anagnost (2006) adopts this phrase from Yan Hairong's (2003) discussion of rural labor migration in China. Yan in turn borrows it from Spivak's (2000) work on the spectralization of "the so-called rural," in an urbanist teleology inherited partly from Marx's accounts of land and labor and the subsequent invisibility of "the rural" despite its centrality to global capitalism.

4. Here I am thinking of Laplanche's (1999) elaboration of "afterwardsness" in psychoanalysis, discussed further in chapter 3.

5. See, for example, Hall and Ames (1995); Kaptchuk (2000); Nisbett (2003); and Descola (2005).

6. See Puett's (2014) discussion of the fragmentary and pluralistic in early Chinese thought on the cosmos and their later misreadings.

7. When I asked mediums in Hexian about souls, they at times evoked the notion of multiple souls belonging to each human, common in Chinese religious thought in various iterations (see Harrell 1979; Yü 1987). But in common usage they did not often mention the multiplicity of the soul.

8. Some similarities with formal colonization include foreign territorial enclaves outside the full jurisdiction of the Chinese state, extraterritorial jurisdiction that placed particular foreign nationals outside of the reach of Chinese law, forcible interventions in Chinese political and economic affairs, monopoly clauses in treaties, and higher education run by foreign missionaries (Osterhammel 1986). Some differences from formal colonization include the distribution of spheres of influence across multiple foreign powers rather than a single colonial power and the seeming continuity of linguistic integrity ("seeming" here points to the radical transition from classical to modern Chinese in spite of shared written characters).

9. See Mullaney and others (2012) for an account of the production of the Han ethnicity and Callahan (2009) for the discursive interplay of civilizational pride and national humiliation mobilized in Chinese identity politics and foreign policy. See Paul Cohen (2010) for a critique of the undue focus of Western historians on the West's influence on Chinese history.

10. *Kanxiang* is also used in Zhao County in Hebei Province to refer to the practice of spirit mediums at the Water Goddess Temple. There three sticks of incense are held in the hand of the medium, in contrast to the batch of twenty to thirty sticks placed in the censer in Hexian (Overmyer 2009, 85).

11. Here I refer to international mental health rather than global mental health, as there remained a strong sense of the politics of national health and the production of national health statistics at that time. See Adams (2016) on the shift from postwar, postcolonial international health development to global health. Whereas the former centered on the unit of the nation-state as a critical response to the imperial reach of colonial medicine, the latter imagines a new transcendence of national, bilateral, and multilateral politics altogether, through new ways of counting—through truly global metrics.

12. This is not to suggest that multiple dimensions of the self do not coexist in and across such boundaries. As Hollan (1992) describes, autonomous approaches to the self are present in contexts assumed in the academic literature to be relationally oriented and vice versa. See also Whitmarsh and Roberts (2016) on the latent religious logics carried within purportedly secular selves.

13. In the writing of ethnography, there is no neutral ground (Clifford and Marcus 1986), and every text risks a production of effects at once overdetermined and unforeseen. Here an encounter that would lead to reflections on the social and political origins of suffering concurrently produced evidence deployed in the crafting of a pharmaceutical self (Jenkins 2011), amid historical forces of political and economic interest (S. Lee 2002).

14. See Lee and Kleinman's (2002) refutation of Munro's characterization of psychiatric abuse in China and Munro's response (2002b).

15. See Oakes (1998) on tourism and ethnic minority identity in China, and Comaroff and Comaroff (2009) on the commodification of ethnicity at large in a neoliberal age.

16. Moral moods, as Throop (2014) puts it, often extend in duration beyond particular morally salient events and moments. Here a sense of loss seems to reverberate across eras near and far.

17. See, for example, debates between Qingping Liu (2007) and Guo (2007) on whether filial piety is a source of morality or corruption.

18. Here, I am thinking of U.S. missionary Arthur Smith's damning diagnostic in *Chinese Characteristics*, in which he argues that China, and the Chinese village in particular, lacks rationality, conscience, and character and that its "manifest needs" can be summarized by a "single imperative need"—that of Christian purification (1894, 168). Many of Smith's condemnations are inherited in the texts discussed here.

19. In Eberhard's (1965) survey of Chinese regional stereotypes taken in 1964, Henanese were described as straight, honest, sincere, mannered, frugal, and gentle, though with a violent temper. The survey was conducted mostly among college students in Taiwan with parents from various regions of the mainland, implying the generation that departed the mainland around the time of the Communist Revolution. This points to the possibility that the caricatures described here are indeed collected effects of Maoist and reform histories.

CHAPTER 1

1. Due to Ban Wang's attempt to traverse the ongoing tensions surrounding the translation of terms across authors on the one hand and his own concepts of history and memory on the other, multiple and at times contradictory usages of the term *history* are employed across his text. Here I refer specifically to his suggestion that "the question of trauma . . . has a significant role to play in the memory-history nexus. . . . Trauma underlies the crisis of

history writing" (2004, 8–9). With regard to the 1980s, Wang writes, "Trauma constitutes the biggest stumbling block and the greatest challenge to rewriting and making sense of the past in modern China. It is also a powerful cataclysm for the shift from history to memory" (114).

2. Anderson (1990) uses terms such as *disenfranchised, disadvantaged,* and *underclass* rather than the *subaltern.*

3. Here Anagnost (1997) cites Barlow's (1991) phrase "localization of the sign."

4. The term *newspeak* was coined in George Orwell's *1984,* originally published in 1949 (2013), the year of Chinese Communist Liberation, as the controlled language of a fictional totalitarian state.

5. Ban Wang himself tends to use the pairing and distinction between *history* and *memory* rather than the term *subjectivity* in his own analytic work. Nonetheless, the question of subjectivity remains relevant, as he writes of the 1980s "root search" *(xungen)* literature: "In the ruins of communist ideology and collectivism, the mere programmatic assertion of a humanistic subjectivity and sensibility would not recover the experience of romantic individuality. . . . The past no longer provided intelligible clues to the present; the sense of history was not available for making affective and ethical links between members of a community" (2004, 105–6). Here I take subjectivity not as a given but as a question posed by history, memory, and trauma.

6. Kleinman notes that the lack of association between wrong political thinking and neurasthenia during the Cultural Revolution was surprising, given the previous campaign against neurasthenia during the Great Leap Forward as an epidemic among "mind workers": intellectuals, including office workers, teachers, and students (1980, 155).

7. Born of British desire for improved trade routes amid the Opium Wars (1839–60), railway construction was once the site of fierce contestation, viewed as infrastructure provision for foreign imperial expansion. While initial opposition led to the Chinese destruction of the first British-built railway less than a year after its completion in 1876, Qing-era policy shifted by 1889, resulting in approximately six thousand miles of tracks by the end of the dynasty. Offered a century later in the Shanghai Railway Museum as evidence of Qing "fatuity and blindness" to the merits of modernization, the history of initial refusal had been restaged as obsolete (X. Wu 2009).

8. In a 1906 translation of the *Communist Manifesto,* the term *proletarians* ("The proletarians have nothing to lose but their chains") was translated into *pingmin* (common people), following the Japanese neologism for proletariat. The Chinese translator noted that the Chinese word for *worker* would not include laboring peasants, unlike *pingmin* (Spence 1990, 260).

9. This comes after a period of Nationalist and Communist cooperation, in which Communist agents were sent to peasant organizations ahead of the army, assisting them in weakening warlord-supporting landlords, followed by a military sweep by Nationalist troops (Karl 2010, 30).

10. The assumption of alignment between class and psychological-political inclination has been critiqued by many and is not my focus here. Rather, I trace the coalescence of value and moral-political significance in the figure of the peasant.

11. In *Futures Past* Koselleck (2004) describes an asymmetrical relationship between what he calls *experience* and what he calls *expectation.* Whereas experience is the past made present—events that can be recalled or preserved unconsciously in "alien" form, expecta-

tion is the future made present—that which is not yet experienced but anticipated and to be revealed. Different modalities of relation and tension between the two, for Koselleck, is what constitutes divergent forms of historical time, one superimposed on another. Any given present, as Tribe (2004) writes in his translator's introduction, is concurrently a former future.

CHAPTER 2

1. The eight trigrams *(bagua)* is a hexagram-based divinatory technique for mapping cosmological correspondences between elements, cardinal directions, seasons, kin relations, and other attributes, subsequent versions of which were later employed in the *Yijing* (also known as the *I Ching*, or *Book of Changes*). See Zhan (2016) for a discussion of contemporary engagements with eight trigrams in nonofficial Daoism and Chinese medicine as "cosmic experiments."

2. See Naquin's (1976) description of White Lotus not as a monolithic organization but rather as smaller scattered groups identified with the name by the state for the sake of governance. In the case of Zhu Yuanzhang, despite the initial centrality of the Maitreyan tradition to the legitimacy of the new dynasty, Zhu harshly suppressed so-called White Lotus groups after his rise to power. Nonetheless, the groups continued underground and raised provocations during Zhu's own reign and beyond (Shek 1990).

3. Some references, such as the county gazetteer and the locally published booklet described later, have been omitted from the reference list for the sake of anonymity.

4. Thanks go to Stuart Earle Strange for encouraging an exploration of the square as public space.

5. Similarly, as Wagner notes of Mao's mausoleum, "the emperors had been embalmed and entombed; the revolutionaries were embalmed and exhibited," starting with the planned crystal coffin of Sun Yat-sen (1992, 392).

6. The original Chinese line is *Weida de Maozedong sixiang yongfang guangmang; Xiongcaidalüe zhen tianxia, fenggongweiji shidai sang.*

7. While temple pilgrimage has had a long history in China and dates back to pre-Buddhist times, pilgrimage had not been a central metaphor when compared with other religious traditions. Buddhism introduced new languages and geographies of pilgrimage through encounters with pre-Buddhist Chinese temples and mountainous sites. But pilgrimage practices were by no means limited to Buddhism proper and crossed official and unofficial religious traditions, monastic and lay life, literati and illiterati (Naquin and Yü 1992).

8. See the introduction for a further elaboration of how I use the term *spirit medium* in this book.

9. Chu (2010) also finds this phrasing among ritual participants she met in Fujian, but she emphasizes the rearticulations of "doing superstition" as congruent with modern progress and mobility (rather than backwardness), while my encounters at the temple square in Hexian differed in tenor. This is not to say it could not be used in both senses under different circumstances in one place.

10. If the tongue-in-cheek reappropriations of Mao's words and images in urban pop culture rings contrary to more serious engagements with his cosmopolitical authority at the

temple square, Taussig reminds us that there is a certain "confluence of the official with the comic that makes kitsch an appropriate aesthetic for the magic of the state" (1997, 94).

11. The "yard" refers to *yuanzi*, which carried a significance well captured in Xin Liu's work in rural Shaanxi, the westerly neighbor of Henan: "*Yuanzi* is what one possesses. As an old man, whose brother had left the community, once said: 'I do not know what I should do. I cannot leave this place, because my *yuanzi* is here. My brother has asked me several times to move to the city where he lives, but I cannot simply leave. What about my *yuanzi*?'" (2000, 39)

12. The original Chinese phrase is *Mao zhuxi dangjia de shihou.*

13. See, for example, Granet (1975), Keightley (1978), Weber (1951), A. Wolf (1974), Freedman (1958), and Ahern (1973).

14. See, for example, Anagnost (1994), Chau (2006), Dean (2003), Duara (1991), Feuchtwang (2010), and M. Yang (2000). The arguments of each of these authors are complex and beyond quick summary, but, as Weller (1994) has noted, the terms of such debates often rely on the notion of the empirical demonstrability of resistance. And, of course, Weber's (1951) work is also inspired by the puzzle of modern capitalism, but there the analytical relation between religion and economy leans instead toward spiritual-religious conditions for the development of capitalism.

15. See Ryang (2012) on the distinction between Kim Il Sung's title of "Great Leader" (Suryeong), which Kim Jong Il, the son, the "Dear Leader" (Chidoja or Ryeongdoja), will never hold, as there is only one possible Suryeong.

16. The original Chinese sentence is *Hengsao yiqie niuguisheshen.*

17. Questions surrounding deification were of course not absent in Christian traditions. See, for example, Christensen and Wittung (2008) and Russell (2004).

18. Although Deng Xiaoping articulated this phrase before Mao's death and his own rule, the slogan came to mark the ethos of the postreform era.

19. At the time of my visit, sixty renminbi was the equivalent of almost ten U.S. dollars and was considered exorbitant, especially for those who needed to pay frequent visits for ritual and cultivation purposes, in contrast with those who visited only occasionally on major holidays or for purposes of tourism. On the first and fifteenth of the lunar month, as well as officially recognized holidays such as Chinese New Year, the ticket price was discounted to twenty renminbi. And some who knew gatekeeping staff entered ticketless with a quiet mutual nod. Nonetheless, many who frequented the temple often decided to simply remain on the temple square.

20. See Strange's (2016) work in Suriname on how pain and protracted anguish can act as messages about one's essential multiplicity in mediumship practices.

21. For Mbembe (2003), thinking alongside Lacan (2007), ghostly sovereignty can also be considered through the notion of the mirror—an apparitional double of the *I* and its shadow, evoking at once the *marvelous* power of the image and the power of *terror*, opened up by a play of proximity and distance, the *luminosity* in between that capacitates distribution and partial visibility. I am of course not saturating the range of reflections on spectrality here. See, for example, Sprinker (1999) for an early set of responses to *Specters of Marx* and Blanco and Peeren (2013) for an overview and collection of writings on spectrality in contemporary cultural theory.

CHAPTER 3

1. In Hexian, cardinal directions are used to refer to a wide range of spatial relations, regardless of whether one is conjuring their cosmic dimension. Designations of north, south, east, and west apply to not only geographies and travel routes but also the location of everyday objects, including parts of the body. In cosmic terms the east is superior to the west, and the north to the south.

2. In Hexian incense money is always laid on the table before a session begins. The amount given is usually volunteered rather than specified and often ranges from ten to fifty renminbi at the village home altar sessions I saw. Compensation in gratitude for the completion of ritual assistance *(huanyuan)* is more likely to be specified and is higher than the initial incense money, often ranging from the low to high hundreds of renminbi. More elaborate rituals or ones that require a medium to visit one's home may reach into the thousands.

3. In contrast to South China and other regions that often use three sticks of incense, most mediums I met in Hexian use a whole bundle, between twenty to thirty sticks. No explanation was offered for this distinction, except from one medium who adopts the southern method after having lived there for some years and simply deems the full batch incorrect and wasteful.

4. Feuchtwang (2010) and Chau (2006) have also discussed this invitational aspect of incense.

5. Honan is the Wade-Giles romanization of Henan, used before the now common pinyin system.

6. Debates arose in the 1960s around "peasant nationalism" amid U.S. interest over why China "fell" to Communism. Framing the peasantry as a previously politically illiterate mass, Johnson posits that it was not "totalitarian instruments of mass manipulation that originally led the Chinese masses into their pact with the Communist elite; it was, rather, the effects of the war and the national awakening that the war induced" (1962, 11). Against Johnson, Gillin (1967) responds, based particularly on prewar materials, that the Communist Party's revolutionary aims and programs were central to their success, rather than the sole impact of anti-Japanese sentiments.

7. Cai Huiqing and I folded the gold ingots across the next several days. Such spirit money *(yinzhi,* lit. "yin paper") is transmitted from the visible human realm to the invisible spirit realm through burning. The reams *(dao)* of yellow spirit money are often said to be used for deities, while more plain, undyed spirit money was said to be used for the deceased. Metallic gold and silver spirit money may be requested by both. When folding and preparing yin spirit money, yang (living human) money—one hundred RMB bills with the face of Mao—are at times pressed onto each slice of spirit money, imprinting value from this world into the next. See Blake (2011) on the burning of paper money as chiasm—as the moment of coincidence and realization between yin and yang worlds.

8. In *Taiwan Min Su* (The customs of Taiwan), Yingtao Wu (1970) describes *tuomeng* as "'dream messages' . . . in which spirits and Buddhas utilize dreams to make revelations either overtly or covertly" (cited in L. Thompson 1988, 75). Writing of rural Shanxi, Zavidovskaya describes *tuomeng* as one method through which deities first reveal their presence to a human: "In many cases, [the deity] speaks to people when they are asleep *(tuomeng)*

and they recognize him" (2012, 184). In Hexian *tuomeng* is used to describe dreams conveyed by both deities and ancestors. Here, though, its potentially deceptive and demonic dimensions come to the fore.

9. Even as mediumship offers vocabularies and techniques for deciphering and attending to spectral collisions, such "quasi-events" may open up a plural universe of doubts beyond one of unified religious-cosmological certainty (Da Col and Humphrey 2012). While I focus here on the traversal of histories major and minor, see also the capacity of not-quite-eventual occurrences to produce shared conditions (Zigon 2015), amplify into events (Povinelli 2011), and make worlds (Tsing 2015).

10. New Culture and May Fourth debates on modernity and tradition pivoted around discourses of individualism through what Lydia Liu (1995) calls "return graphic loans" of individual *(geren)* and self *(ziwo),* classical Chinese terms that reentered modern Chinese by way of a borrowing and radical reconfiguration of meaning elsewhere, particularly Meiji Japan.

CHAPTER 4

1. Formulated as a twenty-character objective, the New Socialist Countryside policy aimed for advanced production, a rich life, a civilized (local) atmosphere, clean and tidy villages, and democratic management. At the level of policy, the framework introduced a new fiscal system to an otherwise old set of issues: rural regions became entitled to receive transfer payments at the county level from central government subsidies. Ahlers and Schubert (2009) find that both township- and county-level cadres cited the increase in fund transfers as a major determinant of recent increases in average rural per capita household income, alongside cash transfers from migrant workers and funds from nonagricultural work.

2. Promises of a prosperity to come also permeated postreform media and state discourses in the language of *xiaokang,* variously translated as "relatively well off," "moderately prosperous," or the more literal "small well-being." In 2013 President Xi Jinping offered a rhyming couplet reiterating the "comprehensive" dimension of prosperity: *xiaokang bu xiaokang, guanjian kan laoxiang,* which might be glossed less poetically as "whether or not moderate prosperity is reached, look to those from the old hometown" (*Renmin Ribao* 2013). The lynchpin to the national vision of a social order buttressed by the sense of a materially adequate life, by this line of reasoning, is whether one could say the same of rural conditions.

3. As Yunxiang Yan (1999) notes of his work in rural Hebei, Shandong, and Heilongjiang, while the perception of urban superiority was shared across generations, older villagers tended to have accepted urban-rural inequities, whereas younger villagers continued speaking of their dreams and emulated urban styles and ideals of individual independence and happiness. Some of the youth Yan spoke to in the late 1980s and 1990s would be nearly the age of the parents of those I met in Hexian, showing that such languages of dreams and ideals shifted not only with reform but also with positions one inhabited across one's life.

4. See Ratigan (2015) for a discussion of this plan, which was first rolled out in the form of pilot projects beginning in 2003. After the collapse of Maoist-era rural healthcare, and prior to 2003, 90 percent of rural residents were uninsured and at times avoided medical care because of the prohibitively high costs. Two new idioms also arose with this new system, Ratigan writes: "poverty due to illness" and "poverty due to catastrophic illness" (2015, 71).

5. Interestingly, rural-based studies in the initial years of the reform era, in contrast to Yunxiang Yan's (2003) work (based on his residence in the 1970s, then after 1989), seem to offer a different portrait: "The relationships between family members are still very close. . . . The commune system has not undermined the family institution" (Baker 1979, 291). Davis-Friedmann writes, "Patterns of interaction between elderly parents and their adult children continue to show high levels of solidarity" (1983, 103). There may have been differences between earlier and later reform years, contextual circumstances, authorial emphases, or what was shared with the authors.

6. Regardless of one's assessment, it seems that filial relations are increasingly articulated in terms of care and support rather than obedience and obligation. Asymmetries have also transformed along age and gender lines. Daughters seem to have been more involved in their parents' lives, with this care seen as optional rather than obligatory (Ikels 2006). In urban contexts care by grandmothers is seen as a resource in the absence or stead of hired service (Croll 2006). In rural contexts daughters increasingly care for their natal families rather than prioritizing the husband's family according to more classic filial expectations (Y. Yan 1996).

CHAPTER 5

1. The Ten Great Marshals of the People's Liberation Army were conferred in 1955, including Zhu De, Peng Dehuai, Lin Biao, Liu Bocheng, He Long, Chen Yi, Luo Ronghuan, Xu Xiangqian, Nie Rongzhen, and Ye Jianying.

2. See Schaberg's (2005) discussion on *ling* and *ming,* commonly used in conjunction and at times used with nearly identical functions in Western Zhou writings. Whereas *tianming* is discussed as "heavenly command," those in Hexian tend to refer to *ling* and *tianling.*

3. The term in Chinese is *yu wenhua miqie xiangguan de jingshen zhang'ai.* The parallel category is referred to as "culture-bound syndrome" in the fourth edition of the *Diagnostic and Statistical Manual of Mental Disorders* (American Psychiatric Association 2000); "cultural concepts of distress" in the fifth edition (2013); and "culture-specific disorder" in the tenth revision of the *International Statistical Classification of Diseases and Related Health Problems* (World Health Organization 2004).

4. As discussed earlier, *xian* is often translated as "immortals" in the context of Daoism and does not always imply evil. Yet in the accounts of many mediums in Hexian, *xian* signals a class of powerful spirits wont to do harm, including old ghosts and corrupted gods. Even more intensely than others, Xu Liying emphasizes their evil *(e);* thus I translate *xian* as "demon" or "demonic entity" here in accordance with her usage. In Chau's work in Shaanxi, mediums possessed by "immortals" *(daxian)* are referred to as *shenguan* (2006, 54–55). But in his text this does not seem associated with corruption and fakery.

5. The original Chinese is *baiwan xiongshi guodajiang* for a "million-strong mighty army crosses the great stream"; *baiwan fengzi naojinduan* for "a million madmen storm the palace"; and *hengsao yichie niugui sheshen* for "sweep out all cow ghosts and snake gods."

6. The phrase was first uttered in 1962, prior to the reform era, in support of an experimental policy contracting land to individual peasant households, which would later be condemned by Mao (Naughton 1993). But it is taken by many in Hexian and more broadly in

China as a slogan that captures the spirit of the post-Mao market reforms of Deng, regardless of the timing of its initial utterance.

7. See N. Chen (2003) for an ethnographic account of qigong deviation psychosis. For an account of the junction between spirit possession, psychiatric interpretation, and a different history of violence and Communist politics in the context of Indonesia, see Lemelson (2014).

8. Some such manifestations may have arisen in their particular form from the history of colonial encounter itself. Whereas *amok* once marked a war cry of a deliberate, honorable form of enemy assassination or political killing, without an association with madness, in the colonial period of the nineteenth century, reports of *amok* episodes came to be marked by sudden, unpremeditated mass killings undertaken in a dissociated state, followed by subsequent amnesia. By 1893 legislation was passed by the British colonial government to try *amok* subjects in court (Tseng 2006).

9. In the early 1990s efforts to address the cultural dimension in the transition from the *DSM III* to the *DSM IV* ended in a compromised synthesis unsatisfactory to many of its creators: an appendix listing twenty-five culture-bound syndromes following more than seven hundred diagnoses in the main text, which "impl[ied] an ontologic status different from that of psychiatrically relevant phenomena" (Hughes 1998, 417; Mezzich et al. 1999). The suggestion by the appointed expert group on culture to include Western culture-bound syndromes—among them obesity, adolescent turmoil and rebellion, premenstrual tension syndrome, and multiple personality disorder—was disregarded.

10. The original Chinese chapter title is "'*Guishen futi' shi shenme yihuishi?*"

CODA

1. Elder uncle *(dashu)* is an address of respect in this case, not a claim to direct kin relation.

REFERENCES

Abraham, Nicolas, and Maria Torok. 1994. *The Shell and the Kernel: Renewals of Psycho-analysis*. Vol. 1. Translated by Nicholas T. Rand. Chicago: University of Chicago Press.

Adams, Vincanne. 1998. *Doctors for Democracy: Health Professionals in the Nepal Revolution*. Cambridge, UK: Cambridge University Press.

———, ed. 2016. *Metrics: What Counts in Global Health*. Durham, NC: Duke University Press.

Agamben, Giorgio. 2002. "The Time That Is Left." *Epoché: A Journal for the History of Philosophy* 7 (1): 1–14.

Ahern, Emily Martin. 1973. *The Cult of the Dead in a Chinese Village*. Stanford, CA: Stanford University Press.

Ahlers, Anna L., and Gunter Schubert. 2009. "'Building a New Socialist Countryside': Only a Political Slogan?" *Journal of Current Chinese Affairs* 38 (4): 35–62.

American Psychiatric Association. 2000. *Diagnostic and Statistical Manual of Mental Disorders*. 4th ed. Washington, DC: American Psychiatric Association.

———. 2013. *Diagnostic and Statistical Manual of Mental Disorders*. 5th ed. Arlington, VA: American Psychiatric Association.

Anagnost, Ann. 1994. "The Politics of Ritual Displacement." In *Asian Visions of Authority: Religion and the Modern States of East and Southeast Asia*, edited by Charles F. Keyes, Laurel Kendall, and Helen Hardacre, 221–54. Honolulu: University of Hawai'i Press.

———. 1997. *National Past-Times: Narrative, Representation, and Power in Modern China*. Durham, NC: Duke University Press.

———. 2004. "The Corporeal Politics of Quality (Suzhi)." *Public Culture* 16 (2): 189–208.

———. 2006. "Strange Circulations: The Blood Economy in Rural China." *Economy and Society* 35 (4): 509–29.

————. 2008. "From 'Class' to 'Social Strata': Grasping the Social Totality in Reform-Era China." *Third World Quarterly* 29 (3): 497–519.

Anderson, Marston. 1990. *The Limits of Realism: Chinese Fiction in the Revolutionary Period.* Berkeley: University of California Press.

Apter, David E., and Tony Saich. 1998. *Revolutionary Discourse in Mao's Republic.* Cambridge, MA: Harvard University Press.

Asad, Talal. 2003. *Formations of the Secular: Christianity, Islam, Modernity.* Stanford, CA: Stanford University Press.

Aulino, Felicity. Forthcoming. "From Karma to Sin: A Kaleidoscopic Theory of Mind and Christian Experience in Northern Thailand." *Journal of the Royal Anthropological Institute,* n.s., 26.

Baker, Hugh D. R. 1979. *Chinese Family and Kinship.* New York: Columbia University Press.

Barlow, Tani. 1991. "Zhishifenzi [Chinese intellectuals] and Power." *Dialectical Anthropology* 16 (3–4): 209–32.

Barmé, Geremie. 1996. *Shades of Mao: The Posthumous Cult of the Great Leader.* Armonk, NY: Sharpe.

Bartlett, Nicholas. Forthcoming. *Recovering Histories: Life and Labor after Heroin in Reform-Era China.* Oakland: University of California Press.

Bataille, Georges. 1993. *The Accursed Share.* Vols. 2–3. Translated by Robert Hurley. Rev. ed. New York: Zone Books.

Baum, Emily. 2018. *The Invention of Madness: State, Society, and the Insane in Modern China.* Chicago: University of Chicago Press.

Benjamin, Walter. 2007. *Illuminations: Essays and Reflections.* New York: Schocken Books.

Berlant, Lauren. 2008. "Thinking about Feeling Historical." *Emotion, Space and Society* 1 (1): 4–9.

————. 2011. *Cruel Optimism.* Durham, NC: Duke University Press.

Bernstein, Anya. 2013. *Religious Bodies Politic: Rituals of Sovereignty in Buryat Buddhism.* Chicago: University of Chicago Press.

Birrell, Anne. 1993. *Chinese Mythology: An Introduction.* Baltimore: Johns Hopkins University Press.

Blake, C. Fred. 2011. *Burning Money: The Material Spirit of the Chinese Lifeworld.* Honolulu: University of Hawai'i Press.

Blanco, Maria del Pilar, and Esther Peeren, eds. 2013. *The Spectralities Reader: Ghosts and Haunting in Contemporary Cultural Theory.* New York: Bloomsbury Academic.

Bo Yang. 1992. *The Ugly Chinaman and the Crisis of Chinese Culture.* Translated by Don J. Cohn and Jing Qing. Sydney: Allen and Unwin.

Brown, Carolyn T., ed. 1988. *Psycho-Sinology: The Universe of Dreams in Chinese Culture.* Ann Arbor: University of Michigan Asia Program, Woodrow Wilson International Center for Scholars.

Brugger, Bill, and David Kelly. 1990. *Chinese Marxism in the Post-Mao Era.* Stanford, CA: Stanford University Press.

Buck-Morss, Susan. 2002. *Dreamworld and Catastrophe: The Passing of Mass Utopia in East and West.* Cambridge, MA: MIT Press.

Butler, Judith. 2004. *Precarious Life: The Powers of Mourning and Violence.* New York: Verso.

Buyandelger, Manduhai. 2013. *Tragic Spirits: Shamanism, Memory, and Gender in Contemporary Mongolia*. Chicago: University of Chicago Press.

Caldwell, John C. 1976. "Toward a Restatement of Demographic Transition Theory." *Population and Development Review* 2 (3–4): 321–66.

Callahan, William A. 2009. *China: The Pessoptimist Nation*. Oxford: Oxford University Press.

Campany, Robert Ford. 1996. *Strange Writing: Anomaly Accounts in Early Medieval China*. Albany: State University of New York Press.

———. 2003. "On the Very Idea of Religions (in the Modern West and in Early Medieval China)." *History of Religions* 42 (4): 287–319.

Cao Jinqing. 2005. *China along the Yellow River: Reflections on Rural Society*. Translated by Nicky Harman and Ruhua Huang. New York: Routledge.

Carrithers, Michael, Steven Collins, and Steven Lukes, eds. 1985. *The Category of the Person: Anthropology, Philosophy, History*. Cambridge: Cambridge University Press.

Caruth, Cathy. 1996. *Unclaimed Experience: Trauma, Narrative, and History*. Baltimore: Johns Hopkins University Press.

Chakrabarty, Dipesh. 1997. "The Time of History and the Times of Gods." In *The Politics of Culture in the Shadow of Capital*, edited by Lisa Lowe and David Lloyd, 35–60. Durham, NC: Duke University Press.

Chan, Alan Kam-leung, and Sor-hoon Tan, eds. 2004. *Filial Piety in Chinese Thought and History*. New York: Routledge.

Chan, Anita, Richard Madsen, and Jonathan Unger. 2009. *Chen Village: Revolution to Globalization*. 3rd. ed. Berkeley: University of California Press.

Chan, Hok-Lam. 2008. "The 'Song' Dynasty Legacy: Symbolism and Legitimation from Han Liner to Zhu Yuanzhang of the Ming Dynasty." *Harvard Journal of Asiatic Studies* 68 (1): 91–133.

Chan, Margaret. 2006. *Ritual Is Theatre, Theatre Is Ritual: Tang-Ki; Chinese Spirit Medium Worship*. Singapore: Singapore Management University.

Chao, Emily. 1999. "The Maoist Shaman and the Madman: Ritual Bricolage, Failed Ritual, and Failed Ritual Theory." *Cultural Anthropology* 14 (4): 505–34.

Chau, Adam Yuet. 2003. "Popular Religion in Shaanbei, North-Central China." *Journal of Chinese Religions* 31 (1): 39–79.

———. 2006. *Miraculous Response: Doing Popular Religion in Contemporary China*. Stanford, CA: Stanford University Press.

Cheah, Pheng. 2003. *Spectral Nationality: Passages of Freedom from Kant to Postcolonial Literatures of Liberation*. New York: Columbia University Press.

Chen, Nancy N. 2003. *Breathing Spaces: Qigong, Psychiatry, and Healing in China*. New York: Columbia University Press.

Cheng, Chuyuan. 1982. *China's Economic Development: Growth and Structural Change*. Boulder: Westview.

Chow, Nelson. 1991. "Does Filial Piety Exist under Chinese Communism?" *Journal of Aging and Social Policy* 3 (1–2): 209–25.

Christensen, Michael J., and Jeffery A. Wittung. 2008. *Partakers of the Divine Nature: The History and Development of Deification in the Christian Traditions*. Grand Rapids, MI: Baker Academic.

Chu, Julie Y. 2010. *Cosmologies of Credit: Transnational Mobility and the Politics of Destination in China.* Durham, NC: Duke University Press.

Clarke, Adele E., Laura Mamo, Jennifer Ruth Fosket, Jennifer R. Fishman, and Janet K. Shim, eds. 2010. *Biomedicalization: Technoscience, Health, and Illness in the U.S.* Durham, NC: Duke University Press.

Clifford, James, and George E. Marcus. 1986. *Writing Culture: The Poetics and Politics of Ethnography.* Berkeley: University of California Press.

Cohen, Myron L. 1993. "Cultural and Political Inventions in Modern China: The Case of the Chinese 'Peasant.'" *Daedalus* 122 (2): 151–70.

Cohen, Paul A. 2010. *Discovering History in China: American Historical Writing on the Recent Chinese Past.* 2nd ed. New York: Columbia University Press.

Collu, Samuele. 2019. "Refracting Affects: Affect, Psychotherapy, and Spirit Dis-possession." *Culture, Medicine, and Psychiatry* 43 (2): 290–314.

Comaroff, John L., and Jean Comaroff. 2009. *Ethnicity, Inc.* Chicago: University of Chicago Press.

Corin, Ellen. 1998. "Refiguring the Person: The Dynamics of Affects and Symbols in an African Spirit Possession Cult." In *Bodies and Persons: Comparative Perspectives from Africa and Melanesia,* edited by Michael Lambek and Andrew Strathern, 80–102. Cambridge: Cambridge University Press.

———. 2007. "The 'Other' of Culture in Psychosis: The Ex-centricity of the Subject." In *Subjectivity: Ethnographic Investigations,* edited by João Guilherme Biehl, Byron Good, and Arthur Kleinman, 273–314. Berkeley: University of California Press.

Crapanzano, Vincent, and Vivian Garrison, eds. 1977. *Case Studies in Spirit Possession.* New York: Wiley.

Croll, Elisabeth. 1984. "Marriage Choice and Status Groups in Contemporary China." In *Class and Social Stratification in Post-revolution China,* edited by James L. Watson, 175–97. Cambridge: Cambridge University Press.

———. 1994. *From Heaven to Earth: Images and Experiences of Development in China.* London: Routledge.

———. 2006. "The Intergenerational Contract in the Changing Asian Family." *Oxford Development Studies* 34 (4): 473–91.

Csikszentmihalyi, Mark. 2006. *Readings in Han Chinese Thought.* Indianapolis: Hackett.

Da Col, Giovanni, and Caroline Humphrey. 2012. "Introduction: Subjects of Luck; Contingency, Morality, and the Anticipation of Everyday Life." *Social Analysis* 56 (2): 1–18.

D'Arcy, Michael. 2019. "'It Tastes Like Order': Psychotic Evidence for Antipsychotic Efficacy and Medicated Subjectivity." *Ethos* 47 (1): 89–107.

Das, Veena. 2006. *Life and Words: Violence and the Descent into the Ordinary.* Berkeley: University of California Press.

———. 2015. *Affliction: Health, Disease, Poverty.* New York: Fordham University Press.

Davis-Friedmann, Deborah. 1983. *Long Lives: Chinese Elderly and the Chinese Revolution.* Cambridge, MA: Harvard University Press.

Day, Alexander F. 2013. *The Peasant in Postsocialist China: History, Politics, and Capitalism.* Cambridge: Cambridge University Press.

Dean, Kenneth. 2003. "Local Communal Religion in Contemporary South-East China." *China Quarterly* 174:338–58.

De Castro, Eduardo Viveiros. 2014. *Cannibal Metaphysics*. Translated by Peter Skafish. Minneapolis: Univocal.

Deng, Zhong, and Donald J. Treiman. 1997. "The Impact of the Cultural Revolution on Trends in Educational Attainment in the People's Republic of China." *American Journal of Sociology* 103 (2): 391–428.

Derrida, Jacques. 1994. *Specters of Marx: The State of the Debt, the Work of Mourning, and the New International*. Translated by Peggy Kamuf. New York: Routledge.

Descola, Philippe. 2013. *Beyond Nature and Culture*. Translated by Janet Lloyd. Chicago: University of Chicago Press.

Desjarlais, Robert. 2018. *The Blind Man: A Phantasmography*. New York: Fordham University Press.

Dorfman, Diane. 1996. "The Spirits of Reform: The Power of Belief in Northern China." *Positions: East Asia Cultures Critique* 4 (2): 253–89.

Duara, Prasenjit. 1991. "Knowledge and Power in the Discourse of Modernity: The Campaigns against Popular Religion in Early Twentieth-Century China." *Journal of Asian Studies* 50 (1): 67–83.

DuBois, Thomas David. 2005. *The Sacred Village: Social Change and Religious Life in Rural North China*. Honolulu: University of Hawai'i Press.

Du Bois, W. E. B. 1996. *The Souls of Black Folk*. New York: Penguin Books.

Dutch, Steven I. 2009. "The Largest Act of Environmental Warfare in History." *Environmental and Engineering Geoscience* 15 (4): 287–97.

Eberhard, Wolfram. 1965. "Chinese Regional Stereotypes." *Asian Survey* 5 (12): 596–608.

Eliade, Mircea. 1964. *Shamanism: Archaic Techniques of Ecstasy*. Rev. ed. New York: Bollingen Foundation.

Fabian, Johannes. 1983. *Time and the Other: How Anthropology Makes Its Object*. New York: Columbia University Press.

Fang Huirong. 1997. *"Wu Shijian Jing" Yu Shenghuo Shijie Zhong de "Zhenshi": Xicun Nongmin Tudi Gaige Shiqi Shehui Shenghuo de Jiyi* ["Nonevent state" and "truth" in the lifeworld: Memories of the social life of Xicun peasants during the period of land reform]. Beijing: Research Center for Oral History of Social Life, Peking University.

Fanon, Frantz. 2008. *Black Skin, White Masks*. Translated by Richard Philcox. Rev. ed. New York: Grove.

Farquhar, Judith, and Qicheng Zhang. 2005. "Biopolitical Beijing: Pleasure, Sovereignty, and Self-Cultivation in China's Capital." *Cultural Anthropology* 20 (3): 303–27.

———. 2012. *Ten Thousand Things: Nurturing Life in Contemporary Beijing*. Brooklyn: Zone Books.

Favret-Saada, Jeanne. 1980. *Deadly Words: Witchcraft in the Bocage*. New York: Cambridge University Press.

———. 2015. *The Anti-witch*. Chicago: HAU Books.

Fei Xiaotong. 1992. *From the Soil: The Foundations of Chinese Society*. Translated by Gary G. Hamilton and Zheng Wang. Berkeley: University of California Press.

Feuchtwang, Stephan. 2001. *Popular Religion in China: The Imperial Metaphor*. Richmond, Surrey, UK: Curzon.

———. 2010. *The Anthropology of Religion, Charisma and Ghosts: Chinese Lessons for Adequate Theory*. New York: De Gruyter.

Foucault, Michel. 1995. *Discipline and Punish: The Birth of the Prison.* New York: Vintage Books.

———. 2006. *History of Madness.* New York: Routledge.

Freedman, Maurice. 1958. *Lineage Organization in Southeastern China.* London: Athlone.

Freud, Sigmund. 2006. "Mourning and Melancholia." In A. Phillips 2006, 310–26.

Fuchs, Thomas. 2005a. "Delusional Mood and Delusional Perception: A Phenomenological Analysis." *Psychopathology* 38 (3): 133–39.

———. 2005b. "Implicit and Explicit Temporality." *Philosophy, Psychiatry, and Psychology* 12 (3): 195–98.

———. 2013. "Temporality and Psychopathology." *Phenomenology and the Cognitive Sciences* 12 (1): 75–104.

Garcia, Angela. 2010. *The Pastoral Clinic: Addiction and Dispossession along the Rio Grande.* Berkeley: University of California Press.

Gillin, Donald G. 1967. *Warlord: Yen Hsi-Shan in Shansi Province, 1911–1949.* Princeton, NJ: Princeton University Press.

Giordano, Cristiana. 2014. *Migrants in Translation: Caring and the Logics of Difference in Contemporary Italy.* Berkeley: University of California Press.

Goffman, Erving. 1961. *Asylums: Essays on the Social Situation of Mental Patients and Other Inmates.* Garden City, NY: Anchor Books.

Good, Byron J., and Mary-Jo DelVecchio Good. 1981. "The Meaning of Symptoms: A Cultural Hermeneutic Model for Clinical Practice." In *The Relevance of Social Science for Medicine,* edited by Leon Eisenberg and Arthur Kleinman, 165–96. Boston: Dordrecht.

Good, Mary-Jo DelVecchio, Sandra Teresa Hyde, Sarah Pinto, and Byron J. Good, eds. 2008. *Postcolonial Disorders.* Berkeley: University of California Press.

Goossaert, Vincent. 2005. "The Concept of Religion in China and the West." *Diogenes* 52 (1): 13–20.

Goossaert, Vincent, and David Palmer. 2011. *The Religious Question in Modern China.* Chicago: University of Chicago Press.

Gordon, Avery. 1997. *Ghostly Matters: Haunting and the Sociological Imagination.* Minneapolis: University of Minnesota Press.

Granet, Marcel. 1975. *The Religion of the Chinese People.* New York: Harper and Row.

Guldin, Gregory Eliyu. 1997. *Farewell to Peasant China: Rural Urbanization and Social Change in the Late Twentieth Century.* Armonk, NY: Sharpe.

Guo, Qiyong. 2007. "Is Confucian Ethics a 'Consanguinism'?" *Dao: A Journal of Comparative Philosophy* 6:21–38.

Haar, Barend ter. 1992. *The White Lotus Teachings in Chinese Religious History.* Leiden: Brill.

Hall, David L., and Roger T. Ames. 1995. *Anticipating China: Thinking through the Narratives of Chinese and Western Culture.* Albany: State University of New York Press.

Harrell, Stevan. 1979. "The Concept of Soul in Chinese Folk Religion." *Journal of Asian Studies* 38 (3): 519–28.

Hart, Roger. 1999. "From Copula to Incommensurable Worlds." In *Tokens of Exchange: The Problem of Translation in Global Circulations,* edited by Lydia H. Liu, 45–73. Durham, NC: Duke University Press.

He, Zengke. 2000. "Corruption and Anti-corruption in Reform China." *Communist and Post-Communist Studies* 33 (2): 243–70.

Hegel, Robert E. 1988. "Heavens and Hells in Chinese Fictional Dreams." In Brown 1988, 1–10.

Hinton, William. 2008. *Fanshen: A Documentary of Revolution in a Chinese Village*. New York: Monthly Review.

Hollan, Douglas. 1992. "Cross-Cultural Differences in the Self." *Journal of Anthropological Research* 48 (4): 283–300.

Hopper, Kim. 1991. "Some Old Questions for the New Cross-Cultural Psychiatry." *Medical Anthropology Quarterly* 5 (4): 299–330.

Howland, Douglas. 2010. "The Dialectics of Chauvinism: Minority Nationalities and Territorial Sovereignty in Mao Zedong's New Democracy." *Modern China* 37 (2): 170–201.

Hsu, Francis L. K. 1971a. "Filial Piety in Japan and China: Borrowing, Variation and Significance." *Journal of Comparative Family Studies* 2 (1): 67–74.

———. 1971b. "Psychosocial Homeostasis and Jen: Conceptual Tools for Advancing Psychological Anthropology." *American Anthropologist* 73 (1): 23–44.

Huang, Hsuan-Ying. 2015. "From Psychotherapy to Psycho-Boom: A Historical Overview of Psychotherapy in China." *Psychoanalysis and Psychotherapy in China* 1:1–30.

———. 2018. "Untamed *Jianghu* or Emerging Profession: Diagnosing the Psycho-Boom amid China's Mental Health Legislation." *Culture, Medicine and Psychiatry* 42 (2): 371–400.

Huang, Philip C. C. 1995. "Rural Class Struggle in the Chinese Revolution: Representational and Objective Realities from the Land Reform to the Cultural Revolution." *Modern China* 21 (1): 105–43.

Hughes, Charles C. 1998. "The Glossary of 'Culture-Bound Syndromes' in DSM-IV: A Critique." *Transcultural Psychiatry* 35 (3): 413–21.

Hui, Yuk. 2016. *The Question Concerning Technology in China: An Essay in Cosmotechnics*. Falmouth, UK: Urbanomic.

Hung, Wu. 1991. "Tiananmen Square: A Political History of Monuments." *Representations* 132 (1): 84–117.

Ikels, Charlotte. 2006. "Economic Reform and Intergenerational Relationships in China." *Oxford Development Studies* 34 (4): 387–400.

Ivy, Marilyn. 1995. *Discourses of the Vanishing: Modernity, Phantasm, Japan*. Chicago: University of Chicago Press.

Jameson, Fredric. 1991. *Postmodernism, or The Cultural Logic of Late Capitalism*. Durham, NC: Duke University Press.

Jenkins, Janis H. 2011. *Pharmaceutical Self: The Global Shaping of Experience in an Age of Psychopharmacology*. Santa Fe, NM: School for Advanced Research Press.

Jenkins, Janis H., and Robert J. Barrett, eds. 2004. *Schizophrenia, Culture, and Subjectivity: The Edge of Experience*. New York: Cambridge University Press.

Johnson, Chalmers. 1962. *Peasant Nationalism and Communist Power: The Emergence of Revolutionary China*. Stanford, CA: Stanford University Press.

Jordan, David K. 1972. *Gods, Ghosts, and Ancestors: the Folk Religion of a Taiwanese Village*. Berkeley: University of California Press.

Jullien, François. 1995. *The Propensity of Things: Toward a History of Efficacy in China*. New York: Zone Books.

———. 2004. *Detour and Access: Strategies of Meaning in China and Greece*. Cambridge, MA: MIT Press.

Kantorowicz, Ernst Hartwig. 1957. *The King's Two Bodies: A Study in Medieval Political Theology*. Princeton, NJ: Princeton University Press.

Kaptchuk, Ted J. 2000. *The Web That Has No Weaver: Understanding Chinese Medicine*. 2nd ed. New York: McGraw-Hill Education.

Karl, Rebecca E. 2006. "Culture, Revolution, and the Times of History: Mao and 20th-Century China." *China Quarterly* 187:693–99.

———. 2010. *Mao Zedong and China in the Twentieth-Century World: A Concise History*. Durham, NC: Duke University Press.

———. 2017. *The Magic of Concepts: History and the Economic in Twentieth-Century China*. Durham, NC: Duke University Press.

Kaske, Elisabeth. 2008. *The Politics of Language in Chinese Education: 1895–1919*. Leiden: Brill.

Keightley, David N. 1978. *Sources of Shang History: The Oracle-Bone Inscriptions of Bronze Age China*. Berkeley: University of California Press.

Kipnis, Andrew B. 2016. *From Village to City: Social Transformation in a Chinese County Seat*. Oakland: University of California Press.

———. 2017. "Governing the Souls of Chinese Modernity." *HAU: Journal of Ethnographic Theory* 7 (2): 217–38.

Kirmayer, Laurence J., and Duncan Pedersen. 2014. "Toward a New Architecture for Global Mental Health." *Transcultural Psychiatry* 51 (6): 759–76.

Kleinman, Arthur. 1977. "Depression, Somatization and the 'New Cross-Cultural Psychiatry.'" *Social Science and Medicine* 11 (1): 3–9.

———. 1980. *Patients and Healers in the Context of Culture: An Exploration of the Borderland between Anthropology, Medicine, and Psychiatry*. Berkeley: University of California Press.

———. 1982. "Neurasthenia and Depression: A Study of Somatization and Culture in China." *Culture, Medicine and Psychiatry* 6 (2): 117–90.

———. 1986. *Social Origins of Distress and Disease: Depression, Neurasthenia, and Pain in Modern China*. New Haven, CT: Yale University Press.

Kleinman, Arthur, and Joan Kleinman. 1994. "How Bodies Remember: Social Memory and Bodily Experience of Criticism, Resistance, and Delegitimation Following China's Cultural Revolution." *New Literary History* 25 (3): 707–23.

———. 1997. "Moral Transformations of Health and Suffering in Chinese Society." In *Morality and Health: Interdisciplinary Perspectives*, edited by Paul Rozin and Allan M. Brandt, 101–18. New York: Routledge.

Kleinman, Arthur, Yunxiang Yan, Jing Jun, Sing Lee, Everett Zhang, Pan Tianshu, Wu Fei, and Guo Jinhua. 2011. *Deep China: The Moral Life of the Person: What Anthropology and Psychiatry Tell Us about China Today*. Berkeley: University of California Press.

Koselleck, Reinhart. 2004. *Futures Past: On the Semantics of Historical Time*. New York: Columbia University Press.

Kwon, Heonik. 2008. *Ghosts of War in Vietnam*. New York: Cambridge University Press.

Lacan, Jacques. 2007. *Écrits: The First Complete Edition in English*. Translated by Bruce Fink. New York: Norton.

Lai, Lili. 2016. *Hygiene, Sociality, and Culture in Contemporary Rural China: The Uncanny New Village.* Amsterdam: Amsterdam University Press.

Lakoff, Andrew. 2006. *Pharmaceutical Reason: Knowledge and Value in Global Psychiatry.* New York: Cambridge University Press.

Laplanche, Jean. 1999. *Essays on Otherness.* Edited by John Fletcher. Translated by Luke Thurston, Philip Slotkin, and Leslie Hill. New York: Routledge.

Larson, Wendy. 2009. *From Ah Q to Lei Feng: Freud and Revolutionary Spirit in 20th Century China.* Stanford, CA: Stanford University Press.

Latour, Bruno. 1993. *We Have Never Been Modern.* Cambridge, MA: Harvard University Press.

Lee, Edward Bing-Shuey. 1930. "The Three Principles of the Kuomintang." *The Annals of the American Academy of Political and Social Science* 152 (1): 262–65.

Lee, Nelson K. 2009. "How Is a Political Public Space Made? The Birth of Tiananmen Square and the May Fourth Movement." *Political Geography* 28 (1): 32–43.

Lee, Sing. 1999. "Diagnosis Postponed: Shenjing Shuairuo and the Transformation of Psychiatry in Post-Mao China." *Culture, Medicine and Psychiatry* 23 (3): 349–80.

———. 2002. "Socio-cultural and Global Health Perspectives for the Development of Future Psychiatric Diagnostic Systems." *Psychopathology* 35 (2–3): 152–57.

Lee, Sing, and Arthur Kleinman. 2002. "Psychiatry in Its Political and Professional Contexts: A Response to Robin Munro." *Journal of the American Academy of Psychiatry and the Law* 30 (1): 120–25.

Leenhardt, Maurice. 1979. *Do Kamo: Person and Myth in the Melanesian World.* Chicago: University of Chicago Press.

Leese, Daniel. 2011. *Mao Cult: Rhetoric and Ritual in China's Cultural Revolution.* New York: Cambridge University Press.

Lemelson, Robert. 2014. "'The Spirits Enter Me to Force Me to Be a Communist': Political Embodiment, Idioms of Distress, Spirit Possession, and Thought Disorder in Bali." In *Genocide and Mass Violence: Memory, Symptom, and Recovery,* edited by Devon E. Hinton and Alexander L. Hinton, 175–94. New York: Cambridge University Press.

Levenson, Joseph R. 1968. *Confucian China and Its Modern Fate: A Trilogy.* Berkeley: University of California Press.

Lévi-Strauss, Claude. 1963. *Structural Anthropology.* New York: Basic Books.

Lewis, I. M. 1971. *Ecstatic Religion: An Anthropological Study of Spirit Possession and Shamanism.* Harmondsworth, UK: Penguin Books.

Lewis-Fernández, Roberto, Neil Krishan Aggarwal, Sofie Bäärnhielm, Hans Rohlof, Laurence J. Kirmayer, Mitchell G. Weiss, Sushrut Jadhav, et al. 2014. "Culture and Psychiatric Evaluation: Operationalizing Cultural Formulation for *DSM-5*." *Psychiatry: Interpersonal and Biological Processes* 77 (2): 130–54.

Liu, Lydia. 1995. *Translingual Practice: Literature, National Culture, and Translated Modernity; China, 1900–1937.* Stanford, CA: Stanford University Press.

Liu, Qingping. 2007. "Confucianism and Corruption: An Analysis of Shun's Two Actions Described by Mencius." *Dao: A Journal of Comparative Philosophy* 6 (1): 1–19.

Liu, Xin. 1997. "Space, Mobility, and Flexibility: Chinese Villagers and Scholars Negotiate Power at Home and Abroad." In Ong and Nonini 1997, 91–114.

———. 2000. *In One's Own Shadow: An Ethnographic Account of the Condition of Post-reform Rural China.* Berkeley: University of California Press.

———. 2009. *The Mirage of China: Anti-humanism, Narcissism, and Corporeality of the Contemporary World.* New York: Berghahn Books.

Liu, Zhenyun. 2012. "Why Won't the Chinese Acknowledge the 1942 Famine?" *New York Times,* November 30, 2012, sec. Opinion/Global Opinion.

Lopez, Donald S., Jr. 1996. *Religions of China in Practice.* Princeton, NJ: Princeton University Press.

Lovell, Anne M. 1997. "'The City Is My Mother': Narratives of Schizophrenia and Homelessness." *American Anthropologist* 99 (2): 355–68.

Lovell, Julia. 2009. Introduction to *The Real Story of Ah-Q and Other Tales of China: The Complete Fiction of Lu Xun.* By Xun Lu, xiii–xxxix. New York: Penguin Books.

Lu Xun. 1977. *Selected Stories of Lu Hsun.* New York: Norton.

Luhrmann, T. M. 2012. "A Hyperreal God and Modern Belief: Toward an Anthropological Theory of Mind." *Current Anthropology* 53 (4): 371–95.

Luo Zhufeng, ed. 2001. *Hanyu Dacidian* [Chinese dictionary]. Shanghai: Hanyu Dacidian Chubanshe.

Lupke, Christopher, ed. 2005. *The Magnitude of Ming: Command, Allotment, and Fate in Chinese Culture.* Honolulu: University of Hawai'i Press.

Ma, Zhiying. 2012. "Psychiatric Subjectivity and Cultural Resistance: Experience and Explanations of Schizophrenia in Contemporary China." In *Chinese Modernity and the Individual Psyche,* edited by Andrew B. Kipnis, 203–27. New York: Palgrave Macmillan.

Major, John S. 1993. *Heaven and Earth in Early Han Thought.* Albany: State University of New York Press.

Mannheim, Karl. 1952. "The Problem of Generations." In *Essays on Sociology and Social Psychology,* edited by Paul Kecskemeti, 276–322. Abingdon: Routledge and Kegan Paul.

Mao, Zedong. 1967. *Selected Works of Mao Tse-Tung.* Vol 1. Beijing: Foreign Languages Press.

———. 2019. "The People's Liberation Army Captures Nanjing." In *Poets of the Chinese Revolution,* edited by Gregor Benton and Chongyi Feng, 478–80. New York: Verso.

Markus, Hazel R., and Shinobu Kitayama. 1991. "Culture and the Self: Implications for Cognition, Emotion, and Motivation." *Psychological Review* 98 (2): 224–53.

Ma Shuo. 2002. *Henan Ren Re Shei Le?* [Who did the Henanese offend?]. Haikou, China: Hainan.

Mauss, Marcel. 1985. "A Category of the Human Mind: The Notion of Person; the Notion of Self." In Carrithers, Collins, and Lukes 1985, 1–25.

Mbembe, Achille. 2003. "Life, Sovereignty, and Terror in the Fiction of Amos Tutuola." *Research in African Literatures* 34 (4): 1–26.

McGranahan, Carole. 2016. "Theorizing Refusal: An Introduction." *Cultural Anthropology* 31 (3): 319–25.

Meyer, Jeffrey F. 1991. *The Dragons of Tiananmen: Beijing as a Sacred City.* Columbia: University of South Carolina Press.

Mezzich, Juan E., Laurence J. Kirmayer, Arthur Kleinman, Horacio Fabrega, Delores L. Parron, Byron J. Good, Keh-Ming Lin, and Spero M. Manson. 1999. "The Place of Culture in DSM-IV." *Journal of Nervous and Mental Disease* 187 (8): 457–64.

Morris, Rosalind C. 2000. *In the Place of Origins: Modernity and Its Mediums in Northern Thailand*. Durham, NC: Duke University Press.

Mueggler, Erik. 2001. *The Age of Wild Ghosts: Memory, Violence, and Place in Southwest China*. Berkeley: University of California Press.

———. 2017. *Songs for Dead Parents: Corpse, Text, and World in Southwest China*. Chicago: University of Chicago Press.

Mullaney, Tom, James Leibold, Stephane Gros, and Eric Vanden Bussche. 2012. *Critical Han Studies: The History, Representation, and Identity of China's Majority*. Berkeley: University of California Press.

Munro, Robin. 2002a. *Dangerous Minds: Political Psychiatry in China Today and Its Origin in the Mao Era*. New York: Human Rights Watch.

———. 2002b. "On the Psychiatric Abuse of Falun Gong and Other Dissenters in China: A Reply to Stone, Hickling, Kleinman, and Lee." *Journal of the American Academy of Psychiatry and the Law* 30:266–74.

Murphy, Rachel. 2002. *How Migrant Labor Is Changing Rural China*. Cambridge: Cambridge University Press.

Naquin, Susan. 1976. *Millenarian Rebellion in China: The Eight Trigrams Uprising of 1813*. New Haven, CT: Yale University Press.

Naquin, Susan, and Chün-fang Yü, eds. 1992. *Pilgrims and Sacred Sites in China*. Berkeley: University of California Press.

Naughton, Barry. 1993. "Deng Xiaoping: The Economist." *China Quarterly* 135:491–514.

Nedostup, Rebecca. 2010. *Superstitious Regimes: Religion and the Politics of Chinese Modernity*. Cambridge, MA: Harvard University Asia Center.

Ng, Emily. 2009. "Heartache of the State, Enemy of the Self: Bipolar Disorder and Cultural Change in Urban China." *Culture, Medicine and Psychiatry* 33 (3): 421–50.

Ngo, Tam T. T. 2019. "The Uncle Hô Religion in Vietnam." In *The Secular in South, East, and Southeast Asia*, edited by Kenneth Dean and Peter Van der Veer, 215–38. Cham, Switzerland: Palgrave Macmillan.

Ngo, Tam T. T., and Justine B. Quijada, eds. 2015. *Atheist Secularism and Its Discontents: A Comparative Study of Religion and Communism in Eurasia*. New York: Palgrave Macmillan.

Nisbett, Richard E. 2003. *The Geography of Thought: How Asians and Westerners Think Differently . . . and Why*. New York: Free Press.

Oakes, Tim. 1998. *Tourism and Modernity in China*. New York: Routledge.

Ong, Aihwa, and Donald M. Nonini, eds. 1997. *Ungrounded Empires: The Cultural Politics of Modern Chinese Transnationalism*. New York: Routledge.

Orwell, George. 2013. *Nineteen Eighty-Four*. London: Penguin Classics.

Osnos, Evan. 2011. "Meet Dr. Freud." *New Yorker* 86 (43): 54–63.

Osterhammel, Jürgen. 1986. "Semi-colonialism and Informal Empire in Twentieth-Century China: Towards a Framework of Analysis." In *Imperialism and After: Continuities and Discontinuities*, edited by Wolfgang J. Mommensen and Jürgen Osterhammel, 290–314. London: Allen and Unwin.

Overmyer, Daniel L. 1972. "Folk-Buddhist Religion: Creation and Eschatology in Medieval China." *History of Religions* 12 (1): 42–70.

———. 2009. *Local Religion in North China in the Twentieth Century: The Structure and Organization of Community Rituals and Beliefs*. Leiden: Brill.

Ownby, David. 1999. "Chinese Millenarian Traditions: The Formative Age." *American Historical Review* 104 (5): 1513–30.

Pandolfo, Stefania. 2018. *Knot of the Soul: Madness, Psychoanalysis, Islam.* Chicago: University of Chicago Press.

Pedersen, Morten Axel. 2011. *Not Quite Shamans: Spirit Worlds and Political Lives in Northern Mongolia.* Ithaca, NY: Cornell University Press.

Phillips, Adam, ed. 2006. *The Penguin Freud Reader.* New York: Penguin Books.

Phillips, Tom. 2016. "'Mega Mao' No More as Ridiculed Golden Statue Destroyed." *Guardian,* January 8, 2016.

Pochu Mixin Wenda [Questions and answers about eradicating superstition]. 1964. Shanghai: Shanghai People's Publishing House.

Poo, Mu-Chou. 1998. *In Search of Personal Welfare: A View of Ancient Chinese Religion.* Albany: State University of New York Press.

Povinelli, Elizabeth A. 2011. *Economies of Abandonment: Social Belonging and Endurance in Late Liberalism.* Durham, NC: Duke University Press.

Price, Jason J. 2016. "A Figure Game." *HAU: Journal of Ethnographic Theory* 6 (2): 345–87.

Puett, Michael J. 2004. *To Become a God: Cosmology, Sacrifice, and Self-Divinization in Early China.* Cambridge, MA: Harvard University Asia Center.

———. 2005. "Following the Command of Heaven: The Notion of Ming in Early China." In Lupke 2005, 49–69.

———. 2014. "Ritual Disjunctions: Ghosts, Philosophy, and Anthropology." In *The Ground Between: Anthropologists Engage Philosophy,* edited by Veena Das, Michael D. Jackson, Arthur Kleinman, and Bhrigupati Singh, 218–33. Durham, NC: Duke University Press.

Rancière, Jacques. 2004. *The Politics of Aesthetics: The Distribution of the Sensible.* New York: Continuum.

Raphals, Lisa Ann. 2003. "Fate, Fortune, Chance, and Luck in Chinese and Greek: A Comparative Semantic History." *Philosophy East and West* 53 (4): 537–74.

Ratigan, Kerry. 2015. "Too Little, but Not Too Late? Health Reform in Rural China and the Limits of Experimentalism." *Journal of Asian Public Policy* 8 (1): 69–87.

Renmin Ribao [People's daily]. 1966. "Hengsao Yiqie Niugui Sheshen [Sweep away all cow ghosts and snake gods]." June 1, 1966.

———. 2013. "*Renmin Ribao* Pinlunyuan: Xiaokang Bu Xiaokang, Guanjian Kan Laoxiang [*People's Daily* commentator: The crux of moderate prosperity is those from the hometown]." *Remin Ribao* [People's daily], December 26, 2013. http://opinion.people.com.cn/n/2013/1226/c1003–23947122.html.

Rofel, Lisa. 1999. *Other Modernities: Gendered Yearnings in China after Socialism.* Berkeley: University of California Press.

Rogaski, Ruth. 2004. *Hygienic Modernity: Meanings of Health and Disease in Treaty-Port China.* Berkeley: University of California Press.

Rongyao Mengping [pseud.]. 2013. "Jinqian Mai Bu Dao Qinqing [Money cannot buy familial affection]" *Xiaohe Zuowenwang.* Accessed December 2, 2013. www.zww.cn/zuowen/html/206/746703.htm.

Rose, Nikolas. 1996. *Inventing Our Selves: Psychology, Power, and Personhood.* Cambridge: Cambridge University Press.

Russell, Norman. 2004. *The Doctrine of Deification in the Greek Patristic Tradition*. Oxford: Oxford University Press.

Ryang, Sonia. 2012. *Reading North Korea: An Ethnological Inquiry*. Cambridge, MA: Harvard University Asia Center.

Sato, Hiroshi, and Li Shi. 2007. "Class Origin, Family Culture, and Intergenerational Correlation of Education in Rural China." Institute for the Study of Labor (IZA). February 2007. https://poseidon01.ssrn.com.

Schaberg, David. 2005. "Command and the Content of Tradition." In Lupke 2005, 23–48.

Scheid, Volker. 2002. *Chinese Medicine in Contemporary China: Plurality and Synthesis*. Durham, NC: Duke University Press.

Scheper-Hughes, Nancy. 2001. *Saints, Scholars, and Schizophrenics: Mental Illness in Rural Ireland*. 20th anniv. ed. Berkeley: University of California Press.

Schmitt, Carl. 2006. *Political Theology: Four Chapters on the Concept of Sovereignty*. Translated by George Schwab. Chicago: University of Chicago Press.

Schwarcz, Vera. 1986. *The Chinese Enlightenment: Intellectuals and the Legacy of the May Fourth Movement of 1919*. Berkeley: University of California Press.

Seaman, Gary. 1974. *Temple Organization in a Chinese Village*. Taipei: Chinese Association for Folklore.

Shek, Richard. 1990. "Sectarian Eschatology and Violence." In *Violence in China: Essays in Culture and Counterculture*, edited by Jonathan N. Lipman and Stevan Harrell, 87–114. Albany: State University of New York Press.

Shen, Yucun, ed. 1982. *Jingshenbingxue* [Psychiatry]. 3rd ed. Shanghai: People's Health.

Shih, Shumei. 2001. *The Lure of the Modern: Writing Modernism in Semicolonial China, 1917–1937*. Berkeley: University of California Press.

Siegel, James. 1978. "Curing Rites, Dreams and Domestic Politics in a Sumatran Society." *Glyph*, no. 3, 18–31.

Simpson, Audra. 2014. *Mohawk Interruptus: Political Life across the Borders of Settler States*. Durham, NC: Duke University Press.

Skafish, Peter. 2016. "The Metaphysics of Extra-Moderns: On the Decolonization of Thought; A Conversation with Eduardo Viveiros de Castro." *Common Knowledge* 22 (3): 393–414.

Smith, Arthur Henderson. 1894. *Chinese Characteristics*. 2nd ed. New York: Revell.

Smith, Graeme. 2010. "The Hollow State: Rural Governance in China." *China Quarterly* 203:601–18.

Smith, Richard J. 1993. "Divination in Ch'ing Dynasty China." In *Cosmology, Ontology, and Human Efficacy Essays in Chinese Thought*, edited by Richard J. Smith and Danny Wynn Ye Kwok, 141–78. Honolulu: University of Hawai'i Press.

Song, Hoon. 2013. "Filiation, Continuous and Discontinuous: Two Recent Anthropological Approaches to North Korea." *Critical Asian Studies* 45 (2): 303–22.

———. 2016. "North Korea's 'Succession' of Marxism." *Boundary 2* 43 (3): 79–104.

Sorace, Christian, Ivan Franceschini, and Nicholas Loubere, eds. 2019. *Afterlives of Chinese Communism: Political Concepts from Mao to Xi*. New York: Verso.

Spence, Jonathan D. 1990. *The Search for Modern China*. New York: Norton.

Spivak, Gayatri Chakravorty. 2000. "From Haverstock Hill Flat to U.S. Classroom: What's Left of Theory." In *What's Left of Theory,* edited by Judith Butler, John Guillory, and Kendall Thomas, 13–51. New York: Routledge.

Sprinker, Michael, ed. 1999. *Ghostly Demarcations: A Symposium on Jacques Derrida's Specters of Marx.* New York: Verso.

Stevenson, Lisa. 2014. *Life beside Itself: Imagining Care in the Canadian Arctic.* Oakland: University of California Press.

Strange, Stuart Earle. 2016. "The Dialogical Collective: Mediumship, Pain, and the Interactive Creation of Ndyuka Maroon Subjectivity." *Journal of the Royal Anthropological Institute* 22 (3): 516–33.

Strassberg, Richard E. 2008. *Wandering Spirits: Chen Shiyuan's Encyclopedia of Dreams.* Berkeley: University of California Press.

Sun, Yan. 2004. *Corruption and Market in Contemporary China.* Ithaca, NY: Cornell University Press.

Taussig, Michael. 1987. *Shamanism, Colonialism, and the Wild Man: A Study in Terror and Healing.* Chicago: University of Chicago Press.

———. 1991. *The Nervous System.* New York: Routledge.

———. 1997. *The Magic of the State.* New York: Routledge.

Teiser, Stephen F. 1988. "'Having Once Died and Returned to Life': Representations of Hell in Medieval China." *Harvard Journal of Asiatic Studies* 48 (2): 433–64.

Terrill, Ross. 1999. *Mao: A Biography.* Stanford, CA: Stanford University Press.

Thaxton, Ralph. 1983. *China Turned Rightside Up: Revolutionary Legitimacy in the Peasant World.* New Haven, CT: Yale University Press.

Thompson, Edward P. 1971. "The Moral Economy of the English Crowd in the Eighteenth Century." *Past and Present* 50:76–136.

Thompson, Laurence G. 1988. "Dream Divination and Chinese Popular Religion." *Journal of Chinese Religions* 16 (1): 73–82.

Throop, C. Jason. 2014. "Moral Moods." *Ethos* 42 (1): 65–83.

Tribe, Keith. 2004. "Translator's Introduction." In Koselleck 2004, vii–xx.

Tseng, Wen-Shing. 2006. "From Peculiar Psychiatric Disorders through Culture-Bound Syndromes to Culture-Related Specific Syndromes." *Transcultural Psychiatry* 43 (4): 554–76.

Tseng, Wen-Shing, and David Y. H. Wu, eds. 1985. *Chinese Culture and Mental Health.* Orlando: Academic Press.

Tsing, Anna Lowenhaupt. 2015. *The Mushroom at the End of the World: On the Possibility of Life in Capitalist Ruins.* Princeton, NJ: Princeton University Press.

Tu, Wei-ming. 1991. "Cultural China: The Periphery as the Center." *Daedalus* 120 (2): 1–32.

———. 1995. *The Living Tree: The Changing Meaning of Being Chinese Today.* Stanford, CA: Stanford University Press.

———. 1998. "Probing the 'Three Bonds' and 'Five Relationships' in Confucian Humanism." In *Confucianism and the Family,* edited by Walter H. Slote and George A. DeVos, 121–36. Albany: State University of New York Press.

Unger, Jonathan. 1993. "Urban Families in the Eighties: An Analysis of Chinese Surveys." In *Chinese Families in the Post-Mao Era,* edited by Deborah Davis and Stevan Harrell, 25–49. Berkeley: University of California Press.

Unschuld, Paul. 1985. *Medicine in China: A History of Ideas*. Berkeley: University of California Press.

Verdery, Katherine. 1999. *The Political Lives of Dead Bodies*. New York: Columbia University Press.

Wagner, Rudolf G. 1988. "Imperial Dreams in China." In Brown 1988, 11–24.

———. 1992. "Reading the Chairman Mao Memorial Hall in Peking: The Tribulations of the Implied Pilgrim." In Naquin and Yü 1992, 378–423.

Wang, Ban. 2004. *Illuminations from the Past: Trauma, Memory, and History in Modern China*. Stanford, CA: Stanford University Press.

Wank, David L. 2001. *Commodifying Communism: Business, Trust, and Politics in a Chinese City*. Cambridge: Cambridge University Press.

Watson, James L. 2010. "Feeding the Revolution: Public Mess Halls and Coercive Commensality in Maoist China." In *Governance of Life in Chinese Moral Experience: The Quest for an Adequate Life*, edited by Everett Zhang, Arthur Kleinman, and Weiming Tu, 33–46. New York: Routledge.

Watson, Rubie. 1995. "Palaces, Museums, and Squares: Chinese National Spaces." *Museum Anthropology* 19 (2): 7–19.

Watters, Ethan. 2010. *Crazy Like Us: The Globalization of the American Psyche*. New York: Free Press.

Weber, Max. 1951. *The Religion of China: Confucianism and Taoism*. Glencoe, IL: Free Press.

Wellens, Koen. 2010. *Religious Revival in the Tibetan Borderlands: The Premi of Southwest China*. Seattle: University of Washington Press.

Weller, Robert P. 1994. *Resistance, Chaos and Control in China: Taiping Rebels, Taiwanese Ghosts and Tiananmen*. Seattle: University of Washington Press.

Wemheuer, Felix. 2014. *Famine Politics in Maoist China and the Soviet Union*. New Haven, CT: Yale University Press.

White, Theodore. 1943. "Until the Harvest Is Reaped." *Time*, March 22, 1943.

Whitmarsh, Ian, and Elizabeth F.S. Roberts. 2016. "Nonsecular Medical Anthropology." *Medical Anthropology* 35 (3): 203–8.

Whyte, Martin K. 2003. "The Persistence of Family Obligations in Baoding." In *China's Revolutions and Intergenerational Relations*, edited by Martin K. Whyte, 85–118. Ann Arbor: University of Michigan Center for Chinese Studies.

Wilhelm, Richard, and Cary F. Baynes, trans. 1967. *The I Ching, or Book of Changes*. Princeton, NJ: Princeton University Press.

Williams, Raymond. 1961. *The Long Revolution*. New York: Columbia University Press.

Winter, Jay. 2014. *Sites of Memory, Sites of Mourning: The Great War in European Cultural History*. Cambridge: Cambridge University Press.

Wittfogel, Karl A. 1957. *Oriental Despotism: A Comparative Study of Total Power*. New Haven, CT: Yale University Press.

Wolf, Arthur P., ed. 1974. *Religion and Ritual in Chinese Society*. Stanford, CA: Stanford University Press.

Wolf, Margery. 1990. "The Woman Who Didn't Become a Shaman." *American Ethnologist* 17 (3): 419–30.

World Health Organization. 2004. *International Statistical Classification of Diseases and Related Health Problems*. 10th rev. Geneva: World Health Organization.

Wou, Odoric. 1994. *Mobilizing the Masses: Building Revolution in Henan.* Stanford, CA: Stanford University Press.

Wu, Xiaoli. 2009. "The Presentation of an Ambivalent History: A Chinese Railway Museum's Perspective." In *Railways as an Innovative Regional Factor,* edited by Heli Mäki and Jenni Korjus, 30–42. Helsinki: University of Helsinki.

Wu, Yingtao. 1970. *Taiwan Min Su* [The customs of Taiwan]. Taipei: Guting Shuwu.

Yan, Yunxiang. 1996. *The Flow of Gifts: Reciprocity and Social Networks in a Chinese Village.* Stanford, CA: Stanford University Press.

———. 1999. "Rural Youth and Youth Culture in North China." *Culture, Medicine and Psychiatry* 23 (1): 75–97.

———. 2003. *Private Life under Socialism: Love, Intimacy, and Family Change in a Chinese Village, 1949–1999.* Stanford, CA: Stanford University Press.

Yang, Jie. 2015. *Unknotting the Heart: Unemployment and Therapeutic Governance in China.* Ithaca, NY: Cornell University Press.

Yang, Mayfair Mei-hui. 1994. *Gifts, Favors, and Banquets: The Art of Social Relationships in China.* Ithaca, NY: Cornell University Press.

———. 2000. "Putting Global Capitalism in Its Place: Economic Hybridity, Bataille, and Ritual Expenditure." *Current Anthropology* 41 (4): 477–509.

———. 2002. "The Resilience of Guanxi and Its New Deployments: A Critique of Some New Guanxi Scholarship." *China Quarterly* 170:459–76.

———. 2008. *Chinese Religiosities: Afflictions of Modernity and State Formation.* Berkeley: University of California Press.

Yang, Zhiyi. 2013. "Classical Poetry in Modern Politics: Liu Yazi's PR Campaign for Mao Zedong." *Asian and African Studies* 22 (2): 208–26.

Yan, Hairong. 2003. "Spectralization of the Rural: Reinterpreting the Labor Mobility of Rural Young Women in Post-Mao China." *American Ethnologist* 30 (4): 578–96.

Yap, Pow-Ming. 1951. "Mental Diseases Peculiar to Certain Cultures: A Survey of Comparative Psychiatry." *Journal of Mental Science* 97 (407): 313–27.

———. 1967. "Classification of the Culture-Bound Reactive Syndromes." *Australian and New Zealand Journal of Psychiatry* 1 (4): 172–79.

Young, Derson. 1989. "Neurasthenia and Related Problems." *Culture, Medicine and Psychiatry* 13 (2): 131–38.

Yü, Ying-Shih. 1987. "'O Soul, Come Back!' A Study in the Changing Conceptions of the Soul and Afterlife in Pre-Buddhist China." *Harvard Journal of Asiatic Studies* 47 (2): 363–95.

Yu Hua. 2012. *China in Ten Words.* Translated by Allan H. Barr. New York: Vintage.

Yurchak, Alexei. 2015. "Bodies of Lenin: The Hidden Science of Communist Sovereignty." *Representations* 129 (1): 116–57.

Zavidovskaya, Ekaterina A. 2012. "Deserving Divine Protection: Religious Life in Contemporary Rural Shanxi and Shaanxi Provinces." *St. Petersburg Annual of Asian and African Studies* 1:179–97. Würzburg: Ergon.

Zhan, Mei. 2009. *Other-Worldly: Making Chinese Medicine through Transnational Frames.* Durham, NC: Duke University Press.

———. 2016. "Cosmic Experiments: Remaking Materialism and Daoist Ethic 'Outside of the Establishment.'" *Medical Anthropology* 35 (3): 247–62.

Zhang, Li. 2002. *Strangers in the City: Reconfigurations of Space, Power, and Social Networks within China's Floating Population.* Stanford, CA: Stanford University Press.

———. 2014. "Bentuhua: Culturing Psychotherapy in Postsocialist China." *Culture, Medicine and Psychiatry* 38 (2): 283–305.

Zigon, Jarrett. 2015. "What Is a Situation? An Assemblic Ethnography of the Drug War." *Cultural Anthropology* 30 (3): 501–24.

Zürcher, Erik. 1982. "'Prince Moonlight': Messianism and Eschatology in Early Medieval Chinese Buddhism." *T'oung Pao* 68 (1–3): 1–75.

Mao, 12, 58; "borrowed" mouth of orator as form of possession, 57; as calling, 62; and images of Mao, 65; and possession, 56–58, 62; ritual behaviors, 64, 65–66; ritual spreads, 64–65; and ten-thousand years of Mao (*wansui*) chant, 65–66

gender: and filial piety, decline of, 167n6; and fortune-tellers, 19; and spirit mediums, 19; of supplicants to spirit mediums, 93

geography, cosmic-symbolic, 65, 80, 83, 127, 133, 141, 165n1

ghosts: abandoned, 84, 93–94; as basis of ancestor worship, 15–16, 84; as form of return, 80–81; gods and ancestors as corrupting into, 16; interchangeability of false gods and, 74–75; melancholic dimension of, 76; traditional view of, 15–16; in triad of the text, 15–16; as uncultivated unbodied souls, 7; *xian* as term for, 16, 83–84. *See also* contemporary cosmology; demonic entities; spectral collisions; spirit mediums

ghost stories, as genre, 16

global mental health, 103–4, 105, 135, 149, 161n11

Goddess of Mercy (Guanyin Pusa), 74

God of the Heavens (Laotianye), 74

gods: classic ethnographic distinction of, from ghosts and ancestors, 16; the cultivated soul as reaching status of, 7, 16, 72; as distant vs. involved in earthly affairs, 7; false, interchangeability with ghosts, 74–75; *xian* as term for, 16, 74, 75, 84. *See also* contemporary cosmology, return of corrupt/false spirits in the postreform era; religion

Gordon, Avery, 55

Great Leap famine ("year '58," 1958–59), 11, 41, 55, 87, 138

Great Leap Forward, and neurasthenia, 162n6

Guangdong Province: posthumous Mao cult in, 13; and vilification of Henan Province, 31. *See also* Shenzhen; South China

Guizhou Province, 28

Haar, Barend ter, 143–44

Hall, David, 75

Han dynasty: charts of elements, 75; and Fuxi/Nüwa, 58; homonymic pairing of *guî* (ghost) and *guî* (to return), 80–81

health insurance, 120, 166n4

heaven-earth distinction: overview, 5–6. *See also* earthly, the; heavenly, the; human realm

the heavenly ("the above"): "cosmic" and "divine" as terms referencing, 6; definition of, 5. *See also* mandate of heaven

Henan Province: apocalyptic imaginary of, 141; as the center of China, 2, 3, 30–31, 141; as the China of China, 30, 150, 161n18; and outmigration as commonplace, 3–4; and postreform rural urbanization, 3; Second Sino-Japanese War and government neglect of, 85–86, 87; and spectralization of the rural, 3–4, 150, 160n3; views of Henanese prior to vilification, 31, 161n19; vilification of, 30–33, 150, 161n19. *See also* Hexian (pseudonym), Henan Province

heterodoxy and orthodoxy, 133–34, 137, 140

Hexian (pseudonym), Henan Province: as the center of the center, 2, 34, 141, 148; and Mao as signifier of rural revolutionary virtue, 41; and Maoist era as irrevocably past but still palpable, 41; peasant as self-referentially chosen term in, 41; as pseudonym, 160n1. *See also* contemporary cosmology; Fuxi Temple; psychiatric unit of the People's Hospital (Hexian); spirit mediums

Hinton, William, 53

historical texts, ghosts and spirits and, 16

historiography, rise of modern, 37

history: cosmic accounts of, xi, 7, 15, 78–79, 133; impact-response approach to, 9, 27; individuation as cosmo-historical collision, 10; mythological "telescoping" of scales of, 48; narrativity as precondition for, 38, 39; oral history and national time, 51; the peasantry and, 46–47, 52, 103; ritual as alternative mode of, 69; shift to memory from, 37, 161–62nn1,5; spectral returns of, 84, 85, 87–88; tradition as symptom of, 30; traumatic disruption of, 37–38

HIV, and blood economy, 3

Ho Chi Minh, 14

holistic. *See* correlative (analogical) cosmology

Hollan, Douglas, 161n12

hollowing: the contemporary cosmology and perception of, 42, 54, 67; the "hollow state," 68; outmigration and, 4, 78

honesty, changing valences of, 112

hospitals: Christian medical missions as first establishing, 128; Japanese puppet government and, 128; Nationalist Party and, 128; and the People's Republic, 128. *See also* psychiatric unit of the People's Hospital (Hexian)

Founded in 1893,
UNIVERSITY OF CALIFORNIA PRESS
publishes bold, progressive books and journals
on topics in the arts, humanities, social sciences,
and natural sciences—with a focus on social
justice issues—that inspire thought and action
among readers worldwide.

The UC PRESS FOUNDATION
raises funds to uphold the press's vital role
as an independent, nonprofit publisher, and
receives philanthropic support from a wide
range of individuals and institutions—and from
committed readers like you. To learn more, visit
ucpress.edu/supportus.